Bonhoeffer

Petra Brown

Bonhoeffer

God's Conspirator in a State of Exception

Petra Brown
Faculty of Arts-Education
Deakin University
Geelong, VIC, Australia

ISBN 978-3-030-05697-1   ISBN 978-3-030-05698-8   (eBook)
https://doi.org/10.1007/978-3-030-05698-8

Library of Congress Control Number: 2018966129

This Palgrave Macmillan imprint is published by the registered company Springer Nature Switzerland AG
The registered company address is: Gewerbestrasse 11, 6330 Cham, Switzerland

This book is dedicated to my children: Ebony, John and Talitha-Hope

In memory of Faith Abigail

how fair are the bright eyes in the grass
[…] for they blossom in all the seasons of the year
and grow where dead men rest
J. R. R. Tolkien

PREFACE

The concept of this book began with an interest in Dietrich Bonhoeffer and his decision to participate in a conspiracy to kill Hitler. As I began research in this area, it very quickly became clear that Bonhoeffer's conspiracy involvement combined with a popular appeal to his 'martyrdom' and unofficial 'sanctification' contained within it the potential to sanctify violent political action beyond classical Christian concepts of martyrdom. Once I became aware of Bonhoeffer's popularity amongst American evangelicals, noting further that Bonhoeffer had *already* been used to justify acts of violence, the need to critically investigate the decision for joining conspiracy became more urgent.

During the research, I discovered two main issues that have become the focus of this book. The first issue is that both mainstream and evangelical Protestants use Bonhoeffer's concept of Christology as the foundation for his decision for conspiracy. I therefore felt compelled to investigate Bonhoeffer's Christology as a problem, rather than a solution to explain Bonhoeffer's decision to become a conspirator. I am not a theologian; my own education and interest lies in philosophy and history of ideas. For this reason, I do not directly critique Bonhoeffer's understanding of Christology, nor do I provide a theological solution that would improve it in some way. Instead, I draw attention to what I argue are potential *political consequences* of that Christology, and how these link to Bonhoeffer's discussion around discipleship and the 'extraordinary situation'.

The second issue that emerged in my initial research was the discovery that a number of American evangelicals (and some mainstream Protestants) show a tendency to interpret Bonhoeffer's decision for conspiracy in terms of the political language of 'last resort' actions in relation to the 'war on terror'. To challenge this use of Bonhoeffer, I began to read the work of the Nazi jurist and political theorist Carl Schmitt, who famously developed the concept of the 'state of exception' as a state of emergency which requires decisive action by the sovereign (in Schmitt's case) or by other actors within the state. By turning to Schmitt as an unlikely ally in my investigation of Bonhoeffer, I was able to use Schmitt's thinking and writing as a critical pressure on Bonhoeffer's own justification for 'last resort' violence, only hinted at in his classic text, *Ethics*, through the concept of the 'extraordinary situation'. Through reading Schmitt and Bonhoeffer together, I draw attention to what the Italian philosopher Giorgio Agamben calls 'violence without reference'. Thus, the final aim of this thesis is not to attack Bonhoeffer, nor is it to disparage the evangelical appropriation of Bonhoeffer's legacy. The final aim is to raise awareness of, and to open up space for, a host of questions that arise from any form of violence that is justified in terms of 'last resort' necessity.

My aim in writing this book is not to justify Bonhoeffer's involvement in conspiracy by other means, such as 'just war theory', and it will become clear in the book why I've chosen not to do this. I also do not aim to try to uncover the possible reasons Bonhoeffer may have had for becoming a conspirator as a kind of biographical exercise, although I do link his emerging ideas to concrete events of his life. I also recognise throughout the book that Bonhoeffer's thinking and writing is a work in progress, written *in situ*, without the benefit of reflection and of being able to present a final *magnum opus* of his ideas after the war. So, I do not attack Bonhoeffer's writing in order to find weaknesses in his arguments. This tends not to be my approach to philosophy in any case, but here in particular it seems not only unproductive but deeply uncharitable.

Chapter 1 introduces the rise of Bonhoeffer as martyr and saint, following his death in the waning days of the Second World War. It introduces some examples of individuals who have claimed Bonhoeffer as inspiration for violent political action. Through considering the case study of Dhanu, a Black Tiger, the basis of Bonhoeffer's martyrdom as political conspirator is problematised. An outline of the problem of contemporary Protestant martyrdom and its connections to political expression, and the contemporary link between religious and political martyrdom concludes this section.

Chapter 2 introduces the different ways Bonhoeffer can be seen to influence a generation of American evangelicals. For the evangelicals, it is not primarily Bonhoeffer's theology but his life and action that are inspiring, and that for some seems to be the basis for a mystical union. Bonhoeffer's involvement in the plot to kill Hitler is understood by evangelicals as an act of courage in the face of the great evil of the Nazi regime and as an example of the faithful disciple who is obedient to Christ, even in her willingness to commit violence in a situation of 'exception' or 'last resort'. The wide range of Bonhoeffer aficionados in this context include violent anti-abortion protestors in the 1980s and 1990s, influential evangelicals, including former President Bush, who sought to recruit Bonhoeffer to harness Christian support in support of a 'war on terror' after 9/11, and more recently the use of Bonhoeffer by some evangelicals in order to harness the Christian vote for Trump.

Chapter 3 begins by considering the concept of the 'extraordinary' in Bonhoeffer's key pacifist text, *Discipleship*. This concept is found in Bonhoeffer's exposition of the Sermon on the Mount, where Christ is considered the exemplar of what it means to be 'extraordinary' and the concrete command to love one's enemy an opportunity to practice Christ's extraordinary love in the world. Yet, by the time *Ethics* is written, a new exposition of the Sermon on the Mount has removed the requirement to love one's enemy, and instead argues that the Christian disciple is called to responsible action that may include political action on behalf of one's neighbour. This chapter therefore draws attention to some of the limitations of Bonhoeffer's famous interpretation of the Sermon on the Mount and further shows that the conceptual tools for Bonhoeffer's later ethical position for violence as a 'last resort' in *Ethics* are already contained in his key pacifist text.

Chapter 4 more fully introduces Bonhoeffer as conspirator and begins to explore the ethical framework that informed Bonhoeffer's decision to become a conspirator, his book *Ethics*, written during his time as a double agent in the *Abwehr*. Through a close examination of a central passage, where Bonhoeffer introduces the concept of the 'extraordinary situation' based on Machiavelli's *necessità*, this chapter investigates the extent to which Bonhoeffer attempts to think through a situation where the Christian is able to act in a situation that may require violence as a last resort. Such actions represent 'borderline cases' understood as requiring ethical decisions without guidance from norms that generally enable discernment of right action. There emerges a tension between the agent who breaks the law in order to affirm the law, but has no basis for doing so that is understandable to the context of law.

Chapter 5 builds a foundation for a critical analysis of the ethical and political implications of Bonhoeffer's concept of the 'extraordinary situation' through an analysis of the concept of exception in what is arguably the most prominent theorist of the 'exception' in the twentieth century, Carl Schmitt. In *Political Theology* (1933), Schmitt introduced the 'state of exception' in connection with strong sovereignty and the event of war. It considers the political and social implications of Schmitt's account of exception, in particular the danger of dictatorship, the loss of a democratic and shared world and the introduction of a force or violence without boundaries.

Chapter 6 critically analyses Bonhoeffer's concept of the 'extraordinary situation' in light of Schmitt's concept of the 'state of exception'. It considers to what extent Bonhoeffer's concept of the extraordinary situation also contains a tendency to encourage decisive action that may come at the expense of democratic and shared common values. It suggests that Bonhoeffer's concept of the extraordinary potentially radicalises Schmitt's concept of exception as it extends to each disciple or follower of Christ, thereby potentially authorising each follower of Christ to enact violence in a 'last resort' scenario.

Chapter 7 deepens the philosophical consequences of the concept of the extraordinary in Bonhoeffer's writing, in conversation with the Danish philosopher Soren Kierkegaard, through a description of the isolated disciple as outlined by Bonhoeffer in *Discipleship*. It suggests that the themes of isolation and obedience to a higher command lead to a narrative in which following Jesus is understood in terms of conflict, struggle and opposition to the world. It outlines the ethical implications of this via the young Bonhoeffer's 1929 Barcelona lecture.

Chapter 8 considers three possible ways to judge action undertaken in the extraordinary situation. The first is the place of the church as the locus of discipleship, which puts a limit to the isolated, existential disciple. The second is Bonhoeffer's ultimate/penultimate distinction, which is considered an important part of Bonhoeffer's political theology and locates existential action in a broader context. Finally, the role of guilt is considered as a limit. Guilt is key to Bonhoeffer's Christological foundation of responsible action, but it is also key to contemporary debates about 'dirty hands' political acts through the work of Michael Walzer.

Chapter 9 turns away from the exegetical and argumentative tasks of the previous chapters in the book. It looks at Bonhoeffer's own intellectual and theological formation in the context of post-war Weimar Germany, through examining the debates between key intellectual figures of the Weimar Republic and Bonhoeffer's place in this. By situating Bonhoeffer in the context of his peers, this chapter seeks to highlight the 'crisis' thinking that pervaded the interwar years and influenced Bonhoeffer's own theology, and demonstrates the danger of too readily justifying actions on the basis of crisis.

The final chapter and conclusion asks to what extent the American evangelical reading of Bonhoeffer as a 'Christian' example of justified last resort violence is legitimate. It suggests that the image of isolated discipleship that endorses violence is not the final Bonhoeffer message for a contemporary age. It draws attention to the dangers of Bonhoeffer's political theology, particularly in light of Schmitt's vision of political life and the current global political climate, including America's own faith-guided political life.

Geelong, Australia   Petra Brown

ACKNOWLEDGEMENTS

The idea for this book became reality thanks to the support of some remarkable people. It is impossible to thank all the people who have contributed in a myriad of ways. But the following in particular stand out as providing encouragement along the journey, which began in 2009, when I commenced my Ph.D.

I thank Dr. Ian Weeks, who supervised my original thesis that was the basis for this book, and provided ongoing encouragement in bringing this work to publication. His breadth of knowledge, extensive library and experience together with a generous spirit of conversation and sharing of ideas have deeply enriched my intellectual life over the last ten years.

I thank my colleague, Dr. Patrick Stokes, for his mentoring during the rather difficult years between completing the Ph.D. and gaining a book contract. His openness in sharing of his own experience in the publishing world during this time was invaluable.

I would also like to take the opportunity to thank all those who originally provided such valuable support and feedback during the Ph.D. research and writing process, in particular Dr. Andrew Vandenberg, Dr. Nick Trakakis and Dr. Jeffrey Hanson.

This book would have been impossible to write, let alone finish, without the unwavering support and steadfast love of my family who have at every stage encouraged my intellectual life. My parents, who frequently provided a quiet place to write, my children, who have survived their often-absent mother remarkably well, and last but not least, my husband for his strength and sense of humour that kept afloat a sometimes-rickety raft to bring this book home.

Contents

CHAPTER 1

Introduction: The Martyrdom of 'Saint' Bonhoeffer

In 2002, in an address to the German *Bundestag*, United States President George Bush mentioned the name of a German theologian, 'one of the greatest Germans of the twentieth century', who 'gave witness to the Gospel of life, and paid the cost of his discipleship' (Bush 2002). This man was Dietrich Bonhoeffer, an ostensibly pacifist theologian who became a double agent for the German Resistance, and a conspirator in the attempted overthrow of Hitler. In the antipodean part of the world, another political leader declared that Bonhoeffer was the person he admired most in the history of the twentieth century. For former Australian Prime Minister, Kevin Rudd, Bonhoeffer demonstrates a 'muscular Christianity', an example of a man who strove for a just world delivered by social action, driven by personal faith (Rudd 2006: 22–30). For Rudd, Bonhoeffer died a peacemaker, a Christian pastor, committed social democrat and passionate internationalist. Such was his admiration of Bonhoeffer that Rudd believed Bonhoeffer held the answers to some of the most pressing problems facing the West today: 'How would Bonhoeffer respond to militant Islam and to the broader challenge of international terrorism today?' (Rudd 2006).

Who is this man who inspires political leaders? Undoubtedly his life as a double agent for the German resistance and his involvement in the plot to assassinate Hitler make for a gripping tale; his death at the hand of the Nazis only days before the liberation of Germany, a tragic end. However, it is not these few biographical details that are significant in and of themselves. Bonhoeffer may very well have remained as little known as Paul

© The Author(s) 2019
P. Brown, *Bonhoeffer*,
https://doi.org/10.1007/978-3-030-05698-8_1

Schneider, a Lutheran Pastor and the first Protestant minister executed by lethal injection at Buchenwald in 1939. But obscurity was not to be Bonhoeffer's fate.

Three months after Dietrich Bonhoeffer was killed on charges of conspiracy against the state, George Bell, his close friend and Bishop of Chichester, declared during a commemoration service that Bonhoeffer belonged to a 'noble company of martyrs' who represent, in the name of God, resistance to evil, and in the name of human conscience, resistance against injustice and cruelty (Bell cited in Middleton 2011: 19). This image of Bonhoeffer as both agent of God and political liberator was quickly taken up into the English-speaking world. The American theologian Reinhold Niebuhr, in an article titled 'The Death of a Martyr', declared that Bonhoeffer was an example of a modern apostle who, through his actions and precepts, provided the hope for a revitalised. Protestant faith—a faith that will have overcome the 'one fateful error of German Protestantism, the complete dichotomy between faith and political life' (Niebuhr cited in Nelson 1999: 22).

In the first comprehensive study of Protestant sainthood in 1968, Bonhoeffer was listed as one of the 'great Protestants who have become canonized' (Harper cited in Haynes 2004: 127). Thirty years later, the Archbishop of Canterbury, George Carey, in the presence of Queen Elizabeth II and Prince Philip, unveiled a Bonhoeffer statue amongst nine other modern-day Christian martyrs, including Martin Luther King and Oscar Romero, in the Western main entrance of Westminster Abbey. In 2008, the United Methodist General Conference named Bonhoeffer a modern martyr (Bloom 2008). Today, devotees of this 'Protestant Saint' can buy Bonhoeffer plaques and prayer cards online[1] and the day of his death is commemorated in Atwell's *Celebrating the Saints* (Atwell 2004: 178–182).

The idea of Bonhoeffer as a Christian martyr has been explored and to some extent encouraged by theologians. In *Bonhoeffer as Martyr*, Craig Slane sees Bonhoeffer as an example of a 'new alphabet' of modern martyrdom. This new alphabet includes Bonhoeffer's freely chosen suffering, rejection of self-sought martyrdom, solidarity of guilt, authentic Christian character and recognition of the authority of death. In an attempt to find a 'theological' epitaph rather than a purely 'moral one', Slane maps Bonhoeffer's death on H.A. Fischel's narrative pattern in his monumental study, *Martyr and Prophet* (1946–1947). Here, he finds a theological rationale for identifying Bonhoeffer as a prophet-martyr identification (Slane 2004: 13, 76). For Slane, martyrdom provides 'the hermeneutic key for interpreting Bonhoeffer's life and thought' (Slane 2004: 13). Slane's theologically grounded analysis interprets Bonhoeffer's life and death as demonstrating 'authentic Christian character'. It is this idea of Christian character that also seems to have inspired Bush and Rudd.

Yet this contemporary prophet-martyr who demonstrates authentic Christian character has inspired more than Western political leaders. The question 'How would Bonhoeffer respond to the drafting of American soldiers in the Vietnam war?' was asked by a Jesuit priest in the 1970s. Father Daniel Berrigan believed he enacted an answer when he protested by burning draft files. Subsequently disappearing underground rather than serve his prison sentence, he wrote:

I begin these notes on 9 April 1970. Two hours ago, at 8:30 a.m. I became a fugitive from injustice, having disobeyed a federal court order to begin a three-year sentence or destruction of draft files two years ago. It is the twenty-fifth anniversary of the death of Dietrich Bonhoeffer in Flossenburg prison, for resistance to Hitler. (Berrigan 1972)

While Berrigan did not resort to violence against another person, his protest was highly political.

Far more willing to resort to violence was Reverend Paul Hill who shot dead Dr. James Britton and security officer James Barrett outside a Florida abortion clinic in 1993. Before his execution in September 2003, Hill claimed Bonhoeffer as the justification for his actions (Haynes 2004: 171). Hill's supporters fervently embraced this Bonhoeffer analogy and Hill became the hero-martyr of violent anti-abortionists. According to supporters, both Bonhoeffer and Hill were 'clergymen who were at odds with the passivity and cowardice of their fellow Christians to resist a holocaust', both 'were determined to defend the defenceless', despite 'the silence of an emasculated church', and both 'laid down their lives gladly for what they believed' (Pavone 2006). In the same vein, Michael Bray, 'the spiritual godfather of anti-abortion violence' forges similar symbolic links to Nazi Germany. His 'definitive book on the ethical justification for anti-abortion violence' names Bonhoeffer as its 'moral exemplar' (Juergensmeyer 2000: 21–22).

The range of individuals inspired by Bonhoeffer shows that his authentic Christian character has the power to inspire a diverse community who have all asked the same question: 'How would Bonhoeffer respond to...?' In asking this question, we must recognise that the Bonhoeffer image that nobly inspires the political leader of a Western democratic nation also seems to inspire the subversive, violent protester within a Western democratic nation. I will now boldly suggest that there is one more candidate who may ask the question, 'How would Bonhoeffer respond to...?'

She is a small, young bespectacled woman, her hair in two plaits. Her appearance designed to inspire trust and confidence, she has carefully prepared for this day. Dressed in the colours of the Indian national flag to ensure she blends into the crowd, she wears a green and orange *salwar kameez* and carries a sandalwood pellet garland, appropriate to a high-value person, with which to honour the Indian President, Rajiv Ghandi (Roberts 2010: 31). She bends down to touch his feet, a sign of respect. With a nod, he acknowledges the gesture. Then, crouched down and kneeling before him, she flicks a manual switch, detonating her belt filled with plastic explosives and ball bearings. Armed with undetectable explosives beneath her guileless, feminine clothing, the angel of death fulfils her appointed task.

In asking the question, 'How should I respond to the aggressive occupation and oppression of my people', 'Dhanu', the 1991 Liberation Tigers of Tamil Eelam (LTTE) female suicide bomber who killed the Indian politician Rajiv Ghandi, answered with a decisive act in the Bonhoeffer spirit.[2] Following her death, the head of the LTTE's political wing declared 'Dhanu' had given the ultimate gift: her act, as all such sacrifices by the Black Tigers, 'a gift of the self...The Person who gives him or herself in full' (Thamilchelvam cited in Hopgood 2005: 74). An act praised by her leader, Prabhakaran on Heroes' Day, July 1993, as the martyrdom of those who have sacrificed their lives for a just cause:

> Their demise does not constitute an ordinary event of death. Rather, their death signifies a profound spiritual aspiration for national freedom. Our martyrs die in the arena of struggle with the intense passion for the freedom of their people, for the liberation of their homeland, and therefore, the death of every martyr constitutes a brave act of enunciation of freedom. (Prabhakaran 1993)

The fervent praise of the self-styled 'sun god', Prabhakaran, echoes the speech given by Bishop Bell in commemoration of Bonhoeffer.

Dhanu's political act was not the act of a solitary, rogue individual manipulated and motivated by religious zeal, as one informed by the popular media might suppose. In the final weeks of her life, Dhanu had been to market, the beach and restaurants, watched six movies at the cinema and enjoyed the luxuries of Madras; altogether, a person who enjoyed the good things in life. According to Robert Pape, Dhanu 'clearly had nerves of steel' (Pape 2005: 230). With her nerves of steel, Dhanu was typical of the Black Tiger mould. For Black Tigers, mental stability and a high level of motivation to complete the mission were amongst the main selection criteria, followed by careful, rigorous and dedicated training. Each individual knew full well what was expected of him or her; each individual was carefully trained to ensure the success of their mission (Pape 2005: 229–230).

Black Tigers were extremely motivated because they were deeply rooted in and committed to their culture and to the dream of a homeland. Each LTTE fighter took an oath, committing themselves to their holy (*punita*) aim: 'The task (or thirst) of the Tigers (is to achieve) Motherland Tamililam' (cited in Roberts 2010: 35). Instead of the Tamil word for suicide, *thatkolai*, the Tigers used *thatkodai*, 'to give yourself' to indicate their commitment to self-sacrifice for their people (Hopgood 2005: 74). Fighting for their Motherland, their people fully supported the Black Tigers in the community. While Tiger leaders had publicly disagreed with the leader of the LTTE, none condemned Tiger suicide attackers (Pape 2005: 146).

In addition to public support of their leaders, the Black Tigers were heroes in their community. After Dhanu's sacrifice, numerous women joined the LTTE to follow in her footsteps. Each year on July 5th, thousands attended the 'Heroes' Day' celebrations, commemorating the first Black Tiger mission in 1987. Hundreds of shrines dotted throughout the countryside were dedicated to individual Black Tigers. With their martyrdom, each Black Tiger was 'counted, mourned, celebrated and added to the swelling pantheon of self-sacrifice' beamed across the world, reminding even expatriate Tamils of those suffering in their homeland (Weiss 2011: 86). The sacrifice of the Black Tiger was also firmly rooted in Tamil folklore and culture, their heroic self-sacrifice understood as an extension of the martial tradition of the ancient Tamil Chola warriors; a myth now put into service for the modern political ambitions of autonomous statehood (Weiss 2011: 76). Dhanu was an educated, integrated individual and supported in her community. Her extreme act may well fall into the category of 'last resort' or 'necessity', since her culture and identity were demonstrably threatened by an aggressor with a superior fighting force.

There are obviously a number of important differences between Dhanu's and Bonhoeffer's respective examples of 'last resort' violence. Dhanu was a highly trained and dedicated fighter in an elite commando unit, whereas Bonhoeffer had to draw upon his courage as a citizen. Unlike the LTTE's missions, the focus of the German resistance remained focused on deposing of Hitler alone. Yet, both Dhanu and Bonhoeffer were required to become something out of the norm, something unexpected. I would even suggest that the account just described makes Dhanu's act of 'self-sacrifice' seems understandable. In light of this account, Slane's praise of Bonhoeffer as a prophet-martyr who demonstrates an 'authentic Christian character' seems far more nebulous and ambiguous. What makes Bonhoeffer's martyrdom specifically 'Christian'? Isn't Schneider, who was executed for refusing to remove his beret in tribute to the Swastika flag on Hitler's birthday, a far better example of courageous martyrdom in the tradition of the early Christians? Bonhoeffer died, not because he was a witness to Christ, but because he was involved in clandestine and politically subversive activities.

It is the ambiguity between his role as a Christian pastor and his political action that has led some theologians and scholars to question the straightforward image of Bonhoeffer as Christian martyr. Slane himself acknowledges the complexity of Bonhoeffer's martyrdom when placed alongside other political/religious martyrs such as Thomas Becket, Thomas More, Charles I and John Brown, each of whom died as a consequence of their 'treason', yet each motivated by faith (Slane 2004: 32). It nevertheless seems that in grounding Bonhoeffer's act of conspiracy in a theological framework, Bonhoeffer's decision for conspiracy becomes less problematic for Slane.

More willing to test the connection between the religious and secular aspects of Bonhoeffer's martyrdom is Frits de Lange. In *Saint Bonhoeffer? Dietrich Bonhoeffer and the Paradox of Sainthood*, de Lange agrees that Bonhoeffer does seem to possess all the classical characteristics of a saint: asceticism, strength of soul, purity and charity (De Lange 2002/2003). For de Lange, Bonhoeffer can be seen as a classical saint because he relocates the centre of his self in God and wants to allow his life to be completely and without reservation determined by the influence of this formative vision. But for de Lange, Bonhoeffer is more than a classical saint: he also qualifies as a modern saint due to his worldly and intense orientation towards the *Diesseitige* (secularistic) worldview in his prison letters. Bonhoeffer, argues de Lange, was not hanged as a pastor, but because of his participation in political resistance. Bonhoeffer is 'to be imitated because of his piety, but also because of his courage' (De Lange 2002/2003). The classical saint, on de Lange's account, is motivated by piety; the modern saint also acts on political conviction.

Paul Middleton sees Bonhoeffer's martyrdom as the embodiment of the difficulty that actually exists at the heart of the creation of martyrs. According to Middleton, the martyr narrative is based on conflict or crisis. Middleton argues that Bonhoeffer can be understood as a martyr against the state, modelled on the struggle, witness and deaths of the early Christians. Yet, Bonhoeffer, in a time of crisis, moves beyond the image of the martyrdom of early Christians: If Bonhoeffer can be regarded as a martyr despite his involvement in the (albeit failed) plot to murder, then murder in itself is not a disqualification to the title 'martyr' (Middleton 2011: 21).

Lacey Baldwin Smith likewise draws direct attention to the political aspect of Bonhoeffer's 'martyrdom':

> Born into a wealthy, well-connected, heel-clicking middle-class German family that believed in God's moral law and social order, he became the spiritual head of a den of political assassins, his ethical concepts in tatters in the face of unprecedented evil. (Smith 2008: 445)

It seems that the aims of modern martyrdom are often grounded in this world, rather than the next. The uniquely modern problem is that the religious orientation of martyrdom has become intricately connected with political potency. The ancient idea of martyrdom as witness unto death in service of divine truth has received a modern reorientation in terms of economic, political and social motivating factors.

Modern motivators fuel modern martyrdom: national liberation and resistance to foreign occupation, for example. This is true, for example, of the LTTE, who did not frame their demand for statehood in religious terms. The LTTE claimed to adhere to four 'cardinal principles' submitted to the Sri Lankan government in 1985: the recognition of the Tamils as a distinct nationality; recognition of an identified Tamil homeland; recognition of the inalienable right of self-determination of the Tamil people; and recognition of the right to full citizenship and other fundamental democratic rights of all Tamils (Pape and Feldman 2010). These were distinctly secular concerns—issues of autonomous political identity.

This is not to say that religion does not have a place in the fight for self-determination and statehood. Robert Pape argues that the tap-root of suicide terrorism is usually nationalism, where religion plays an important secondary role as it encourages demonisation, thereby isolating the enemy outside the faith (Pape 2005). In this context, religion can be recruited for political ends. The nation or state interacts with that of a religious community of believers, and martyrdom is awarded for those who make the supreme sacrifice for their fellow citizens, as much as for their fellow believers. However, modern martyrdom retains the focus on the actors, on the individuals who give courageous public testimony in the face of force, torture and execution, and who are rewarded at their death with the epitaph 'martyrdom' by the community (Smith 2008: 345). In this sense, each religion determines its own cause as to what constitutes a martyr: 'It takes two to create a martyrdom; the actor who sacrifices life and the community that offers the title' (Smith 2008: 458).

Clearly, there are a number of troubling questions around the 'martyrdom' and sanctification of Dietrich Bonhoeffer. On the one hand, if Bonhoeffer is admirable because he exhibits qualities praiseworthy of a religious martyr in his decision to conspire, then the new alphabet, to borrow Slane's term again, provides an example of martyrs who are willing to kill in the name of religion for political causes. On the other hand, if the theological and religious justifications for Bonhoeffer's political actions are avoided, and he is judged admirable because he embodied the cultural values that shaped Western civilisation, where civilised sensibilities, education and reason led him to make a rational choice in the face of an irrational regime that usurped power, then he is a political martyr. But then Dhanu might have equal status with Bonhoeffer as an educated, socially integrated and highly capable young woman who sought to defend her own nation from usurping powers. There spans a seemingly unbridgeable gulf between Bonhoeffer as martyr, who died as the result of faithful witness to Christ, and Bonhoeffer as political conspirator, who participated in an assassination attempt.

Drawing together these various threads, it now seems that the modern Christian saint is not unique because of the connection between piety and political conviction, but is unique because political assassination does not disqualify the modern Christian saint from the title of 'martyr'. This means that the modern Christian who is looking for a saint who demonstrates authentic Christian character can see this character displayed in those who would oppose the state through violent means. This of course shows that there is no reason to exclude individuals such as Revered Paul Hill or Michael Bray from the pantheon of twentieth-century Christian saints. Indeed, if the modern Christian saint is unique precisely because they are willing to resort to violence, Hill and Bray may well become quintessential exemplars of modern sainthood. Similarly, de Lange referred to Bonhoeffer as a 'unique Protestant saint' who becomes a unique model for our time by bringing together piety and political conviction.

It is this reference to the Protestant saint that hints at an important difference between classic trajectories of sainthood and the modern secular, or Protestant, version. This is not the place for an in-depth analysis of the differences between classic, or Catholic and Orthodox sainthood, and the more modern Protestant development. However, central to the modern Protestant saint lies a theological and philosophical point of orientation that is radically different from the classic understanding of sainthood. The epitaph of martyrdom was granted to individuals by the religious institution—the church. While stories of martyrdom may have grown amongst individual believers in the church and may contribute to the process of recognition or legitimation, nevertheless the church determined the legitimacy of the title through pronouncing martyrdom and subsequently integrated the individual martyr into the wider narrative of the believing community. Aspects of this authorisation by the institution and integration into a wider believing community can be seen in the development of Bonhoeffer as saint—for example, through his inclusion at Westminster Abbey.

Protestant theology and history have, however, at their nucleus a radically iconoclastic and institutionally destabilising element: the place of the church is always subordinated to the direct relationship between God and the believer. The political and social institutions that organised believers, the church, were removed as the source of authority between God and individuals. Instead, all believers had direct access to the Bible, the sole source of authority, which was, to a large extent, self-interpreting for each believer (Bruce 1990: 45).

What are the consequences of this for the various appropriations of Bonhoeffer? If the relationship between the Protestant and the church is secondary to the relationship between the Protestant and God, or Christ, the Protestant who centres herself in God and is shaped by this formative vision of her identity may find herself in conflict with the ethical expectations of both the wider society and/or the church. Likewise, the individual who is inspired by the Protestant saint does not rely on interpretive authorities such as the church or Christian scholarship to mediate her unique relationship to the Protestant saint. Thus, while various Protestant denominations have made of Bonhoeffer a Christian martyr, Bonhoeffer as a Protestant saint does not require the mediation of church tradition, but inspires believers through a sense of mystical union.

The Christian disciple exists in her own unique relationship to this Protestant saint. The consequences of this in the most recent market of Bonhoeffer admirers results in an astounding new form of praise for Bonhoeffer, where individuals such as Hill and Bray represent only the extreme form. A mystical relationship between the German theologian, pastor and political conspirator, and every individual evangelical American who is inspired by the heady mix of piety and patriotism is made possible. As will become clear in the next chapter, it is the adoption of Bonhoeffer as an evangelical American that has the potential to create a highly politically potent Protestant saint.

NOTES

1. See for example—https://www.trinitystores.com/?detail=390&artist=11 accessed 04/03/2010.
2. The Bonhoeffer/Dhanu comparison was first raised in an unpublished paper by Richard Gillingham (MA), who identified several areas of similarity between Bonhoeffer and his place in the Abwehr anti-Hitler conspiracy, and Dhanu and the LTTE (2007).

REFERENCES

Atwell, Robert. 2004. *Celebrating the Saints: Daily Spiritual Readings to Accompany the Calendars of the Church of England the Church of Ireland the Scottish Episcopal Church and the Church in Wales.* Norwich, Norfolk: The Canterbury Press Norwich.

Berrigan, Daniel. 1972. *America Is Hard to Find.* Garden City, NY: Double Day.

Bloom, Linda. 2008. United Methodists give Bonhoeffer martyr status. United Methodist News Press Release. http://archives.gcah.org/handle/10516/3563. Accessed 19 December 2018.

Bruce, Steve. 1990. *A House Divided: Protestantism, Schism, and Secularization.* London and New York: Routledge.

De Lange, Frits. 2002/2003. Saint Bonhoeffer? Dietrich Bonhoeffer and the Paradox of Sainthood. *Zeitschrift für dialektische Theologie* 37: 245–269.

Gillingham, Richard. 2007. The Problem of Dietrich Bonhoeffer, Or, The Martyr and the Suicide Bomber. http://subrationedei.files.wordpress.com/2007/02/themartyrandthesuicidebomber.pdf. Accessed 22 July 2009.

Haynes, Stephen R. 2004. *The Bonhoeffer Phenomenon—Portraits of a Protestant Saint.* Minneapolis: Fortress Press.

Hopgood, Stephen. 2005. Tamil Tigers—1987–2002. In *Making Sense of Suicide Missions,* ed. Diego Gambetta, 43–76. Oxford: Oxford University Press.

Juergensmeyer, Mark. 2000. *Terror in the Mind of God: The Global Rise of Religious Violence.* Berkeley: University of California Press.

Middleton, Paul. 2011. *Martyrdom: A Guide for the Perplexed.* London and New York: Continuum.

Nelson, Burton. 1999. The Life of Dietrich Bonhoeffer. In *The Cambridge Companion to Dietrich Bonhoeffer,* ed. John W. De Gruchy, 22–49. Cambridge and New York: Cambridge University Press.

Pape, Robert A. 2005. *Dying to Win: The Strategic Logic of Suicide Terrorism.* New York: Random House.

Pape, Robert A., and James K. Feldman. 2010. *Cutting the Fuse: The Explosion of Global Suicide Terrorism and How to Stop It.* Chicago: The University of Chicago Press.

Pavone, Joe. 2006. Men of Courage: Dietrich Bonhoeffer and Paul Hill Prolife America. http://lifediscussions.org/view/?id=2392. Accessed 19 December 2018.

Prabhakaran, Velupillai. 1993. Maha Veerar Naal Address 1993 Heroes Day.

President Bush Thanks Germany for Support Against Terror. 2002. Office of the Press Secretary. http://georgewbush-whitehouse.archives.gov/news/releases/2002/05/20020523-2.html. Accessed 13 June 2012.

Roberts, David. 2010. Killing Rajiv Ghandi: Dhanu's Sacrificial Metaphorsosis in Death. *South Asian History and Culture* 1 (1): 25–41.

Rudd, Kevin. 2006. Faith in Politics. *The Monthly—Australian Politics, Society & Culture* 17: 22–30.

Slane, Graig J. 2004. *Bonhoeffer as Martyr: Social Responsibility and Modern Christian Commitment.* Grand Rapids: Brazos Press.

Smith, Lacey Baldwin. 2008. Can Martyrdom Survive Secularization? *Social Research* 75 (2): 435–460.

Weiss, Gordon. 2011. *The Cage: The Fight for Sri Lanka & the Last Days of the Tamil Tigers.* London: Bodley Head.

CHAPTER 2

Bonhoeffer: All American Hero?

From the moment Bishop Bell brought Bonhoeffer to the attention of the English-speaking world, Bonhoeffer's life and writings have been interpreted through the lens of his death and the subsequent epitaph of martyrdom. However, it is not just the death itself that is significant, it is the magnitude of the enemy that has made Bonhoeffer a heroic martyr. Stephen Haynes, in *The Bonhoeffer Phenomenon: Portraits of a Protestant Saint* (2004), describes a number of Bonhoeffer images and argues that one of the most commanding is the 'universal Bonhoeffer' who is the opponent of Nazism. According to Haynes, Bonhoeffer is seen as a mythic warrior because he stands against Nazism. As such, the symbolic Bonhoeffer speaks the language of sacrifice, morality, spirituality and mature faith. Bonhoeffer's participation in a violent coup against Hitler is incorporated into the story of the last good man in 'mortal conflict with the epitome of human evil' (Haynes 2004: 94). As such, Bonhoeffer's actions as a conspirator come to be seen not only as permissible, but uncritically accepted as righteous and justified because of the magnitude of the enemy.

This chapter considers the significance of the image of Bonhoeffer as a mythic warrior who stands against evil in light of Bonhoeffer's Anglo-American readership that emerged in the 1980s. Up until this time, Bonhoeffer had been the inspiration and motivation for progressive liberals, so-called death of God theologians and liberation theologians, who all found inspiration in his writings and actions as pacifist protestors. But in the 1980s, Bonhoeffer gained a new audience, one

© The Author(s) 2019
P. Brown, *Bonhoeffer*,
https://doi.org/10.1007/978-3-030-05698-8_2

more enamoured with his subversive actions as a double agent in the *Abwehr*, and less inclined to explore the theological intricacies and complexities of Bonhoeffer's writings. Bonhoeffer's new readership was the sizeable American evangelical population, which in the 1980s began to leave the pews of the church, in order to exercise its political voice in the public sphere of politics and policies. Bonhoeffer proved amenable to this new audience in ways that would disturb the carefully guarded legacy as bequeathed by Bonhoeffer's friend and biographer, Eberhard Bethge, and the mainstream and liberal Bonhoeffer scholarship that had grown over time. In particular, Bonhoeffer's involvement in the plot to kill Hitler was now seen as an act of courage in the face of the great evil of the Nazi regime and as an example of the faithful disciple who is obedient to Christ, even in her willingness to commit violence. The Bonhoeffer image that emerges serves two functions. First, he appears as a political and decisive figure who endorses evangelical values of love of family, God and country, and the American ideal of a rugged individualism, and does not hesitate to act decisively in a situation of last resort. Second, what further emerges amongst more radical Bonhoeffer aficionados is an image of the Christian disciple at war with the world, in which the task is to claim the world as a legitimate sphere of obedience to the sovereignty of Christ.

Bonhoeffer as Opponent of Nazism: The Pro-life Movement

Both radical and moderate elements of the pro-life movement in 1980s and 1990s readily saw a parallel between the Nazi policy of genocide and the killing of babies in wombs, as evidenced by Randall Terry, founder of the pro-life protest group Operation Rescue, whose first book, *Operation Rescue*, carried the slogan 'You can stop the abortion holocaust in America!' (Kaplan 1995: 142). For Michael Bray, who served 46 months in prison for destroying seven abortion facilities in the mid-1980s, the Nazi analogy was so powerful that he believed Christianity gave him the right to use force to defend innocent 'unborn children', even if it involved 'destroying the facilities that they are regularly killed in, or taking the life of one who is murdering them' (Bray in interview with Juergensmeyer 2000: 23). The image of Bonhoeffer as the heroic and courageous opponent to Nazism was eagerly taken up in this context. To support the anti-abortion cause while he was imprisoned for setting fire to two abortion clinics and attempting to blow up a third, John Brockhoeft wrote and published the Brockhoeft Report. In one issue, Brockhoeft invokes Bonhoeffer in defence of Mike Griffin, who in 1993 killed Dr. David Gunn, the first act of lethal force in the anti-abortion movement. Brockhoeft rationalises the comparison as follows: 'abortionist David Gunn's victims were exactly as human as were Hitler's', both Bonhoeffer and Griffin 'decided to fight, literally fight, for the lives of the innocent people' and that Griffin's approach was exactly the same as Bonhoeffer's in his use of lethal force against the killer. Brockhoeft concludes that therefore 'Mike Griffin is exactly the Dietrich Bonhoeffer figure for our generation' (Brockhoeft, n.d.-a).

American pro-life protestors, arrested and prosecuted during the mid to late 1980s at the height of the anti-abortion protest movement, not only turned to Bonhoeffer for justification of their action, but for spiritual support. In one particular issue, Brockhoeft published a fictional story written by a friend, Joe Bartlett, in which Brockhoeft is the protagonist who meets Bonhoeffer with the aid of a time machine (Brockhoeft, n.d.-b). The story is set in the USA, with Bonhoeffer's return to Europe and war imminent. Bonhoeffer and Brockhoeft develop a deep 'spiritual bond', a bond that 'transcends time' when 'the two flew together in an embrace'. In the story, Bonhoeffer's life and death is framed in a wider narrative of the unfolding of a divine plan, as Brockhoeft is told by a third person warned not to interfere with the course of history.

> It might be within your power to save Bonhoeffer's life, but is that what we would actually want? The Lord our God has always been ultimately in control! Bonhoeffer was executed before you were born. The Lord could have kept him from it. Bonhoeffer was willing to die defending others. He volunteered to die! He became more powerful in death than in life! Had he survived the war, Christianity and the world may have forgotten him. Do not rob him of his voluntary and glorious sacrifice! Do not rob us of the legacy he handed down to us! (Brockhoeft, n.d.-b)

Bonhoeffer played the part assigned to him by God and in so doing he became more powerful in his death than in life, what Brockhoeft calls a 'voluntary and glorious sacrifice'. It is his death in defending others that becomes an example for the oppressed American husbands and wives imprisoned as a result of their role in defending America's purported 'unborn children'. Pro-lifers who hear about the encounter in the story are in awe; Bonhoeffer appears to have foreknowledge of Brockhoeft; Bonhoeffer shows no fear when his own death is revealed to him, instead praising God because he still has 'almost six years to work!'; he accepts his death 'in peace of spirit'; Bonhoeffer is humble and does not see himself as 'a martyred saint', but only 'as an ordinary man'; he prays directly to Jesus; and he affirms the evangelical belief in 'the whole Bible to be the [true] word of God' (Brockhoeft, n.d.-b). All this serves to create an image of a man who is on the side of the anti-abortion protestors. Like them, he is courageous and faithful, and importantly, on the side of the righteous.

MYSTICAL UNION

The deep identification between the protestors and the unborn, who are seen as the victims of evil, and Bonhoeffer as a hero who opposed evil, suggests a strong symbolic identification that Jeffrey Kaplan refers to as a 'mystical sense of unity' (Kaplan 1995: 146). Kaplan uses this term in reference to the symbolic identification between the protestors and the unborn, where 'some of the imprisoned rescuers were convinced that they had heard the cries of unborn babies from within the walls of the abortion clinic' (Kaplan 1995: 146–147). The belief was that each baby saved was a miracle, and a confirmation of God's blessing on the rescuers. According to Kaplan, it was this identification with the babies that led Brockhoeft to become one of the early clinic bombers (Kaplan 1995: 147). This sense of mystical unity is also seen in the movement's wider appropriation of Bonhoeffer.

This sense of mystical identification was not confined to the radical elements of the anti-abortion movement—those willing to be arrested and prosecuted. It also extended to the broader pro-life movement. Charles Colson, evangelical Christian leader, cultural commentator and special counsel for former President Richard Nixon, drew a direct link between the establishment of the Confessing Church under Niemöller and Bonhoeffer, and the American evangelical church, which Colsen argued ought to support pro-life protestors who sought to overturn a 1994 ruling that prevented them from demonstrating in certain places and distances outside clinics that performed abortions.[1] The choice for Christians was clear, argued Colson: either they will turn a 'blind eye to America's moral decline [...] or they will withdraw from mainstream society' (Colson 1996: 64). Unless American Christians stood up with the same courage as that shown by the Confessing Church (and Bonhoeffer), 'American civil religion' will become a loved memory (Colson 1996).

Influential psychologist and evangelical leader Dr. James Dobson echoed Colson's stance when he called for pro-lifers to stand firm, to not remain silent while 'tiny brains were being sucked from the heads of viable babies' (1999: 56). This created a more direct link between Bonhoeffer's conspiracy involvement and the challenge facing the pro-life movement: 'Since when did being outnumbered and underpowered justify silence in response to evil? Dietrich Bonhoeffer, a Lutheran pastor and theologian, stood against the Nazi regime and its oppression of the Jews, for which he paid with his life' (Dobson 1999: 57). George Grant, a prolific evangelical writer and Presbyterian Church of America pastor, drew similar connections between Bonhoeffer's conspiracy involvement and the pro-life movement, but actually claimed to find support for this in Bonhoeffer's own writing. In *Third Time Around: A History of the Prolife Movement*, Grant argued that Bonhoeffer opposed the Nazi eugenic programme on the basis of the regime's active promotion of abortion. In Grant's account, Bonhoeffer was 'banned from preaching and teaching and was thus forced to continue his discipling and prolife ministries covertly. In 1944, he was implicated in a conspiracy that had been linked to the German resistance ...' (1991: 145). The reader gets the impression that it was his opposition to abortion, rather than National Socialism, that brought Bonhoeffer to the attention of the authorities, and eventually led him to conspiracy and death.

Neither Colson, Dobson nor Grant advocated direct violence against abortion clinics or doctors who perform abortions. Yet, each of these authors created links between Bonhoeffer's resistance to Nazism and the pro-life movement's resistance to what they call the 'Holocaust sweeping America'. Each of these authors also approved of Bonhoeffer's conspiracy involvement and suggested, at least indirectly, that his decision to participate in a violent overthrow was justified by the situation in which he found himself. Yet the radical elements of the pro-life movement, including Paul Hill, Michael Bray and John Brockhoeft, were more than willing to connect Bonhoeffer's conspiracy involvement with their own claims and acts of violence against American institutions and citizens.

It may seem a stretch to suggest there is a connection between the moderate pro-life supporters, who tend to speak on behalf of mainstream evangelicals on the issue of abortion, and those who advocate for violent protest. Yet, the decision to act violently as Christians against other American citizens is not without explanation. Kaplan has identified two significant factors that led to the willingness to use violence amongst anti-abortion protesters. These were an apocalyptic worldview and the image of war. The rescue movement held an apocalyptic view that did not allow of any compromise with America's 'death culture'—the language is that of a battle between good and evil, between God's people and Satan's 'murderous henchmen', the abortionists (Kaplan 1995: 152). The image of war was also invoked, with the servants and collaborators of abortion culture on one side, and the people of God on the other (Kaplan 1995: 135, 144). Kaplan argues that it was in part the apocalyptic millenarian worldview and imagery of war that led to a new level of violence. This is evident in both Brockhoeft and Hill. Brockhoeft saw abortion as a war crime and developed a position of 'absolutism', which grew from Brockhoeft's identification with 'the unborn children', a consequence of which was that every person, every act was judged with reference to the abortion issue (Kaplan 1995: 152). Brockhoeft's absolutism was at once pragmatic and willing to justify 'homicide intended solely for self defence and the defence of family members or neighbours from imminent, deadly peril' (Kaplan 1995: 151). His absolutism was also deeply informed by an apocalyptic view that interpreted all events in terms of an 'Abortion War' between Christians and Satan. This view led to the use of violence in the anti-abortion movement (Brockhoeft cited in Kaplan 1995: 152).

Similar to Brockhoeft, Paul Hill relied on a blend of pragmatism and apocalyptic imagery. His Defensive Action statement issued after Michael Griffin killed David Gunn, declared that 'whatever force is legitimate to defend the life of the born child is legitimate to defend the life of an unborn child' (Hill cited in Kaplan 1995: 154). Then, in a 1994 essay, Hill framed the actions of anti-abortionists in more apocalyptic terms: 'Though sin has fanned God's righteous anger to a searing blaze, the shedding of guilty blood has cooled the flame and saved the people from destruction' (Hill cited in Kaplan 1995: 155). The implication is that individuals like Griffin are not only justified because they have shed 'guilty blood' in defending innocent lives, they are part of a bigger battle in which they have saved America from the wrath of God.

For the pro-life protestors, the images of apocalypse and war led to a heightened sense of crisis that required a form of action generally believed forbidden for Christians. Thus, the narrative of war, fuelled by an apocalyptic mindset, led to a sense of crisis in this radicalised group in which following Christ can require killing. Kaplan points to Dietrich Bonhoeffer as 'the undisputed model for emulation of the Defensive Action wing of the rescue movement' (Kaplan 1995: 143). Bonhoeffer's opposition to Nazism is a particularly important narrative for radical pro-lifers as it enabled them to endure suffering at the hands of the state and to justify their violent action in terms of Bonhoeffer's own action against the Nazi state. As shown, it was the language and imagery of apocalypse and war that fuelled an increasing inclination towards violent action, and here too Bonhoeffer served as a role model. While not all in the pro-life movement supported the use of force, middle-of-the-road pro-life groups also drew direct comparisons between the Second World War Holocaust and the 'abortion epidemic' sweeping America; moderate pro-lifers were equally willing to create connections with Bonhoeffer that were more symbolic than real.

BONHOEFFER AS OPPONENT OF NAZISM: MAINSTREAM EVANGELICALISM

Having looked in detail at the evangelical pro-life appropriation of Bonhoeffer, both the violent and more moderate groups, it is time now to turn to the wider evangelical readership. What is their relationship to Bonhoeffer? Does the image of Bonhoeffer as opponent of Nazism still apply? And how do mainstream evangelicals[2] understand their connection to Bonhoeffer? Stephen Haynes has thoroughly chronicled Bonhoeffer's conservative reception and considers Bonhoeffer's reputation amongst conservative Christians as the clearest marker of his unique status in the world of modern theology (2004: 68). The broad and popular evangelical readership of Bonhoeffer arguably began in 1991, when *Christian History*, then published by the flagship evangelical periodical *Christianity Today*, dedicated an entire issue to Bonhoeffer, with highly respected and established Bonhoeffer scholars contributing articles.[3] In the years that followed, Bonhoeffer appeared in various forms of inspirational literature marketed to evangelicals. These included articles of discussion in popular magazines, biographies, a radio theatre biography and Christian fiction.[4] Haynes argues that there are a number of things that evangelicals admire about Bonhoeffer. These include family background, values found in 'familiar-sounding phraseology', 'Bonhoeffer's presumed philosemitism', an 'ambivalence towards religious institutions' and, most importantly, 'evangelicals are heartened by Bonhoeffer's attention to familiar Christian practices – especially Bible reading, prayer, devotion to Christ, obedience, discipleship, and life in community' (Haynes 2004: 75–76).

Evangelicals believe they find many of these important practices supported by Bonhoeffer in his text, *Discipleship*, voted by evangelicals as one of the ten 'best devotional books of all time' in a 2007 issue of the periodical *Christian Reader* (Haynes 2004: 77). *Discipleship* certainly discusses devotion to Christ, obedience and discipleship, as I will show in later chapters, but not necessarily in the 'familiar Christian way' that evangelicals would appreciate. Instead of dealing with more complex scholarship matters, evangelicals read *Discipleship* as a devotional text, rather than a scholarly work, seeking to derive from it encouraging spiritual wisdom. Indeed, this tendency to mine Bonhoeffer for inspiration seems to be prevalent amongst evangelical authors, often at the cost of accuracy.

Mark Devine, in his book, *Bonhoeffer Speaks Today: Following Jesus at All Costs* (2005), praises Bonhoeffer's apparent disciplined reading of the Scriptures and his obedience to the will of God.

> Bonhoeffer's quest for the will of God drove him to the Bible and to prayer. Because Bonhoeffer expected the Bible to answer all crucial questions for the Christian and the church, he embraced a daily discipline of Bible study and meditation on the Word of God. (Devine 2005: 46)

It does not seem to matter to Devine, who is an associate professor at the Southern evangelical institution Beeson Divinity School, that he is contradicted by Bonhoeffer himself. The latter, over a period of three years, wrote to his friend Eberhard Bethge various statements such as—'Sometimes there are weeks in which I read very little of the Bible'.[5] This lack of accuracy can also be seen in Eric Metaxas' popular Bonhoeffer biography, *Bonhoeffer: Pastor, Martyr, Prophet, Spy* (2010).[6] Metaxas saw Bonhoeffer as 'more like a theologically conservative evangelical than anything else' (cited in Hansen 2010). As with Devine's portrait, the Bonhoeffer who appears in Metaxas' biography demonstrated key evangelical values; he 'maintained the daily discipline of scriptural

meditation and prayer' even throughout prison; 'once he got his Bible
back he read it for hours a day' (Metaxas 2010: 438). As with many
evangelical authors, Metaxas concentrates on the events of Bonhoeffer's
life, rather than the writings. His biography of Bonhoeffer reads like a
Hollywood action blockbuster. Chapter headings such as 'The Church
Battle Heats Up', 'Mars Ascending' and 'The Great Decision' create a spectacular Bonhoeffer narrative that far surpasses Eberhard
Betghe's earlier biographical efforts, or Ferdinand Schlingensiepen's
more recent biography *Dietrich Bonhoeffer 1906–1945: Martyr, Thinker,
Man of Resistance* (2010). However, instead of accurately describing
Bonhoeffer's own context, critics argue that Metaxas' biography is 'lit-
tered with historical mistakes' and demonstrates a serious 'lack of theological and philosophical understanding' (Weikart 2011: 73–74).[7]
Devine also demonstrates this lack of historical, theological and philosophical understanding. Indeed, he specifically claims he is not interested in Bonhoeffer's theology in its own historical context but wants
'to exploit aspects of Bonhoeffer's life and work that speak to concerns
relevant to evangelical Christians' (Devine 2005: 1).

Lack of accuracy and historical understanding does not seem to dis-
suade evangelical interpretations of Bonhoeffer's life and thought. More
comfortable with lifting encouraging slogans from his life and writings,
evangelical readers are less concerned with the finer theological details
of Bonhoeffer's complex writings. Indeed, the theological or historical context of Bonhoeffer's writings tends to be overlooked. Yet, as I
showed earlier, this propensity to read Bonhoeffer for inspiration is also
part of the more radicalised elements of the pro-life movement. Both
mainstream evangelical readers and radical pro-lifers show a tendency to
read Bonhoeffer for immediate spiritual edification rather than education, or sustained growth in spiritual knowledge. This is not entirely sur-
prising. As Haynes points out, for many evangelicals there is a dichotomy
between matters of the head and matters of the heart, between scholarly
work and the life of faith and spirituality (Haynes 2004: 79).

For evangelicals, commitment to Christ and the Bible must come
first and inform all aspects of life, including education and political
organisation. This commitment to Christ as ordering all other aspects
of life is clearly seen in Devine, who stresses the centrality of Christ in
Bonhoeffer's life. 'For Bonhoeffer, in Jesus Christ and in him alone we
belong to one another, not in Gandhi, or Buddha, or anyone else, just
Jesus Christ and him alone' (2005: 86–87). The Christ of the evangelical

Bonhoeffer demands obedience and loyalty against competing gods. Yet Christ also brings the freedom to live 'within the world as his witnesses', a freedom that extends to the church for it too must 'claim the world as the legitimate sphere for obedience to its Lord, the Lord of this world, Jesus Christ' (Devine 2005: 115–116). The lordship of Christ, according to Devine's reading of Bonhoeffer, leads to a call for the disciple to work within the world to actively bring the world to Christ. Devine views Bonhoeffer's 'willingness to die in obedience to the command of his Lord' as a salutary lesson for contemporary American evangelicals who have become enamoured by 'secularization, urbanization, and technological innovation' that is hostile to community building of any kind (2005: 100, 123). Certainly, this prophetic warning against the disintegrative effect of modernity on human forms of community is laudable; it places Devine in a tradition of theologians and philosophers who provide a critique on the excesses of modernity. However, Devine's use of Bonhoeffer is not limited to a prophetic critique of modernity. He connects Bonhoeffer's martyrdom for Christ with a more concrete, pressing political problem of the USA post-September 11: that of dealing with terrorism.

When faced with the 'human atrocities' caused by Saddam Hussein and Al Qaida, Devine suggests that evangelical Americans can draw on Bonhoeffer's legacy for courage and inspiration: 'What does the legacy of Bonhoeffer's life and work have to say in the face of the targeting of innocents, the maintenance of rape rooms, torture chambers, and mass graves?' (Devine 2005: 139). Similar to the pro-life movement's symbolic connection between Nazi Germany and the 'abortion holocaust' in America, Devine suggests an analogy between Hitler's Nazi regime and Saddam Hussein and Al Qaida. The criterion of 'last resort' introduced by Devine directly links Hitler's assassination attempts and the 'war on terror and Saddam Hussein' (2005: 138).

Devine asks American evangelicals to consider whether similar action might be required by them in a situation of last resort:

> Without taking a dogmatic position, perhaps we can say that Bonhoeffer fairly consistently maintained a strong Christian aversion to the use of violence, accepting its inevitability only as a last resort. This still leaves aside the question of the criteria by which believers recognise whether last resort conditions are met. What we can say with real confidence is that

Bonhoeffer found retreat from the concrete problems of human kind on supposed Christian or theological grounds intolerable. (2005: 138)

While himself certainly not advocating political violence, Devine believes Bonhoeffer provides a salutary example of how Christians who refuse to 'retreat from the concrete problems of human kind' might overcome their 'strong Christian aversion' to the use of violence. Devine believes that there are times when Christians must get their hands dirty, even if it means that the Christian 'sins' or engages in violence, on 'Christian or theological grounds'. He continues:

> Better to sin boldly and let grace abound (Luther) than to welcome and enjoy the benefits of Hitler's assassination by others while smugly adoring and displaying one's own ostensibly clean hands! Bonhoeffer's pacifism accepted agonising participation in violence, asking for forgiveness all along the way but refusing to stand by and let non-believers do the dirty work. (2005: 138)

The implication for evangelical readers is that, while other Christians may hide behind their theology, true Christians refuse to 'let nonbelievers do the dirty work' and accept 'agonizing participation in violence'. That is, Christians should be willing to become politically dirty, alongside the secular world, but should do so in a way that causes the individual believer deep pain and suffering, leading to a feeling of deep guilt and driving the believers to their knees, begging for forgiveness.

The metaphor of dirty hands is not unique to Devine. It is a metaphor that has also been used by mainstream Bonhoeffer scholars. Larry Rasmussen argues that Bonhoeffer shows that '[w]hile the man of private virtue refuses to dirty his hands in the public arena, injustice will roll on' (2005: 66). Using a similar metaphor, Eberhard Bethge argued that Bonhoeffer decided that it was 'no longer a matter of keeping one's reputation clean as a Christian, a pastor and an individual, but of sacrificing everything, even one's reputation as a Christian' (Bethge 1975: 123). The willingness to become unclean or guilty was even used by Randall Terry who declared to his pro-life members that 'we will have to leave the comfort and safety of our church pews. We are going to have to get our hands dirty and be active in society' (cited in Ginsburg 1993: 574). The metaphor of dirty hands or guilty conscience is thus a recurring theme amongst both scholars defending Bonhoeffer and other Christian believers contemplating forms of political action that do not sit comfortably with their Christian values.

However, not all evangelicals agonise over the use of force as a last resort. As already shown in the previous chapter, former US President, George W. Bush believed Bonhoeffer to be the greatest German of the twentieth century. Bush readily created a link between Bonhoeffer's decision for conspiracy against an evil regime and America's 'war on terror' on at least two occasions. In a 2002 address to the German *Bundestag*, President Bush invoked a hero who would unite two nations against a new force of evil. Bonhoeffer

> gave witness to the Gospel of life, and paid the cost of his discipleship [...]
> 'I believe,' said Bonhoeffer, 'that God can and wants to create good out of everything, even evil'... In America, very recently, we have also seen the horror of evil and the power of good. (2002)[8]

For Bush, Bonhoeffer could serve as a mediator to cement the friendship of Germany and America, friends who, together, build 'that house of freedom for our time and for all time' (2002). Two years later, in a university address, Bush linked the courage of Bonhoeffer, 'a solitary soul, condemned and stripped of all power', with the Abu Graib prison scandal where 'the cruelty of a few has brought discredit to their uniform and embarrassment to our country' (2004). Bush declared that Abu Graib shows that the choices of individual men and women have a great impact. Bonhoeffer demonstrates a form of life that 'holds the possibility of serving God ... in service' to others (2004). By inference, those individuals involved in Abu Graib demonstrated the wrong kind of individual power. Jeffrey Pugh argues that Bush's admiration of the solitary Bonhoeffer was typical of a wider trend that appropriated Bonhoeffer in terms of a last resort, an appeal that extended beyond the Iraq war into the wider context of the war on terror. Bonhoeffer in this context is used to justify a certain kind of action that vindicates itself by overthrowing and removing tyrants (Pugh 2009: 3–4).

Yet, in using Bonhoeffer's involvement in conspiracy as a model for a war on terror, Bush goes further than Devine. For while Devine claims Christians must accept *agonized* participation asking for forgiveness, Bush speaks to all Americans. And for Bush, the decision to declare war on terror is *not* about agonised participation and a willingness to become guilty, but an example of the power of good. That is, America is judged righteous in its decision to embark on this war, and therefore has no need to ask for forgiveness. This is a disturbing use of Bonhoeffer in support of a political agenda that seemed to be fuelled by national pride rather than agonised participation by Christians willing to dirty their hands. Yet, Devine's own claim that Bonhoeffer accepted the need for political violence as inevitable and a last resort dovetails comfortably with more secular political language of last resort as justification to engage in a war on terror. Thus, there is little critical space between Devine's call for Christians to consider supporting the war on terror and Bush's own call to Germany to stand alongside America.

Finally, in examining the appropriation of Bonhoeffer by American evangelicals, some mention must be made of more recent uses of Bonhoeffer as part of the 'culture-wars' between the politically conservative right and the progressive left that have taken place in the US over the last ten years and are echoed across the globe. In this context, the term that most frequently appears is that of a 'Bonhoeffer moment' in divisive social issues such as same-sex marriage[9] and conversion therapy (Broyles 2018). Most memorable was Metaxas' call to Christians that they must vote for Trump (Metaxas 2016).[10] It is important to note that the recent turn to the 'Bonhoeffer moment' is not explicitly linked to a call for violent resistance against the state. In this way, it is unlike either the radical pro-life movement of the 1980s and 1990s, or the 'last resort' violence in the post 9/11 context of the war on terror. However, against the backdrop of the current political divide between the left and the right, evangelicals who vocally support Trump may inadvertently also support Trump's secular messianism and a turn to violent rhetoric in the service of a nationalism now decoupled from its conservative religious origins (Gorski 2017; Morris 2017). I will return to this in the final chapter of the book. Suffice it to say that invoking Bonhoeffer to support not only the concerns of white nationalist Christians, but also secular messianic political projects, should be of deep concern to Bonhoeffer scholars, and Bonhoeffer readers more generally.

Bonhoeffer as 'Church Father' for Evangelicals

One further figure is worth mentioning at this point. In the early 1990s, a somewhat peculiar book emerged on the evangelical market. The book itself was intended to confirm that Bonhoeffer was 'very close in spirit to the evangelicals' for whom he would be 'a church father in the future' (Huntemann 1993: 12). So argued Georg Huntemann, professor of Protestant theology in Louvain Belgium and the Free Protestant Academy of Theology at Basel, in *Der Andere Bonhoeffer* (1989), translated and published four years later as *The Other Bonhoeffer*. Until Huntemann's book, Bonhoeffer's more conservative views, seen in his identity as an aristocrat from the Prussian tradition and his patriarchal views on marriage and ethics, lay relatively dormant. Now a new Bonhoeffer emerged. This Bonhoeffer was not a 'church father of the progressives, the feminists, or the emancipators' but a patriarch and 'an ethicist of order who held conservative values' (Huntemann 1993: 87, 235). These conservative values were reflected in the fact that Bonhoeffer was 'a man of order and inner discipline' who 'believed in the primacy of the family before the state' (Huntemann 1993: 26, 25). As with many evangelicals, Huntemann believed Bonhoeffer's struggle against National Socialism could be readily carried over to the social and political world of the late 1980s, where many showed a willingness to carry on the work of the 'anti-Christian elements of the Nazi period', in particular the 'progressive Left-wing scene' (1993: 11). Strangely echoing the former Australian Prime Minister Kevin Rudd's praise of Bonhoeffer as exemplifying a 'muscular Christianity', Huntemann argued 'Bonhoeffer's piety was manly, bracing, and rugged in every way', and he was not afraid to unflinchingly consider 'the violent removal of Hitler' (1993: 26, 286). As well as emphasising the masculinity and heroism of Bonhoeffer, Huntemann advocated for a strong sovereign in Christ, who should not be mistaken for the 'feminized God who is the victim of the powerful, healthy and the strong' but is 'the Master of order and law' who also condemns and judges (1993: 163, 167). Huntemann argues that Christ commands Bonhoeffer with an order that is 'clear, definite and concrete to the last detail' and 'comes from above' (1993: 233, 234). This command counters the 'permissive, hedonistic, purely emotionally oriented' morality of this world (Huntemann 1993: 338). It seems to be intended to endorse the kind of social and family values favoured by many evangelicals. But Huntemann does more than this, for he links Christ as the Master of order and law to an apocalyptic vision: Christ 'at his second coming at the end of time will ride the white horse and tread the winepress of wrath' (1993: 197). It this apocalyptic imagery combined with a strong claim to sovereignty that creates a powerful combination of sovereign commander and obedient disciple who is 'responsible not to a law, but to the Lord who gives the command' (Huntemann 1993: 239). Huntemann's Bonhoeffer does not seem to agonise over his participation in the coup d'état. His Bonhoeffer appears as a hero who seems to overthrow evil in a herculean effort, aided by a powerful divine being and secure in his confidence that he acts on behalf of righteousness.

At the time of the release of the book, scholars tended to see Huntemann as 'gerrymandering' with Bonhoeffer's prison writings, the latter forming the basis of Huntemann's hermeneutic efforts (Marty 2011: 170). But Huntemann's concept of 'Christ-mysticism', a term he borrowed from Albert Schweitzer, was particularly noted as one way in which Huntemann attempted to 'rescue Bonhoeffer for those in Evangelical circles who had been frighted away by the radicals', which at the time referred to the various Marxist or Christian-atheist interpretation that were in vogue (Marty 2011: 170, 174).[11] I would suggest that it is the combination of conservative values and Christ-mysticism that links Huntemann's interpretation of Bonhoeffer to favourite evangelical themes and concepts, and the apocalyptic imagery favoured by both radical pro-lifers and more mainstream evangelicals. In Huntemann's account, these merge with a powerful image of Christ as a sovereign commander who stands against the weakened morality of a secular, humanist age.

Just as Huntemann had his critics, so Bonhoeffer scholars have spoken out against what they suggest are inaccurate and extreme interpretations of Bonhoeffer by radical pro-lifers. Clifford Green explicitly rejects the appropriation of Bonhoeffer by violent anti-abortion protestors. Unlike Paul Hill, declares Green, Bonhoeffer was not an individual acting on a self-appointed mission, he was part of a resistance group including top military officers, lawyers and government officials who all shared the judgement that Hitler's regime must be overthrown, a judgement shared by a significant part of the international community. None of these criteria, concludes Green, apply to Paul Hill (Green 2003, 2005: 42).[12] Scholars have likewise rejected aspects of the mainstream evangelical dissemination of Bonhoeffer, particularly what they see as Metaxas' attempt to turn Bonhoeffer into an American evangelical (Marty 2011: 163).[13] In the recent culture wars, scholars were vocal in their critique of Metaxas' use of Bonhoeffer in his own political activism (Haynes 2017; Marsh 2016).

Finally, in this overview of the political uses of Bonhoeffer, it should be noted that American evangelicals are not the first to link Bonhoeffer to political protests. In the 1970s, Protestant liberation theologians in South America were encouraged in their reading of Bonhoeffer to leave their ecclesiastical enclaves and to take action in the cultural, economic, political and trade union life of their countries (Kelly and Nelson 2003). In the 1980s, British theologian and author Keith Clements saw Bonhoeffer as an example to Christians who should counter the resurgence of British nationalism connected with the Falklands war (Clements 1986). Respected and long-standing Bonhoeffer scholar, John de Gruchy pointed to Bonhoeffer as having more influence on South African Protestant theologians in their fight against apartheid than any other twentieth-century European theologian (1997). In these cases, Bonhoeffer was seen as an example of civil disobedience, and most found inspiration in his exposition of the Sermon on the Mount, in *Discipleship*.[14] Yet something new has emerged with the American evangelical reception of Bonhoeffer. This is not only their explicit admiration of Bonhoeffer's conspiracy involvement. It is the fact that they link this to what Colson calls a 'civil religion' that is also the foundation of a 'two-hundred year tradition of religious patriotism' (Colson 1996: 64). Bonhoeffer is no longer invoked as a critic of nationalism, but has come to be seen as an advocate for religious patriotism. The latter is grounded in mystical identification and apocalyptic visions and valorises an uncompromising stance against perceived cultural immorality, in which violence (whether understood as agonising or heroic action) is seen as a legitimate expression of Christian faith and discipleship.

As explored in this chapter, both mainstream evangelical readers and radical pro-lifers show a tendency to read Bonhoeffer for immediate spiritual edification. The evangelical Bonhoeffer who prays and studies Scripture diligently, who acts decisively and professes faith in Christ alone may seem a caricature to scholarship, but for an audience undaunted by the theological or historical intricacies of Bonhoeffer's life and situation, this political and decisive Bonhoeffer appears as an authentic Christian saint and hero who endorses evangelical values of love of family, God and country, and the American ideal of a rugged individualism that does not hesitate to act decisively in a situation of last resort. The language and imagery of apocalypse and war has had a tendency to fuel an increasing inclination towards violent action, particularly amongst radical pro-lifers, and here too Bonhoeffer served as a role model. While not all in the pro-life movement supported the use of force, moderate pro-lifers were equally willing to create symbolic connections with Bonhoeffer that relies on apocalyptic language and imagery. Huntemann's image of Bonhoeffer as the anti-radical revolutionary who acts in accordance with Christ's command to return a world to Christian order exacerbates such a reading. It is in turn echoed by Devine's emphasis on Christ as a figure who commands exclusive obedience against competing gods; both view Bonhoeffer as Christ's disciple who must claim the world as a legitimate sphere of obedience to Christ.

The political repercussions for this could be significant, as the Bonhoeffer image that emerges is of the faithful disciple who experiences themselves as being at war with the world, and must claim the world as a legitimate sphere of obedience to Christ. Christ's sovereignty and notions such as discipleship and obedience lead evangelicals to identify with a universal Bonhoeffer who is contemporaneous to the admirer and inspires the latter with an uncritical and unreflective emotional connection transcending historical context, secure in the knowledge that God is in control. The significance of the evangelical appropriation of Bonhoeffer's involvement in conspiracy in this context is twofold: it provides the ethical/political justification of last resort force for one's nation and unites this with the theological justification of obedience to Christ in an act of discipleship. Thus, Bonhoeffer's involvement in the plot to kill Hitler is understood by evangelicals both as an act of courage in the face of the great evil of the Nazi regime and as an example of the faithful disciple who is obedient to Christ, even in her willingness to commit violence. It is the fusion of political action and religious devotion, exacerbated by the epitaphs of 'martyr' and 'Protestant saint', that urgently requires Bonhoeffer scholars to ask the question: Could someone who believes themselves to be a Christian with a relationship to Christ, and believes themselves to be at war with the world, find in Bonhoeffer's writing something that would enable them to justify violence in the name of Christ? It is to this task that I now turn.

NOTES

1. Madsen v. Women's Health Center Inc., 1994.
2. What is means to be an evangelical American has arguably been never more scrutinised or contested than the last five years. It is important to note that not all evangelical Christians are American. Indeed, evangelical

Christianity is a worldwide phenomenon, where the number of evangelicals in Africa, Latin America and Asia exceeds the total in Europe and North America combined (Noll 2014: 17). Evangelicals are considered to share an identity based on a broad set of characteristics. These include the idea that ultimate meaning is found in the person of Jesus Christ, that the Bible is the sacred text that provide authoritative guidance, that all Christians are joined with other believers through history, back to the time of Christ, most practice water baptism, and celebrate the Lord's Supper as a way to memorialise the death and resurrection of Christ (Noll 2014: 19). In the USA, the term has come to designate believers who have fundamentalist tendencies (infallibility of Scripture, substitutionary atonement and the return of Christ at the end of history) with a sense of moral mission is increasingly connected to politically conservative movements (Noll 2014: 22–23). Yet, not all who call themselves 'evangelicals' or use a related term hold to these traditional evangelical beliefs, and there is an 'increasing vagueness in the use of terminology about evangelicalism, both by scholars and among evangelicals themselves' (Noll 2014: 25).

3. This included J.D. Godsey, G.B. Kelly, and E. Bethge.
4. See for example (Gushee 1995: 24–30), Paul McCusker, *Bonhoeffer, the Cost of Freedom*, Colorado Springs: Focus on the Family, 1997; Michael R. Phillips, *The Eleventh Hour* (Wheaton, Ill.: Tyndale House, 1993); Michael Van Dyke, *Dietrich Bonhoeffer: Opponent of the Nazi Regime* (Uhrichsville, Ohio: Barbour Pub., 2001).
5. In a letter dated 31 January 1941 (Bonhoeffer 2006: 133). Also letters dated 25 June 1942, 'I am astonished I can live for days without the Bible' and 'I feel resistance against everything "religious" growing in me' in (Bonhoeffer 2006: 326); and 19 March 1944, 'Once again I'm having weeks when I don't read the Bible much' in (Bonhoeffer 2010: 326).
6. Charles Marshs's biography, *Strange Glory*, is considered to share a similar lack of historical accuracy or understanding. Schlingensiepen argued both Marsh and Metaxas 'have dragged Bonhoeffer into cultural and political disputes that belong in a U.S. context. The issues did not present themselves in the same way in Germany in Bonhoeffer's time, and the way they are debated in Germany today differs greatly from that in the States' (Schlingensiepen 2015).
7. Richard Weikart, who was inspired by Bonhoeffer as a young evangelical, describes his own move away from his uncritical acceptance of Bonhoeffer in his youth, as he identifies features in Bonhoeffer's thought and theology that he believes should concern evangelicals. These include Bonhoeffer's views about Scripture, salvation and other crucial doctrines:

'Bonhoeffer was not the theological conservative I had earlier assumed him to be' (Weikart 2012). So concerned is Wiekart that he suggests that it is not safe to allow believers to read even *Life Together* or *The Cost of Discipleship*, texts that have proved popular amongst the Evangelical readership.

8. The quote is from Bonhoeffer's essay, 'Ten Years'—'I believe that God can and will let good come out of everything, even the greatest evil' (Bonhoeffer 2010: 46).

9. Such as former Southern Baptist minister and leader of Vision America Action, Rick Scarborough who reportedly stated that: 'This is a Bonhoeffer moment ...What will we do and how will we respond?' (Johnson 2015); Rev. Ronnie Floyd of the Southern Baptist Convention: 'This is a Bonhoeffer moment for every pastor in the United States [...] While some evangelicals ... may be bowing down to the deception of the inclusiveness of same-sex marriage or marriage in their churches, we will not bow down, nor will we be silent' (Viviano 2015); and Conservative Commentator Larry Tomczak: 'We are facing a "Dietrich Bonhoeffer Moment." [...] Brace yourself and prepare to face new challenges requiring risk-taking as the new normal in an increasingly secular society' (Tomczak 2015). Likewise, the progressive left draw on similar metaphors. Mark Edington, higher-education executive, social entrepreneur, writer and editor, and ordained Episcopalian minister, understood the 'Bonhoeffer Moment' as the requirement to challenge the appeal of a restored American civil religion suggested by Trump's slogan, 'Make America Great Again' (Edington 2017).

10. Up to 80% of American evangelicals actively supported Trump during the 2016 election, following a political campaign that caused deep division within the American evangelical community (Morris 2017: 17).

11. Both the 1960s Marxist readings of Bonhoeffer such as David Müller, and so-called death-of-god theologians from the 1960s such as John Robinson, Thomas J. J. Altizer, and Paul Van Buren shared fundamental convictions regarding the role of Christian theology in the secular world, each determined to ensure the relevance of Christianity to modern culture, each claiming in Bonhoeffer a 'seer', prescient to the changing face of modernity (Haynes 2004: 20).

12. For Green, 'Bonhoeffer's position was supported by the tyrannicide tradition in Christian ethics. He presented a moral consensus and was not a self-appointed vigilante' (Green 2009: 25, fn. 98). This is further discussed in Chapter 4.

13. Not all scholars rejected Metaxas' biography of Bonhoeffer. Timothy Larsen argues it should be welcomed 'with gratitude and joy. If America were to launch a "One Nation, One Book" program and were seeking

a volume written in this millennium, I would be thrilled if Metaxas's Bonhoeffer was selected' (Larsen 2011).
14. This will be explored further in Chapter 3.

References

Bethge, Eberhard. 1975. *Bonhoeffer: Exile and Martyr*. London: Collins.

Bonhoeffer. 2006. *Conspiracy and Imprisonment, 1940–1945*, trans. Lisa E. Dahill. Dietrich Bonhoeffer Works English. Minneapolis: Fortress Press.

Bonhoeffer. 2010. *Letters and Papers from Prison*, trans. Isabel Best, Lisa E. Dahill, Reinhard Krauss, and Nancy Lukens. Dietrich Bonhoeffer Works English. Minneapolis: Fortress Press.

Brockhoeft, John. n.d.-a. The Brockhoeft Report Vol. 1 Issue IV. http://www.armyofgod.com/Brock4.html. Accessed 10 Apr 2015.

Brockhoeft, John. n.d.-b. The Brockhoeft Report Vol. 1 Issue IX. http://www.armyofgod.com/Brock9.html. Accessed 10 Apr 2015.

Broyles, Dean. 2018. To Pastors—This Is a Bonhoeffer Moment: The State Is About the Declare Gospel a Fraud. California Family Council.

Bush, George W. 2002. President Bush Thanks Germany for Support Against Terror. Office of the Press Secretary.

Bush, George W. 2004. *Commencement Address at Concordia University Wisconsin in Mequon*. In The American Presidency Project: Wisconsin.

Clements, Keith. 1986. *A Patriotism for Today: Love of Country in Dialogue with the Witness Dietrich Bonhoeffer*. London: Collins.

Colson, Charles. 1996. Christian v. America. *Christianity Today* 40 (5): 64.

de Gruchy, John. 1997. The Reception of Bonhoeffer in South Africa. In *Bonhoeffer for a New Day: Theology in a Time of Transition*, ed. John de Gruchy, 353–372. Grand Rapids, MI: Eerdmans.

Devine. 2005. *Bonhoeffer Speaks Today: Following Jesus at All Costs*. Nashville: Broadman & Holman.

Dobson, James. 1999. The New Cost of Discipleship. *Christianity Today* 43 (10): 56.

Edington, Mark. 2017. Our Bonhoeffer Moment. Huffpost. https://www.huffingtonpost.com/entry/our-bonhoeffer-moment_us_5895eaa0e4b061551b3dff0b. Accessed 2 April.

Ginsburg, Faye. 1993. Saving America's Souls: Operation Rescue's Crusade Against Abortion. In *Fundamentalisms and the State*, ed. Martin E. Marty and R. Scott Appleby, 557–588. The Fundamentalism Project. Chicago and London: University of Chicago Press.

Gorski, Philip. 2017. Why Evangelicals Voted for Trump: A Critical Cultural Sociology. *American Journal of Cultural Sociology* 5 (3): 338–354. https://doi.org/10.1057/s41290-017-0043-9.

Grant, George. 1991. *Third Time Around*. Brentwood, Tennessee: Wolgemuth & Hyatt.

Green, Clifford J. 2003. Bonhoeffer: No! To Paul Hill. *International Bonhoeffer Society Newsletter* 83: 10.

Green, Clifford J. 2005. Pacifism and Tyrannicide: Bonhoeffer's Christian Peace Ethic. *Studies in Christian Ethics* 18: 31–47.

Green, Clifford. 2009. Editor's Introduction to the English Edition. In *Act and Being: Transcendental Philosophy and Ontology in Systematic Theology*, ed. Dietrich Bonhoeffer. Dietrich Bonhoeffer Works. Minneapolis: Fortress Press.

Gushee, David P. 1995. Following Jesus to the Gallows. *Christianity Today* 39 (4): 26.

Hansen, Collin. 2010. The Authentic Bonhoeffer. *Christianity Today* 54: 55.

Haynes, Stephen R. 2004. *The Bonhoeffer Phenomenon—Portraits of a Protestant Saint*. Minneapolis: Fortress Press.

Haynes, Stephen R. 2017. Has the Bonhoeffer Moment Finally Arrived. https://www.huffingtonpost.com/stephen-r-haynes/has-the-bonhoeffer-moment_b_13275278.html. Accessed 4 July 2018.

Huntemann, George. 1993. *The Other Bonhoeffer: An Evangelical Reassessment*. Grand Rapids: Baker Publishing Group.

Johnson, Ben. 2015. 'A Bonhoeffer Moment': Evangelical Leaders Vow Civil Disobedience If Supreme Court Redefines Marriage. *LifeSite*.

Juergensmeyer, Mark. 2000. *Terror in the Mind of God: The Global Rise of Religious Violence*. Berkeley: University of California Press.

Kaplan, Jeffrey. 1995. Absolute Rescue: Absolutism, Defensive Action and the Resort to Force. *Terrorism and Political Violence* 7 (3): 128–163. https://doi.org/10.1080/09546559508427309.

Kelly, Geoffrey, and F. Burton Nelson. 2003. *The Cost of Moral Leadership: The Spirituality of Dietrich Bonhoeffer*. Grand Rapids: Eerdmans.

Larsen, Timothy. 2011. Bonhoeffer: Pastor, Martyr, Prophet, Spy: A Righteous Gentile vs. the Third Reich/Dietrich Bonhoeffer's. *Fides et Historia* 43 (2): 138–141.

Marsh, Charles. 2016. Eric Metaxas's Bonhoeffer Delusions. In *Religion & Politics*. Washington University, John C. Danforth Center on Religion and Politics.

Marty, Martin E. 2011. *Dietrich Bonhoeffer's Letters and Papers from Prison: A Biography*. Princeton, NJ and Oxford: Princeton University Press.

Metaxas, Eric. 2010. *Bonhoeffer: Pastor, Martyr, Prophet, Spy*. Nashville: Thomas Nelson.

Metaxas, Eric. 2016. Should Christians Vote for Trump. *The Wall Street Journal*.

Morris, Daniel A. 2017. Religion in the Age of Trump. *Intersections* 2017 (45): 16–20.

Noll, Mark A. 2014. Defining Evangelicalism. In *Global Evangelicalism: Theology, History and Culture in Regional Perspective*. Downers Grove, IL: InterVarsity Press.

Pugh, Jeffrey C. 2009. *Religionless Christianity: Dietrich Bonhoeffer in Troubled Times*. London: Continuum.

Rasmussen, Larry. 2005. *Dietrich Bonhoeffer: Reality and Resistance*. Louisville, KY: Westminster John Knox Press.

Schlingensiepen, Ferdinand. 2015. Making Assumptions About Dietrich: How Bonhoeffer Was Made Fit for America. In *Book Review*. The Bonhoeffer Centre.

Tomczak, Larry. 2015. Church Is Facing a Dietrich Bonhoeffer Moment. *Charisma News*.

Viviano, JoAnne. 2015. Southern Baptists Kick Off Conference with Call for Leadership. The Columbus Dispatch. http://www.dispatch.com/content/stories/local/2015/06/16/southern-baptists-convene-in-columbus.html. Accessed 13 June 2018.

Weikart, Richard. 2011. So Many Different Dietrich Bonhoeffers. *Trinity Journal* (32 NS): 69–81.

Weikart, Richard. 2012. The Troubling Truth About Bonhoeffer's Theology. *Christian Research Journal*. http://www.equip.org/PDF/JAF5356.pdf. Accessed 19 December 2018.

CHAPTER 3

Pacifism: The 'Extraordinary' Sermon on the Mount

In addressing the question of Bonhoeffer's political involvement as a conspirator, it is tempting to omit his earlier writings, and to engage directly with what is considered his key conspiracy involvement text, *Ethics*. Yet, this would be a mistake. Scholars have long argued over a possible connection between Bonhoeffer's earlier vocal but non-violent political protest, and his later, secretive and violence-endorsing work as a double agent for the *Abwehr*. There are those who argue for a rupture between Bonhoeffer's pacifist and conspirator phases, and others who see connections or continuity between the two forms of protest. While not entering directly into this debate, this chapter presents a close reading of a central section of *Discipleship*, considered to be Bonhoeffer's key pacifist text. I am interested in the explication of a particular term that emerges as a central identifier of what it means to follow Christ in *Discipleship*: 'extraordinary'. Bonhoeffer's explication of what being 'extraordinary' might mean is based on two passages in the Sermon on the Mount: Matt 5:20 and Matt 5:47. Both passages use a variation of the Greek περισσός (*perissos*) that is central to Bonhoeffer and for which he uses the term *Außerordentliche*.[1]

The concept of the 'extraordinary' is significant for two reasons. First, as I will show in this chapter, an exposition of this term challenges the concrete applicability of the Sermon on the Mount. This will to some extent support those who see a separation between the pacifist and conspirator phases of Bonhoeffer's political involvement. However, as I will show in the next chapter, this term will re-emerge in *Ethics*, in a

© The Author(s) 2019
P. Brown, *Bonhoeffer*,
https://doi.org/10.1007/978-3-030-05698-8_3

completely different context, as Bonhoeffer engages in direct political resistance. Thus, I will also suggest there is a continuity to be found between Bonhoeffer's pacifist and conspiracy phases, and it can be found in the use of this concept of the 'extraordinary'. Yet, this continuity does not explain but rather problematises those who seek to justify last resort violence as they believe it is found in Bonhoeffer's own writing. This is a theme that will be pursued throughout the remaining book. Starting with *Discipleship* is therefore not only essential in providing insight into Bonhoeffer's own gradual immersion into direct resistance, it will also bring to light challenges for those who would seek to model their own political involvement using 'last resort' justification, based on Bonhoeffer's example and writings.

DISCIPLESHIP, PACIFISM AND THE SERMON ON THE MOUNT

Discipleship is based on Bonhoeffer's seminars, sermons, study groups and lecture series given throughout the 1930s. Its original function was primarily a training manual aimed at the Confessing Church (*Bekennende Kirche*) students of the underground seminary, Finkenwalde. It was published in 1937 with the closing of the seminary. Like most of Bonhoeffer's writings, *Discipleship* is a response to concrete events and circumstances that demanded Bonhoeffer's attention. The background to this is the establishment of the Confessing Church as the Christian church that remained faithful to its calling. Thus, the book was a call to the true church to remain obedient to Christ, against the pressure of the 'heretical' church that has fallen away from the lordship of Christ, in this case, the German Evangelical Church (*Deutsche Evangelische Kirche* or the *Reichskirche*). Bonhoeffer's *Discipleship* must therefore be first and foremost understood as a text addressed to a church-community (*Gemeinde*) that struggled to remain true to what Bonhoeffer believed was the Christian call to peace in the face of an emerging totalitarian political regime.

Beyond its own context, *Discipleship* has been widely read as a classic devotional text offering a 'Christ-centred spirituality' in both Protestant and Catholic circles, challenging the Christian reader to consider what it might mean to declare oneself a follower of Jesus Christ (Kelly and Godsey 2003: 1). What following Christ might mean is understood in diverse ways, depending on the readership. Evangelical readers are encouraged by Bonhoeffer's tone of conviction, his call to discipleship, prayer, obedience and devotion to Christ, voting *Discipleship* one of the ten 'best devotional books of all time' (cited in Haynes 2004: 77). Yet, as briefly noted in the previous chapter, others have been inspired by Bonhoeffer's vision of Christian community and the call for radical love in *Discipleship* that extends to the world, beyond one's own spirituality, to include civil disobedience as an act of political resistance. In this context, pacifism is understood as 'a serious and enduring commitment of Bonhoeffer during the 1930s' that was also a public witness to others, and a political commitment as a non-violent way to protest a hostile government (Green 2005: 37). Beatriz Melano, who had studied under Bonhoeffer's personal friend, Professor Paul Lehmann and was one of the founding members of the South American ecumenical group Church and Society in Latin America (ISAL), notes that the pacifist writings in *Discipleship* proved helpful on the question of participation in their struggle against repression:

> It was Bonhoeffer's example, mediated to us through Paul Lehmann, that gave us faith and courage when the police interrogated us in our homes and in the jails, inventoried our personal libraries, and falsely accused many of us of being 'subversives' and 'communists'. (Melano 2001: 83)

Thus, Melano and other believers within ISAL found encouragement to resist authoritarian violence, based on Bonhoeffer's writings such as *Discipleship*.[2] Similarly, John de Gruchy describes Bonhoeffer as playing an important role for Christians in the Apartheid struggle in South Africa in the late 1980s. As in South America, here again it was the appropriation of Bonhoeffer by those who were actively involved in the struggle for justice who found encouragement in his theology, even if in this situation the group consisted of a relatively small circle of privileged, elite, and often white, academics who stood in solidarity with those who struggled for liberation (de Gruchy 1997: 354–355). While not invoking Bonhoeffer in the context of similar acts of concrete pacifist resistance, Stanley Hauerwas has understood Bonhoeffer's primary task as reclaiming 'the visibility of the church as the necessary condition for the proclamation of the Gospel in a world that no longer privileged Christianity' (2004: 137). Thus, Hauerwas views Bonhoeffer's *Discipleship* as a call to the church to occupy a visible place within the secular world, an act that he considers political in its orientation.

The Sermon on the Mount is one of the key themes of *Discipleship*, and central to Bonhoeffer's own commitment to pacifist protest. The example of how to live out the Sermon on the Mount had been Bonhoeffer's friend, the French pacifist Jean Lassere, whom Bonhoeffer met as a fellow student at Union Theological Seminar, while in the USA (1930–1931). As Keith Clements notes, Bonhoeffer 'was deeply challenged by the pacifism of Lassere [...] [which was] centred on how to receive Jesus' teaching in the Sermon on the Mount. Jesus quite clearly enjoins non-violence to his disciples' (1999: 155).[3] A further important influence was Bonhoeffer's encounter with the black spirituality at Abyssian Baptist Church, during the New York 'Harlem Renaissance'.[4] Thus, Bonhoeffer's experience in the USA proved important in his own developing understanding of the Sermon in terms of concrete application in lived reality, not simply as an abstract idea of an ideal future. Following his new understanding of the Sermon on the Mount, Bonhoeffer began to live out the meaning of the Sermon through his teaching, preaching, growing ecumenical work and church resistance in the 1930s (Stassen 2005). Bonhoeffer's interpretation of the Sermon was therefore already political, in the sense that it led to his direct engagement with events of his time.

Key aspects of Bonhoeffer's interpretation of the Sermon the Mount can be found in Martin Luther, whose exposition of the Sermon in turn differs from significant interpreters within the Christian tradition.[5] For Luther, the Sermon on the Mount was primarily addressed to Christians, but precisely Christians living in society, rather than those seeking to flee it (Pelikan 2000: 129–130). DeJonge identifies Bonhoeffer's 'peace statements' as firmly belonging to the Lutheran theological tradition, rather than Anabaptist informed tradition (2015).[6] Yet, Bonhoeffer's understanding of the Sermon on the Mount departs from the traditional Lutheran interpretation, which arguably did not see the commands of the Sermon on the Mount as having application in the 'temporal kingdom' of the world.[7] That is, Luther's two-kingdoms doctrine meant that the Sermon had no application to the governing of the secular world, where law, justice and force prevailed (Pelikan 2000: 146). In a sermon delivered in 1938, Bonhoeffer seemed to directly criticise Luther as he rejects the division between one's Christian life and one's temporal life, seeing this as 'wholly alien to the teaching of Jesus [...] the precept of non-violence applies equally to private life and official duty. [Jesus] is the Lord of all life and demands undivided allegiance' (cited in Hindman 2016: 194).[8]

In *Discipleship*, Christ is described not only as the exemplar of non-violence, but understood by Bonhoeffer as the entire rationale for the Sermon on the Mount. In contrast to other interpretations that might emphasise the role of the Sermon as character formation, inspiration or as ethical injunctions, Bonhoeffer's understanding fits in the scholarship tradition that views the Sermon as profoundly Christological in orientation:

> [F]ar from being a philosophical discourse on ethics, this is a messianic manifesto, setting out the unique demands and revolutionary insights of one who claims an absolute authority over other people and whose word ... will determine their destiny. (France cited in Trout 2015: 3)

As Jordan Redding notes, the Sermon on the Mount in *Discipleship*, 'is above all else, a Christological statement – a statement that places Jesus at the centre of the church-community and which calls us to be with each other in the life of Christ: a concrete living out of the coming kingdom' (2013: 15). Bonhoeffer's Christological understanding of the Sermon was intended to be practical in its orientation, based on what Stassen refers to as a 'concrete hermeneutic, in which the teachings are meant for our regular practice' (Stassen 2005: 92).[9] Moreover, Bonhoeffer came to see the Sermon on the Mount as a call to discipleship by Jesus Christ that encompasses the world more broadly. In this way, some have seen Bonhoeffer's reading of the Sermon on the Mount as prescient to Martin Luther King Jr's later use of the Sermon in the civil rights movement, particularly the idea that justice is 'the core way of Jesus' and 'that the love of God implores us to serve our neighbour' (Williams 2014: 188, 190).[10]

When *Discipleship* was published as it was on the eve of war, it was seen by many in the midst of the church struggle as a 'call to arms pointing in the right direction' with its clear demand for concrete action (Kuske and Tödt 2003: 304).[11] Yet, despite his belief that the Sermon required concrete action, and his own attempts to put this into practice, key themes emerge in his interpretation of the Sermon that seem to counter Bonhoeffer's desire for a 'concrete hermeneutic' that is able to integrate the commands of the Sermon with everyday practice, and this lies precisely in a concept that is central to Bonhoeffer's exposition of the Sermon on the Mount: 'the extraordinary'.

THE CONCEPT OF THE 'EXTRAORDINARY'

The concept of the 'extraordinary' is found in Bonhoeffer's exegesis of the Sermon on the Mount, in Chapter 6, subtitled 'Matthew 5: On the "Extraordinary" of Christian Life' (*Vom „Außerordentlichen" des Christliche Leben*). In his analysis, Bonhoeffer argues that the Sermon on the Mount doesn't offer general principles of ethical behaviour, as is often supposed, but is actually a commentary on the category of the Christian life as 'extraordinary'. Here Bonhoeffer introduces the concept as a uniquely Christian category based on the 'extraordinary' love modelled by Christ that calls the disciple into relationship, and commands love of the enemy as a visible expression of obedience. Bonhoeffer does this through a discussion of the concept of the extraordinary in three different contexts.

The first appearance of the concept of the extraordinary highlighted by Bonhoeffer is Matthew 5:20: 'For I say to you, that unless your righteousness exceeds the righteousness of the scribes and Pharisees, you will by no means enter the kingdom of heaven'. Bonhoeffer argues that this is the first time the concept of '*perissos*', translated by Bonhoeffer into *das Außerordentliche* appears, and it does so in reference to the righteousness of Christ that for the disciple means following Christ to the cross, thereby demonstrating obedience to the will of God and fulfilment of the law (Bonhoeffer 2003: 119). Because of their obedience to the call of Christ, their hearing of the call, the righteousness of the disciples 'towers over' the scribes[12]; it surpasses the righteousness based on law in a way that is 'extraordinary' and 'distinctive', suggests Bonhoeffer (2003: 119). What does this mean? According to Bonhoeffer, both Christians and those who follow the law and do what is right need forgiveness, since *all* are unable to keep the law as they ought. But Christ 'is righteousness personified', and in forgiving the disciples, in *calling* his disciples, the disciples are declared righteous through participation in Christ's righteousness (2003: 119–120). This is not through their own effort, but because they surpass the law through Christ's pronouncement. Therefore, declares Bonhoeffer:

> The disciples' righteousness is 'better' than that of the Pharisees in that it rests solely on the call into the community of Jesus, who alone has fulfilled the law. The disciples' righteousness really is righteousness because they themselves now truly do the will of God and fulfil the law. (2003: 120)

Christ has fulfilled the requirement of the law; those who are in relationship with Christ thereby participate in Christ's righteousness. In Bonhoeffer's reading of the 'better' righteousness, the disciple is now separated from the Pharisees.

Invoking the term 'Pharisee' at this point is fraught with difficulty. While it can simply be read as a representative of religious custom and law or the authority of law, as Stephen Haynes points out, Bonhoeffer's use of the term Pharisee fits within the specific anti-Jewish conventions of German theology (2006: 98).[13] As readers, we must be wary of this. For Bonhoeffer, Pharisees 'intended to be doers of the law. Their righteousness consisted of their immediate, literal obedience to what was commanded in the law' (2003: 118). As such he can be seen to stand in the Lutheran theological tradition of a division between the Jewish faith based on works or adherence to law, and the Christian faith based on the grace of Christ; the latter tending to view itself as superseding the 'Old Testament' covenant and promises to the Jewish people.[14] Yet, Biblical scholars also note that the theme of righteousness in Matthew 'is profoundly a matter of doing [...] the disciple is called above all else to do what is ethical [...] the disciples' righteousness is not to appear as that which is popularly expounded' (Charles 2002: 5). In this context, the deficiency of the Pharisees in the Sermon is not a theological shortcoming, but an ethical one. This fits with Bonhoeffer's later definition of the Pharisee in *Ethics*, which is more explicitly framed in terms of the ethical failure of persons more broadly who are 'dominated by the knowledge of good and evil' and 'the epitome of the human being in the state of disunion' (Bonhoeffer 2009: 310).

In this chapter and my exposition of the Sermon on the Mount, my interest in Bonhoeffer's references to the law, or those who live by the law is intended to indicate people more generally who live by conventions and institutions established through moral norms and laws that are considered in some way natural to human beings. This is in contrast to those who act on the basis of their extraordinary relationship with Christ, where the latter is not to be understood as an extension of natural or earthly norms. Pennington points to the radical nature of Jesus' teachings in the Sermon on the Mount, in which the followers of Jesus are called to live 'with a God-hoping ethical standard that is counter-intuitive and counter-cultural', emphasising that the ways of God, or heaven, challenge the ways of humanity and the earth (Pennington 2007: 346). Bonhoeffer's exposition of the Sermon very much follows this understanding of a radical Christ confronting the world and challenging the established norms of humanity. Thus, in this first appearance of the concept of the extraordinary in his explication of the Sermon on the Mount, Bonhoeffer emphasises the separation of the Christian from the those who live by ethical norms, declaring that the Christian participates in *true* righteousness, as pronounced by Christ.

The separation is further emphasised in the second appearance of the concept of the extraordinary highlighted by Bonhoeffer, Matt 5:47: 'And if you greet your brethren only, what do you do *more* than others? Do not even the tax collectors do so?' (my emphasis). Commenting on this verse, Bonhoeffer states that:

> At this point the word appears toward which the whole fifth chapter is pointed, in which everything already said is summarized: what is Christian is what is 'peculiar' [...] the extraordinary [*das Außerordentliche*], irregular, not self-evident. (2003: 144)

In his exposition of this verse, Bonhoeffer refers back to Matt 5:20 and the separation of the disciple from what is regular, now reframed in terms of the natural category of the ordinary person, or the non-believer:

> How are disciples different from non-believers? What does 'being Christian' consist of? [...] what is Christian is what is 'peculiar' περισσόυ, the extraordinary, the irregular, not self-evident. This is the 'better righteousness' which 'outdoes' that of the Pharisees, towers over them, that which is more, beyond all else. (2003: 143–144, 147)

Bonhoeffer contrasts what is 'extraordinary' (*perissos*) with what is 'natural' or 'one and the same' (*to auto*) for Christians and non-Christians; the distinctly Christian begins with the extraordinary, which is what finally places the natural in 'the proper light' (Bonhoeffer 2003: 144). For Bonhoeffer, the concept of the extraordinary signifies the distinctive nature of Christianity; 'What is Christian does not take place in naturally given circumstances, but in stepping beyond them' (2003: 144). This stepping beyond means that the category of the extraordinary can never be allowed to dissolve into what seems natural to human beings. The stepping beyond in terms of Matt 5:20 concerns the forgiveness of the disciple through which she enters into relationship with Christ and thereby exceeds in righteousness to the category of the natural, or those who are not part of Christ.

The third appearance of the concept of the 'extraordinary' arrives in Bonhoeffer's exposition of Matt 5:47, extending the exegesis of the earlier passage to firmly connect the original sense of separation between Christians and non-Christians, to a concrete command. While the first reference to the extraordinary was interpreted to mean that Christians exceed the righteousness of those who live by the law because of Christ's proclamation of forgiveness, now the Christian must demonstrate that justification through obedience to Christ. This obedience must be visible to the world through living a life that is visibly marked as extraordinary:

> It is the existence of those blessed in the Beatitudes, the life of the disciples [...] the way of self-denial, perfect love, perfect purity, perfect truthfulness, perfect non-violence. Here is undivided love for one's enemies, loving those who love no one and whom no one loves. It is love for one's religious, political, or personal enemy. (Bonhoeffer 2003: 144)

Here the concept of the 'extraordinary' is understood as the love of the disciples that must surpass the love of the publicans, of those who, in Matt 5:20, are said to 'greet their brethren' only. The Christian must do more than this and love in a way that exceeds or surpasses the 'natural' love of the publican and demonstrates the extraordinary love of Christ; this is shown through loving her enemies. Natural love, Bonhoeffer states, is the love shown towards one's own, whether friends, family or associations, and as such is 'self-evident, regular, natural, but not distinctly Christian' (2003: 142). The significance of the extension from natural to extraordinary love is that the natural love for one's own is extended to include enemies, the 'one who hates me', or the person who refuses to reciprocate the love offered. Indeed, the disciple is required to be 'fond' of her enemies and serve and help her enemies in all things (2003: 139).

Bonhoeffer's exposition of Matt 5:20 and Matt 5:47 requires that the Christian not only loves those like herself, but does more than that, because the extraordinary exceeds the natural. It is in connection with the Beatitudes and the love of one's enemies that the meaning of 'stepping beyond' is brought into sharp relief with the category of what is considered natural moral behaviour. Christians are recognised as obedient to Christ by their willingness to love their enemies. The Christian demonstrates love and remains faithful to it through prayer, in the moment in which the Christian stands alongside her enemy:

We are with them, near them, for them before God [...] Every insult from our enemy will only bind us closer to our enemy. Every persecution can only serve to bring the enemy closer to reconciliation with God, to make love more unconquerable. (2003: 140)

In prayer, Christ's love helps the disciple to act towards her enemy as she does towards her kindred (Bonhoeffer 2003: 139). Bonhoeffer emphatically states that such extraordinary love is impossible for the natural person:

> Loving one's enemies is not only an unbearable offense to the natural person. It demands more than the strength a natural person can muster, and it offends the natural concept of good and evil [...] loving one's enemies appears to people living according to the law to be a sin against God's law itself. (Bonhoeffer 2003: 138)

Here again is a strong division. This time it is between those who are Christian in name but act in accord with natural moral sensibilities, and those who demonstrate their obedience to Christ through their willingness to transgress against the same moral sensibilities by exceeding in their loving towards others, even their enemies. Bonhoeffer emphasises that no natural person can muster the strength to love their enemy. Only the person who looks to Christ is able to fulfil this demand. Christ himself makes the task possible for he is the exemplar of the extraordinary:

> It is the love of Jesus Christ himself, who goes to the cross in suffering and obedience. It is the cross. What is unique in Christianity is the cross, which allows Christians to step beyond the world in order to receive victory over the world. The *passio* is the love of the crucified one – that is the 'extraordinary' mark of Christian existence. (2003: 144–145)

Now Bonhoeffer argues that the most perfect category of the extraordinary is the cross, or the love of Christ demonstrated to the disciple through his own suffering and death. The disciple is only able to love her enemy if she herself stands in the love of Christ. The righteousness of the disciple is the perfect righteousness of Christ's forgiveness; the love of the disciple is the perfect love of Christ extended to her enemy. Loving one's enemy becomes the visible (exterior) evidence of the disciple's interior love of Christ. Clifford Green describes Bonhoeffer's interpretation of the command to love one's enemies as the theological kernel at the heart of Christian faith:

For Bonhoeffer, love of enemies is not just a single discrete command of Jesus in the Sermon on the Mount. Love of enemies belongs to the heart and substance of the gospel. Without God's love of enemies there is no reconciliation, no grace, no forgiveness, no salvation [...] For Bonhoeffer, the Christian peace ethic is at the centre of the Gospel. (Green 2005: 38–39)

Thus, the concept of the extraordinary is deeply connected to the requirement to love one's enemies as a *marker* of Christian discipleship.

Although extended scholarship on Bonhoeffer's interpretation of the Sermon on the Mount using the concept of the 'extraordinary' is scarce, there have been some references to it. Phillip Ziegler briefly notes the place of the 'extraordinary' in *Discipleship* as connected to the love of Christ (2009: 287). David Gides suggests that the references to the *perissos* in the context of Bonhoeffer's wider themes in *Discipleship* indicates that Bonhoeffer wants to show how different and separate Christians are from the world. Joseph McGarry describes the meaning of *perissos* in *Discipleship* as 'the gift of Christ's own righteousness [...] [that] becomes visible to the world through the disciples' actions' (2014: 114). Such actions are extraordinary deeds that visibly separate disciples from those who would only follow Christ in word.[15] Christine Tietz similarly links 'the extraordinary' to the radical demand of discipleship: 'The disciple has to step beyond the naturally given conditions. Put concretely, loving Christ is not wrapped up in loving one's country, but demands love for one's enemy' (Tietz 2012). Stephen J. Nichols links the concept of the extraordinary as it emerges from *Discipleship* to the lives of contemporary Christians: 'The ethics of the Sermon on the Mount are nothing less than extraordinary. To look at them as something that can be fulfilled within the ordinary and by ordinary means is foolish [...] [O]nly by living from the cross can the ethical demands of Jesus come to pass in our lives' (2013: 169). Thus, each of these scholars identifies specific characteristics that flow out of the concept of the extraordinary, yet none have connected the various aspects of discipleship that emerge through Bonhoeffer's use of the extraordinary as a key hermeneutical concept.

The three aspects of Bonhoeffer's concept of the extraordinary began with the place of the disciple as declared righteous through her participation in Christ's righteousness, through which she becomes extraordinary or the disciple. Yet, the requirement now is to live an extraordinary life in the natural world. This she does by obedience to Christ's command in

the Sermon on the Mount: the extraordinary command to love her enemies. This extraordinary love appears as an offence to, or transgression
of, the ethical norm that requires love of one's own and hatred of one's
enemies. This form of love is not possible on human strength alone; it is
not a natural phenomenon but steps beyond what is the natural foundation of human relationship: the category of the enemy.

THE IMPOSSIBILITY OF THE COMMAND TO BE 'EXTRAORDINARY'?

For all those who were encouraged by Bonhoeffer's Sermon on the
Mount exposition in *Discipleship*, there were also those who felt it had
limitations. Melano found that the early pacifism of ISAL was gradu-
ally influenced by outside revolutionary influences and some Christians
began to take up arms as revolutionaries. de Gruchy likewise noted that
in the South African context, too, Bonhoeffer was invoked in a more
complex way than a straightforward support of pacifism. de Gruchy gives
examples such as the young, white males who refused to serve in the
South African army because they rejected the moral authority and legitimacy of the state in defending Apartheid, and debate about the use of
violence in recognition of the illegitimacy of the apartheid regime (1984:
358).[16] According to Melano, the revolutionary call to take up arms was
mistakenly based on Bonhoeffer's participation in conspiracy:

> This option to use violence [...] seduced many Latin American Christians,
> and unfortunately some chose to the see the death of Dietrich Bonhoeffer
> [...] and his earlier participation in the plot to assassinate Hitler, as a
> kind of inspiration and legitimization of violence as a possible Christian
> recourse. (2001: 82)

Melano argues that Bonhoeffer's decision to join conspiracy was a choice
that Bonhoeffer knew was not Christian, therefore he should not be used
as an example of the legitimisation of violence on Christian grounds
(2001: 82). Kelly and Nelson similarly claim that even when Bonhoeffer
abandoned his non-violence to join the conspiracy, 'pacifism always
remained his ideal. Only with a troubled conscience and the acceptance of guilt could he abandon pacifism' (2003: 100). For de Gruchy
Bonhoeffer's conspiracy involvement was on the basis of the higher
obedience owed to God, all the while recognising that such action may
have put him outside the boundaries of the church itself (1984: 96).

Thus, those who drew on Bonhoeffer's pacifist teaching see his later actions as running counter to his earlier theologically informed protest, and even as outside the Christian faith of the church.[17]

There's some suggestion that Bonhoeffer himself came to regret his earlier call to passive resistance. While reflecting on *Discipleship* some years later, Bonhoeffer wrote the following:

> I thought I myself could learn to have faith by trying to live something like a saintly life. I suppose I wrote *Discipleship* at the end of this path. Today I clearly see the dangers of that book, though I still stand by it. Later on I discovered, and am still discovering to this day, that one only learns to have faith by living in the full this- worldliness of life. (2010: 486)

Scholars suggest that this reflection from Bonhoeffer, written during his imprisonment and following his actions as a double agent for the *Abwehr*, indicates that *Discipleship* marks the conclusion of a particular chapter of his journey that led him from the 'spiritual exercises' of a church-community, back to his family and involvement in conspiracy (Kuske and Tödt 2003: 309). For David Gides, there is a tension between Bonhoeffer's understanding of the church-world relationship in *Discipleship*, and Bonhoeffer's own later political position (2011: 250). *Discipleship* presents a 'church-against-world vision' in which disciples demonstrate their commitment through visible suffering, which according to Gides is a 'prescription for political passivity' (2011: 251–252). Similarly emphasising the political failure of the spirituality advocated in *Discipleship*, Glen Stassen describes Bonhoeffer as developing a 'renunciation ethic', which ultimately failed as it prevented Bonhoeffer from acting adequately on behalf of others (2005).

It would seem that Bonhoeffer's attempt to interpret and apply the Sermon on the Mount as a concrete ethic failed. Part of this failure may be precisely because Bonhoeffer's rhetoric in *Discipleship* is one of separation from the world. By emphasising the extraordinary call to discipleship, Bonhoeffer appears to promote an other-worldly identity for Christians; the key hermeneutic concept of Bonhoeffer's interpretation of the Sermon on the Mount in *Discipleship* itself encourages a separation from what is ordinary and worldly. As I've shown, the concept of the extraordinary exceeds or is beyond what is regular or everyday. Thus, it fails to fully affirm the concrete reality that includes ethical norms such as loving one's own in preference to loving one's enemies. Far from engaging with their historical contexts, Christians seem to be required to step beyond what appears to be natural, or the norm; they are required to be visible exemplars of a counter-cultural love as demonstrated by Christ that nevertheless seems an impossible demand in concrete life where the enemy threatens the very life of one's neighbour. This radical separation between the disciple and the world, an exposition that appeared absolute, also seemed to have been regretted by Bonhoeffer himself, and subsequently necessitated a 'stark change' in how he viewed the relationship between church and world (Gides 2011: 280).

In addition to his later reflection on *Discipleship*, there is further evidence in his own writing that Bonhoeffer's perspective changed. Until 1939, the theme of 'loving one's enemy' was prevalent throughout Bonhoeffer's work. Throughout the 1930s, it appeared in sermons and addresses. As late as 1938, Bonhoeffer still preached on the gospel requirement to love one's enemies. Yet, by the appearance of *Ethics* in 1942, it had departed altogether (Hale 2007: 83). Likewise, the centrality of the Sermon on the Mount recedes in Bonhoeffer's later writings. As Stassen writes:

> [S]omething strange occurs in Bonhoeffer's *Ethics*, written just a few years later. The concrete way of discipleship as seen in the Sermon on the Mount [...] that he devoted years to writing and teaching – makes almost no appearance in his *Ethics*. (2005: 92–93)[18]

Yet, while there are fewer references overall to the Sermon on the Mount in *Ethics*, there is one section that deals more extensively with the Sermon, and this new exposition points precisely to the limitations of an other-worldly Christianity, as advocated in *Discipleship*. In this new exegesis of the Sermon, the concept of the 'extraordinary' has disappeared. Instead, Bonhoeffer argues:

> [T]he Sermon on the Mount [....] confronts a person with the necessity of responsible historical action. It addresses the individual, not to give status to individuals as such, but so they may be what they already are before God, namely, persons with historical responsibility. (2009: 242)

A new term is introduced that was not found in the *Discipleship* exposition but will become key in *Ethics*: the notion of responsibility [*Vertantwortung*].[19] Bonhoeffer's earlier demand that loving one's enemies is the visible marker of discipleship seems to be set aside, as he now describes discipleship as 'persons charged with historical responsibility'. With this, the extraordinary command understood in terms of loving of one's enemies is also reframed. Now the Sermon on the Mount 'calls individuals to love, which proves itself in responsible action toward the neighbor and whose source is the love of God that encompasses all reality' (Bonhoeffer 2009: 243). Responsible action shows love towards one neighbour, rather than one's enemy. Yet, Bonhoeffer seems unclear as to how this might manifest in practice. In the final few paragraphs of his new exposition of the Sermon, Bonhoeffer suggests that:

> [...] God's love for the world also includes political action, and that the worldly form of Christian love is therefore able to take the form of a person fighting for self-assertion, power, success, and security. It is here that the limits, or, rather, the ultimate foundations of the law of self-assertion in political action become evident. (2009: 245)

This proposes that God's love not only includes political action, but Christian love in this instance may take the form of a person fighting for what seem to be worldly or secular goals for most Christians, such as power, success and security. A number of revisions occur at this point, including a deleted paragraph that suggests that the person fighting in a 'worldly form of Christian love' could be either a government authority or the 'Christian who is faced with the necessity to act politically' (Bonhoeffer 2009: 245, fn. 103).[20] It is in these final pages that it seems Bonhoeffer has dramatically reconsidered his position on the call to love one's enemy. He mentions that he intends to deal in a later section with the 'validity of the sayings concerning self-denial and love of enemies ... for one who acts politically', an intended section that was never written (2009: 244).[21]

The concept of the 'extraordinary' in *Discipleship* is found in a text that is considered key to Bonhoeffer's understanding of discipleship and is directly linked to his commitment to pacifist protest during the 1930s as an outworking of following Christ, and a visible and public expression of faith. In the narrative of Bonhoeffer's opposition to National Socialism, his writings on visible but passive resistance have been interpreted as a stage that proved inadequate to the concrete, historical events in which he found himself embroiled. Bonhoeffer's own later reflections on the *Discipleship* writings seem to confirm this. His attempt to implement the Sermon on the Mount to develop a new concrete hermeneutic failed, in part due to his tendency to abstract discipleship from the world. As noted at the start of the chapter, the historical context of *Discipleship* was that of training pastors to be shepherds and leaders in the Confessing Church, the latter itself established as a protest against the acquiescence of the *Reichskirche* to National Socialist doctrine that ran counter to the gospel of Jesus. One can read the separation from the world as a call to for Christians to visibly separate from nationalist expansionist propaganda. Yet, by emphasising the extraordinary call to discipleship, Bonhoeffer seemed to promote an other-worldly identity for Christians that seems an impossible demand in concrete life where the enemy threatens the very life of one's neighbour.

In the new interpretation of the Sermon on the Mount in *Ethics*, Bonhoeffer's other-worldly exposition in *Discipleship* changes towards a stronger focus on action in this world. With this comes a conceptual shift from the call for Christians to be witness to Christ's extraordinary love through obedience to the command of the Sermon on the Mount, to Christians called to responsible action in the world, in which they are no longer separate but are required to become politically involved and ready to act beyond the command of the Sermon on the Mount. Thus, we see the disappearance of the concept of the extraordinary as it is understood in terms of key *Discipleship* themes, including the requirement to love one's enemy, to a new interpretation of the Sermon on the Mount in *Ethics*, where now the faithful disciple is required to engage in responsible historical action that may well include overt political action. Yet, while the concept of the extraordinary as a marker of faith has disappeared in Bonhoeffer's explication of the Sermon on the Mount in *Ethics*, it re-emerges in a new context as Bonhoeffer engages in direct political resistance. This will have profound implications on how we should understand Bonhoeffer's various forms of resistance, and what discipleship might involve, once a Christian chooses the path of active resistance.

NOTES

1. The two Greek terms are περισσός, perissos (Matt 5:47) adj—'beyond the regular number; superabundant (in quantity) or superior (in quality)'; περισσεύω, perisseuo (Matt 5:20) verb—'to be over and above, to superabound (in quantity or quality), be in excess, be superfluous; also (transitively) to cause to superabound or excel'—Strong's Greek Lexicon

Numbers: G4053 περισσός (Strong 1890b) and G4052 περισσεύω (Strong 1890a; Kittel and Friedrich 1985).

2. Geffrey Kelly and Matthew Kirkpatrick identify four themes of liberation theology in Bonhoeffer's work, including solidarity with the oppressed, the 'suffering God', a radical hermeneutical shift and, the demand that the church live up to its promise to be Christ in the world (Kelly and Kirkpatrick 2016).

3. Further important influences on Bonhoeffer's pacifist turn were American friend and Reformed theologian, Paul Lehmann, and the German theologian Franz Hildebrandt, as well as others (Green 2005: 35–36).

4. This period introduced a culture that sought to develop authentic black self-perception in public life. As it took place in Harlem New York, it can also be seen as 'the urbanization of black life', and as a 'sophisticated, educated and cultured' black identity emerged a 'seedling of a theology of civil disobedience' emerged alongside. Bonhoeffer's involvement in African American life in 1930–1931 came at a critical moment of African American history (Williams 2013: 60).

5. There is a 'clear line from Luther to Bonhoeffer; a clear influence of one on the other [...] [n]owhere is this link clearer than in Bonhoeffer's most enduring work, *Discipleship*' (Montover 2013: 351).

6. DeJonge suggests that contemporary Mennonite and pacifist interpretations such as those offered by Stanley Hauerwas, and more recently Mark Nation, Anthony Siegrist and Daniel Umbel in *Bonhoeffer the Assassin?*, read Bonhoeffer as though he belongs to an Anabaptist theological context, rather than a Lutheran context, and are mistaken in doing so (DeJonge 2015: 162–163).

7. The extent to which this is Luther's view, or a subsequent perversion of Luther by various interpretations of Lutheranism remains contentious. Frank Matera suggests Luther's interpretation meant that Christians were required to observe the commands of the Sermon on the Mount in their private lives, but they were 'not necessarily obligated to do all of its prescriptions in the public sphere of life where they hold particular offices such as being a soldier or magistrate' (Matera 2013: 10). Lisa Cahill similarly suggests Luther did not 'interpret Christian love streaming into the world as a force for social change' (Cahill 2016: 276), yet she also notes that contemporary Lutheran theologians point to a distortion of Luther's theology by later Lutheranism, and that faith according to Luther includes participation in Christ's nature that leads to doing good works (Cahill 2016: 279–280). Thorsten Prill similarly suggests that even though Luther did not advocate applying the Sermon on the Mount in politics, as it would 'endanger peace in society and lead to destruction', nevertheless for Luther the Christian has obligations and responsibilities towards both kingdoms (Prill 2005: 18–19).

8. The sermon 'Christ's Love and Our Enemies' was delivered on 23 Jan 1938 (the Third Sunday after Epiphany) at the secret seminary, Gross-Schlonwitz.

9. Stassen himself explores how the Sermon on the Mount helps to live one's life in *Living on the Sermon on the Mount*, as a 'readable book' that can be applied to life, and free us 'from being stuck in the vicious cycles that trap us in our lives' (Stassen 2006: xvii). Written for a lay audience, Bonhoeffer features throughout this book.

10. Although Bonhoeffer did not appear to have directly influenced King, as Williams points out, both Bonhoeffer and King 'wrestled with the efficacy of Christ-like love in their context, to resist injustice and to encourage social transformation' (Williams 2014: 186). See also Wilson (2015), Roberts (2005).

11. Kuske and Tödt further note that it discouraged mere intellectual engagement and consequently no extensive reviews were published at the time. These did not appear until after 1945. Nevertheless, the wider readership was such that Bonhoeffer found himself listening to a reading from the book by the monks at the Benedictine Monastery in Dec 1940, while composing his manuscript for *Ethics* (Bethge 1977: 371).

12. Kittel and Friedrich translate *perisseuo* as *Überschießen* or 'overshoot' (Kittel and Friedrich 1985). Luther uses '[being] better than' while Bonhoeffer uses 'tower over' (Editor's note in Bonhoeffer 2003: 119, fn. 78).

13. Haynes points out that little scholarly work has been done on *Discipleship's* potential contributions to a post-Holocaust theology, noting that Bonhoeffer's exposition on the Sermon on the Mount in particular has a lot to contribute to an understanding of Christianity's relationship to Judaism (Haynes 2006: 89). Haynes finds that Bonhoeffer's relationship to Judaism in *Discipleship* shows 'expressions of solidarity with suffering Jews and an implied obligation to respond that few if any Christians in Germany were articulating at the time' yet it also shows the 'recirculation of some of the very anti-Jewish canards that were used to rationalize this suffering' (Haynes 2006: 91).

14. Luther saw the Sermon as 'an argument for the necessity of divine grace' in the face of the reality of human sin (Clarke 2003: 62).

15. McGarry highlights the visibility of the 'extraordinary' deed, but also notes that being extraordinary itself should never be the goal, lest one becomes a spiritual enthusiast who only covets the effects of being seen as set apart.

16. For de Gruchy, Bonhoeffer's conspiracy involvement should be seen as a result from his high regard for the state whose authority is given by God, arguing that it was only on the basis of the higher obedience owed to

God that Bonhoeffer was willing to act against the state in his own situation, all the while recognising that such action may have put him outside the boundaries of the church itself (de Gruchy 1984: 96).

17. Stanley Hauerwas takes a different approach, arguing Bonhoeffer's decision to become a conspirator may simply have been a way to avoid conscription and its associated oath of loyalty to Hitler. Hauerwas' analysis of Bonhoeffer's decision for conspiracy suggests it was not theologically informed in a positive way. Rather it was a pragmatic decision, theologically informed to the extent that Bonhoeffer would see military conscription and the associated oath to the Fuhrer as incompatible with his pacifist commitment. For Hauerwas, Bonhoeffer's theological commitment remained with pacifism. Hauerwas concludes that the secrecy required by conspiracy means 'we have no way to determine how Bonhoeffer understood his work with the *Abwehr*' (Hauerwas 2004: 138).

18. *Ethics* has 358 references to New Testament passages, and only sixteen of them refer to the Sermon on the Mount (Stassen 2005: 94).

19. De Jonge notes that Bonhoeffer turned to the concept of responsible action in terms of the individual from 1939 onwards (DeJonge 2017: 259).

20. 'Deleted, new paragraph: "The one who acts politically in exercise of a governing office [replaces: 'The Christian who is faced with the necessity to act politically'] is commissioned with [deleted: 'a'] concrete responsibility. This person, is, for example, charged to protect the security, property, or the peace of the people"' (Editor's note in Bonhoeffer 2009: 245, fn. 103). The final lines are as follows: 'Political action means taking on responsibility. This cannot happen without power. Power is to serve responsibility' (Bonhoeffer 2009: 245).

21. For Stassen, this unfinished reassessment of the Sermon on the Mount in *Ethics* shows Bonhoeffer's struggle in applying his 'concrete hermeneutic' developed in *Discipleship* to his own historical context; Bonhoeffer's 'hermeneutic ethic of renunciation' needed to be reframed into a hermeneutic that enabled 'transforming initiatives' (Stassen 2005: 104).

REFERENCES

Bethge, Eberhard. 1977. *Dietrich Bonhoeffer: Theologian. Christian. Contemporary*, trans. Eric Mosbacher, Peter and Betty Ross, Frank Clarke, and William Glen-Doepel. London: Fountain Books.

Bonhoeffer, Dietrich. 2003. *Discipleship*, trans. Barbara Green and Reinhard Krauss. Dietrich Bonhoeffer Works English. Minneapolis: Fortress Press.

Bonhoeffer, Dietrich. 2009. *Ethics*, trans. Reinhard Krauss, Charles C. West, and Douglass W. Stott. Dietrich Bonhoeffer Works English. Minneapolis: Fortress Press.

Bonhoeffer. 2010. *Letters and Papers from Prison*, trans. Isabel Best, Lisa E. Dahill, Reinhard Krauss, and Nancy Lukens. Dietrich Bonhoeffer Works English. Minneapolis: Fortress Press.

Cahill, Lisa Sowle. 2016. Global Health Justice: Love as Transformative Political Action. In *Love and Christian Ethics: Tradition, Theory, and Society*, ed. Frederick V. Simmons and Brian C. Sorrells, 274–289. Washington, DC: Georgetown University Press.

Charles, J. Daryl. 2002. Garnishing with the "Greater Righteousness": The Disciple's Relationship to the Law (Matthew 5:17–20). *Bulletin for Biblical Research* 12 (1): 1–15.

Clarke, Howard W. 2003. *The Gospel of Matthew and Its Readers: A Historical Introduction to the First Gospel*. Bloomington: Indiana University Press.

Clements, Keith. 1999. Ecumenical Witness for Peace. In *The Cambridge Companion to Dietrich Bonhoeffer*, ed. John de Gruchy, 154–172. Cambridge: Cambridge University Press.

de Gruchy, John. 1984. *Bonhoeffer and South Africa: Theology in Dialogue*. Grand Rapids, MI: Eerdmans.

de Gruchy, John. 1997. *Bonhoeffer for a New Day: Theology in a Time of Transition—Papers Presented at the Seventh International Bonhoeffer Congress, Cape Town, 1996*. Grand Rapids: Eerdmans.

DeJonge, Michael. 2015. How to Read Bonhoeffer's Peace Statements: Or, Bonhoeffer Was a Lutheran and Not an Anabaptist. *Theology* 118 (3): 162–171. https://doi.org/10.1177/0040571x14564933.

DeJonge, Michael. 2017. *Bonhoeffer's Reception of Luther*. Oxford: Oxford University Press.

Gides, David M. 2011. *Pacifism, Just War, and Tyrannicide: Bonhoeffer's Church-World Theology and His Changing Forms of Political Thinking and Involvement*. Eugene, OR: Pickwick Publications.

Green, Clifford J. 2005. Pacifism and Tyrannicide: Bonhoeffer's Christian Peace Ethic. *Studies in Christian Ethics* 18: 31–47.

Hale, Lori Brandt. 2007. From Loving Enemies to Acting Responsibly: Forgiveness in the Life and Theology of Dietrich Bonhoeffer. *Word & World* 27 (1): 79–87.

Hauerwas, Stanley. 2004. Dietrich Bonhoeffer. In *The Blackwell Companion to Political Theology*, ed. Peter Scott and William T. Cavenaugh, 136–149. Malden and Oxford: Blackwell.

Haynes, Stephen R. 2004. *The Bonhoeffer Phenomenon—Portraits of a Protestant Saint*. Minneapolis: Fortress Press.

Haynes, Stephen R. 2006. *The Bonhoeffer Legacy: Post-Holocaust Perspectives*. Minneapolis: Fortress Press.

Hindman, Caleb M. 2016. Bonhoeffer's Dilemma. *Faulkner Law Review* 7 (2): 191–230.

Kelly, Geffrey B., and John D. Godsey. 2003. Editors' Introduction to the English Edition. In *Discipleship*, ed. Geffrey B. Kelly and John D. Godsey, 1–33. Minneapolis: Fortress Press.

Kelly, Geffrey B., and Matthew D. Kirkpatrick. 2016. Dietrich Bonhoeffer and Liberation Theologies. In *Engaging Bonhoeffer: The Impact and Influence of Bonhoeffer's Life and Thought*, ed. Keith W. Clements, Guido De Graaff, Peter Frick, T.O.M. Greggs, Brian Gregor, Christopher R.J. Holmes, Geffrey B. Kelly, et al., 139–168. Minneapolis: Augsburg Fortress.

Kelly, Geoffrey, and F. Burton Nelson. 2003. *The Cost of Moral Leadership: The Spirituality of Dietrich Bonhoeffer*. Grand Rapids: Eerdmans.

Kittel, Gerhard, and Gerhard Friedrich. 1985. *Theological Dictionary of the New Testament*. Grand Rapids: Eerdmans.

Kuske, Martin, and Ilse Tödt. 2003. Editor's Afterword to the German Edition. In *Discipleship*, ed. Geffrey B. Kelly and John D. Godsey, 289–314. Minneapolis: Fortress Press.

Matera, Frank J. 2013. *The Sermon on the Mount: The Perfect Measure of the Christian Life*. Collegeville, MN: Liturgical Press.

McGarry, Joseph. 2014. Formed While Following: Dietrich Bonhoeffer's Asymmetrical View of Agency in Christian Formation. *Theology Today* 71 (1): 106–120. https://doi.org/10.1177/0040573613518644.

Melano, Beatriz. 2001. The Influence of Dietrich Bonhoeffer, Paul Lehmann, and Richard Shaull in Latin America. *The Princeton Seminary Bulletin* 22 (1): 64–84.

Montover, Nathan. 2013. From Luther to Bonhoeffer: A Clear Line. *Currents in Theology and Mission* 40 (5): 351.

Nichols, Stephen J. 2013. *Bonhoefffer on the Christian Life*. Wheaton, IL: Crossway.

Pelikan, Jaroslav. 2000. *Divine Rhetoric: The Sermon on the Mount as Message and as Model in Augustine, Chrysostom and Luther*. Crestwood, NY: St. Vladimir's Seminary Press.

Pennington, Jonathan T. 2007. *Heaven and Earth in the Gospel of Matthew*. Supplements to Novum Testamentum. Leiden: Brill NV.

Prill, Thorsten. 2005. Martin Luther, the Two Kingdoms, and the Church. *Evangel* 23 (1): 17–21.

Redding, Jordan. 2013. The "Light on the Hill" Paradox: Hearing the Sermon on the Mount with Dietrich Bonhoeffer. *Stimulus: The New Zealand Journal of Christian Thought & Practice* 20 (2): 14.

Roberts, J. Deotis. 2005. *Bonhoeffer and King: Speaking Truth to Power*. Louiseville, KY: Westminster John Knox Press.

Stassen, Glen Harold. 2005. Healing the Rift Between the Sermon on the Mount and Christian Ethics. *Studies in Christian Ethics* 18 (3): 89–105. https://doi.org/10.1177/0953946805058800.

Stassen, Glen Harold. 2006. *Living the Sermon on the Mount: A Practical Hope for Grace and Deliverance*. San Francisco: Jossey-Bass—A Wiley Imprint.

Strong. 1890a. G4052 – perisseuō – Strong's Greek Lexicon (KJV). *Strong's Greek Dictionary*. Accessed 20 December 2018.

Strong. 1890b. G4053 – perissos – Strong's Greek Lexicon (KJV). *Strong's Greek Dictionary*. Accessed 20 December 2018.

Tietz, Christiane. 2012. Dietrich Bonhoeffer: Standing "in the Tradition of Christian Thinking". In *Kierkegaard's Influence on Theology Tome I: German Protestant Theology*, ed. Jon Stewart, 43–64. Kierkegaard Research: Sources, Reception and Resources. Surrey, UK and Burlington, USA: Ashgate.

Trout, Bradley M. 2015. The Nature of the Law's Fulfilment in Matthew 5:17: An Exegetical and Theological Study/Die aard van die vervulling van die Wet in Matteus 5:17: 'n eksegetiese en teologiese studie. *In die Skriflig* (1). https://doi.org/10.4102/ids.v49i1.1910.

Williams, Reggie L. 2013. Dietrich Bonhoeffer, the Harlem Rennaisance and the Black Christ. In *Bonhoeffer, Christ and Culture*, ed. Keith L. Johnson and Timothy Larsen, 59–72. Downers Grove, IL: InterVarsity Press.

Williams, Reggie L. 2014. Christ-Centered Concreteness: The Christian Activism of Dietrich Bonhoeffer and Martin Luther King Jr. *Dialog: A Journal of Theology* 53 (3): 185–194. https://doi.org/10.1111/dial.12115.

Wilson, Paul E. 2015. Between Berlin and Birmingham: A Comparison of Resistance in the Lives of Dietrich Bonhoeffer and Martin Luther King, Jr. *Appraisal* 10 (4): 20–27.

Ziegler, Philip G. 2009. 'Not to Abolish, but to Fulfil': The Person of the Preacher and the Claim of the Sermon on the Mount. *Studies in Christian Ethics* 22 (3): 275–289. https://doi.org/10.1177/0953946809106233.

CHAPTER 4

Bonhoeffer's Turn to Conspiracy: The 'Extraordinary Situation'

The reader who hopes to find either an explanation or justification for the turn to conspiracy in the main text written during Bonhoeffer's conspiracy involvement, *Ethics*, will be disappointed (Bethge 1977: 625). There is perhaps one oblique autobiographical reference to suggest how Bonhoeffer viewed his conspiracy involvement.[1] Obviously, there were practical reasons for silence on this matter. As Larry Rasmussen points out, the lack of commentary is 'obvious to anyone who understands the dangers of the written word to an underground movement in a totalitarian state' (2005: 131). Similar to his own decision for conspiracy, Bonhoeffer makes very few direct references to tyrannicide in his writings, although the terms 'tyrant' and 'tyranny' occur several times in *Ethics*, particularly the title 'tyrannical despiser of humanity' reserved for Hitler himself (2009b: 85). However, a number of essays in *Ethics* do impact directly on Bonhoeffer's own thinking and decision-making regarding his conspiracy involvement, although careful reading is needed to draw out these ideas.

Unlike Bonhoeffer's earlier books, *Ethics* remained an unfinished work, a collection of essays and manuscripts spanning 1941 to Bonhoeffer's arrest in 1943.[2] At the time of Bonhoeffer's death, most of the manuscripts remained in first draft stage.[3] One notable exception to this is the 'History and Good' manuscript, composed during the height of Bonhoeffer's resistance involvement.[4] In addition to the historical situation in which it was composed, this manuscript is particularly interesting because it was the only one rewritten by Bonhoeffer,[5] and it was

© The Author(s) 2019
P. Brown, *Bonhoeffer*,
https://doi.org/10.1007/978-3-030-05698-8_4

the only manuscript he sought help with.[6] As Clifford Green points out: 'Because of the content of this material, plus Bonhoeffer's reworking of it and his effort to secure Barth's help, I believe that we are dealing here with the core ethical concerns which Bonhoeffer engaged in his ethical reflection on the *coup d'etat* and tyrannicide' (2009: 312). Thus, these two key manuscripts in *Ethics* can be read as an ongoing outworking by Bonhoeffer, where he seeks to integrate the reality of his life and actions with the ongoing development of his theology.[7]

CONSPIRACY, *ETHICS* AND THE 'EXTRAORDINARY SITUATION'

While Bonhoeffer is primarily known as a theologian, in the second draft of the History and Good manuscript (HG2) Bonhoeffer's writing strikes a new, far more political tone in a key passage *not found* in the earlier draft of the manuscript (HG1). Here Bonhoeffer makes a direct reference to the political philosopher Machiavelli's concept of *necessitá*. The dense passage is worth quoting in full in order to get a sense of both the political tone and to introduce a number of important key ideas:

> There are occasions when, in the course of historical life, the strict observance of the explicit law of a state, a corporation, a family, but also of a scientific discovery, entails a clash with the basic necessities of human life. In such cases, appropriate responsible action [*verantwortliches sachgemäßes Handeln*] departs from the domain governed by laws and principles, from the normal and regular, and instead is confronted with the extraordinary situation [*Außerordentliche Situation*) of ultimate necessities (*letzter Notwendigkeiten*) that are beyond any possible regulation by law (*Gesetz).* In his political theory Machiavelli coined the term *necessitá* for such an occasion. For politics this means that the craft of political governance becomes political necessity. (Bonhoeffer 2009b: 272–273)

Here, the 'extraordinary situation' is introduced as a concept that appears when a person or a group of people might find themselves in a situation that is no longer governed by law and are driven to act by what Bonhoeffer calls 'ultimate necessities'. Bonhoeffer invokes the fifteenth-century political theorist, Machiavelli, as the exemplar of this situation. Machiavelli suggested there were two ways of ruling: law and force; law being appropriate to humans, and force to animals. But, according to Machiavelli, because law is often ineffective, the ruler must have recourse to force, which means that 'a ruler must know well how to imitate beasts as well as employing properly human means' (Machiavelli 1988: 61). For Machiavelli, the skill of the prince or authority figure is to be able to be both lawful and forceful; to know when to behave 'virtuously' and when to be 'beastly', as the circumstances require. While the prince should 'not deviate from right conduct if possible', he should be 'capable of entering upon the path of wrongdoing when this becomes necessary' (1988: 62). The prince responds to the necessity of conditions surrounding him and violates the state's good in response to *necessitá*. The passage continues:

> There can be no doubt that such necessities (*Notwendigkeiten*) actually exist. To deny them would mean ceasing to act in accordance with reality [*wirklichkeitsgemäßes Handeln*]. It is equally certain, however, that these necessities, as primordial facts [*Urtatsachen*] of life itself, cannot be captured by any law and can never become laws themselves. They appeal directly to the free responsibility of the one who acts, a responsibility not bound by any law. They create an extraordinary situation, and are in essence borderline cases (*Wesen nach Grenzfälle*). They no longer permit human reasoning to come up with a variety of exit strategies, but pose the question of the *ultima ratio*. In politics this *ultima ratio* is war but it can also be deception or breaking a treaty for the sake of one's own life necessities [...] The *ultima ratio* lies beyond the laws of reason; it is irrational action. (Bonhoeffer 2009b: 273)

Several key features of the extraordinary situation emerge from this passage. First, for Bonhoeffer, ultimate necessities exist as 'primordial facts' of life itself that escape the boundaries of law. The prefix *Ur* is used in German to indicate something that is originary, primary or first, suggesting that extraordinary situations not only escape the boundaries of law, but are in some sense prior to the categories established by law. Second, ultimate necessities are borderline cases. In his analysis of the 'extraordinary situation' passage in *Ethics*, Matthew Puffer argues that Bonhoeffer's reference to a *Grenzfall* belongs in a broader tradition of thinkers that include Carl Schmitt, Karl Jaspers, and the later Karl Barth. In this context, Bonhoeffer's unique exploration of the concept of *Grenzfall* lies in 'the uncommon occurrence of a conflict between ethical norms', suggests Puffer (2014: 260).[8] Puffer describes extraordinary situations as: 'uncommon experiences that nevertheless can and do occur whenever life's necessities are threatened by the intrinsic law of human existence itself' (2014: 262). This is the borderline case or the question of the *ultima ratio*, which Bonhoeffer describes as beyond the *laws of reason*: it appears as irrational action, suggests Bonhoeffer in this passage.

There are significant implications to Bonhoeffer's idea of action undertaken in a borderline scenario, particularly in the way he frames this as somehow outside or inaccessible to the rational, law bound or regulative state of the norm. Puffer notes the difficulty of making ethical decisions in a borderline case:

> Once confronted by a borderline case, [...] ethical decisions are beyond appeal to intrinsic laws for the purposes of discerning right action, even though the ethical agent must acknowledge the validity of the laws he or she breaks. (2014: 263)

There emerges here a tension between the agent who breaks the law in order to affirm the law, but who has no basis for so doing that is understandable to the context of law. This tension will be explored further in later chapters. For now, it is enough to note that Bonhoeffer envisions a scenario in which the agent must engage in action beyond established ethical norms or laws, in a way that cannot be explained within existing frameworks. By linking the extraordinary situation with Machiavelli, Bonhoeffer looks to find a form of action that he believes is appropriate to the primordial experiences or encounters which are not only beyond any possible regulation by law, but also described as beyond reason itself. Bonhoeffer takes for granted that such extraordinary situations exist. Bonhoeffer does not argue *for* an extraordinary situation; in his mind such as situation had already presented itself. The primordial facts of life to which he refers *raise* or enable the 'extraordinary situation' to emerge as a scenario where law is suspended because the extraordinary situation cannot be addressed or contained by the law. What would constitute such a situation? Here, Bonhoeffer names three scenarios: war [*Krieg*], deception [*Betrug*] or breaking a treaty [*Vertragsbruch*]. All three are permissible in such a situation if done 'for the sake of one's own life necessities', suggests Bonhoeffer.

The concept of the extraordinary that appeared in Bonhoeffer's classic pacifist text *Discipleship* as the 'extraordinary' command to love one's enemies, has re-emerged in his conspiracy text, *Ethics*, in the 'extraordinary situation' that may require killing. Yet, while the two imperatives may seem widely divergent, there are in fact a number of important conceptual similarities. The previous chapter identified several key features of the concept of the extraordinary in *Discipleship*. First, the concept functioned to separate the disciple from those who would claim righteousness (or justification for their actions) on the basis of their adherence to moral norms and laws. This division was deepened by Bonhoeffer's claim that the extraordinary 'does not take place in naturally given circumstances, but in stepping beyond them' (2003: 144). Just as in *Discipleship* the individual was separated from the regular or self-evident by Christ, and subsequently required to act in a new way, now in *Ethics* she is confronted with the extraordinary situation of ultimate necessities that similarly requires that she acts in a new reality, beyond ethical norms. In *Discipleship*, the final appearance of the concept was in relation to the command to love one's enemies, which was considered the most visible marker of the extraordinary nature of discipleship. The extraordinary love extended to one's enemies appeared as an offence to natural love in *Discipleship*; in *Ethics*, action is now described as beyond the laws of reason and therefore similarly appears as an offence to reason, as irrational, which for Bonhoeffer means it 'is a deed which can no longer be decided by the laws of reason' or through calculation (2009b: 273, fn. 102).[9] Thus, the theologically framed identity of the disciple who transgresses moral norms in obedience to the command to love one's enemies has reappeared as the person who is confronted with the extraordinary situation in which they are required to act against previously held moral norms and also laws.

Considered critically, the connections that I've pointed out can seem tenuous at best. But there is a further strong link between the concept of the 'extraordinary' love of Christ in *Discipleship* and the concept of the 'extraordinary situation' in *Ethics*. This link is found in Bonhoeffer's idea of responsible action. In the previous chapter, I noted that the new interpretation of the Sermon on the Mount in *Ethics* introduced the concept of 'responsible action' as the framework of action that replaced *Discipleship*'s emphasis on love of one's enemies as the most visible marker of Christian love. This new interpretation of the Sermon on the Mount is found in the first draft of the History and Good manuscript (HG1). Thus, HG1 can be seen as an attempt to link Bonhoeffer's reflections on Christology and discipleship from his pacifist writings, to a transformed understanding of what following Christ and discipleship might mean in the new scenario of conspiracy involvement. Responsible action shows love towards one's neighbour, suggested Bonhoeffer in his interpretation of the Sermon on the Mount in HG1. Such love may include political action. As noted in the previous chapter, a number of revisions occur at this point, including a deleted paragraph that suggests a person 'fighting in a 'worldly form of Christian love' could be either a government authority or the 'Christian who is faced with the necessity to act politically' (Bonhoeffer 2009b: 245, fn. 103). Any reference to the Sermon on the Mount has disappeared in the second draft of the History and Good manuscript (HG2). Instead, the Christian who is faced with the necessity to act politically appears in connection with the 'extraordinary situation', based on Machiavelli's *necessità*. Thus, Machiavelli's prince who must be capable of entering on the path of wrongdoing is here linked to Bonhoeffer's idea of the Christian required to act politically on the basis of love for their neighbour. The Christian or agent in HG2 is now described as acting on the basis 'appropriate responsible action' [*verantwortliches sachgemäßes Handeln*] (Bonhoeffer 2009b: 272). The term 'responsible action' that emerged in Bonhoeffer's reinterpretation of the Sermon on the Mount in HG1 is now described as guiding action in borderline scenarios based on Machiavelli's concept of *necessità*.

RESPONSIBLE ACTION IN THE EXTRAORDINARY SITUATION

While action in the HG2 takes place in a political context, it is not Machiavelli who guides what constitutes or demarcates 'appropriate responsible action' in the 'extraordinary situation'. Bonhoeffer's parameters at to what constitutes responsible action in an extraordinary situation are still theologically, or more specifically, Christologically grounded: it is modelled on Christ's own example of 'vicarious representative action' [*stellvertretend verantwortliches Handeln*]. 'All human responsibility is rooted in the real vicarious representative action of Jesus Christ on behalf of all human beings. Responsible action is vicarious representative action', writes Bonhoeffer in the first draft of the History and Good manuscript (2009b: 232). Vicarious representative action has both a theological and legal meaning. Its theological meaning is the sum and substance of Christology, and it is specifically Lutheran in its orientation to sin and punishment: 'Though innocent, Jesus takes the sin of others upon himself, and by dying as a criminal he is accursed, for he bears the sins of the world and is punished for them', writes Bonhoeffer in his dissertation, *Sanctorum Communio*, where he extends this central

Lutheran idea of salvation of the individual from sin, to the corporate body of the church-community (*Gemeinde*) (2009a: 156).[10] Its legal meaning indicates a person, or agent, acting on behalf of another person in a legal context. It has been variously described as 'deputyship' (Muller 1997) and 'representational being' (Palmisano and Krauss 2016: 132). Bonhoeffer likens it to secular relationships in which a person is required to act on behalf of others, 'such as a father, as a statesman, or as the instructor of an apprentice' (2009b: 257).[11] Indeed, in the second draft of the History and Good manuscript, Bonhoeffer prefaces the theological example with the more secular examples, just noted (Bonhoeffer 2009b: 257–258). In a section titled 'The Structure of Responsible life', in the redrafted History and Good manuscript, Bonhoeffer outlines key features of the ethical characteristics that accompany 'vicarious representative action'. These are 'action in accord with reality', 'willingness to become guilty', and 'acting in freedom'. It is important to examine these in more detail, as it shows just how Bonhoeffer tries to bring together Christlike character and action in an extraordinary situation in which previously understood ethical boundaries are deeply challenged.

Responsible action is 'action in accord with reality', which is action in accordance with 'the God who became human, Jesus Christ, who took on humanity, and who has loved, judged and reconciled humanity, and with it the world [...] action in accordance with Christ is action in accord with reality [...] As *the* Real One he is the origin, essence, and goal of all reality' (Bonhoeffer 2009b: 263). The redemptive love of God shown in Christ is the foundation of reality, and reality is understood as the ongoing reconciliation of God to the world within history. This understanding of reality limits action undertaken in an extraordinary situation. Bonhoeffer argues that 'human beings are place in a position of concrete and thus limited, i.e., created, responsibility that recognizes the world as loved, judged and reconciled by God, and acts accordingly within it' (2009b: 267). Our created nature entails the limitation of our actions: 'We do not create the conditions for our action but find ourselves already placed within them', and we can only act on the basis of our historicity, the limitations of the past and the future that cannot be avoided (Bonhoeffer 2009b: 267). Christ is the real one who establishes reality and with this, the limits of what constitutes responsible action.

Closely connected is the idea that responsible action demonstrates a 'willingness to become guilty' [*Bereitschaft zur Schuldübernahme*], which is modelled on the example of Christ whose 'sinless-guilt' (*sündlos-schuldig*) is the foundation of all vicarious representative action (Bonhoeffer 2009b: 275). In German, the concept of *Schuld* carries with it an objective meaning grounded in a juridical context. It refers to both being judged guilty by a court, and personal obligation or culpability. In theological parlance, it refers both to the fact of sin, and the personal consequences of sin (Krauss and Lukens 2009: 114, fn. 12). Responsible action is therefore recognisable to the extent that it shows a readiness to become guilty under law. Yet, it is not enough to choose to become guilty through intentional transgression, it must be done on behalf of others, as it is modelled on the example of Christ. Acting responsibly incurs guilt and Christ demonstrates this through entering human historical existence. For Bonhoeffer, action undertaken on behalf of others in an extraordinary situation is undertaken by an innocent person willing to become guilty under law on behalf of others, accepting the guilt that comes with such action.

Finally, Bonhoeffer names freedom as part of the structure of responsible life:

> Responsibility and freedom are mutually corresponding concepts. Responsibility presupposed freedom substantively – not chronologically – just as freedom can exist only in the exercise of responsibility. Responsibility is human freedom that exists only by being bound to God and neighbor. (2009b: 283)

Those who act responsibly, act in freedom, insofar as they act without the support of people, conditions or principles. There is nothing to defend or exonerate those who act on the basis of responsibility: 'They themselves have to observe, judge, weigh, decide and act on their own' (Bonhoeffer 2009b: 283). Such action Bonhoeffer describes as a venture [*Wagnis*] that cannot be justified by any law, nor can such actors rely on self-justification; such actors can only surrender to God 'the deed that has become necessary'; it is God who 'weighs the deed, and guides history' (2009b: 284). As Clifford Green notes, such freedom is not to be understood as 'the freedom of secular modernity, namely, freedom of choice regardless of what is chosen', rather it is freedom based on God becoming human in Christ (2009: 14). It is freedom to act on behalf of others, and therefore it is tied intimately to responsibility, and is able to advocate for risk insofar as it is action undertaken for others. Because such action is undertaken on behalf of others, the actor considers the support of people, conditions or principles in decision-making, even if these cannot be used as the basis for responsible action. Thus, three key ideas have emerged that help to make sense of action in an extraordinary situation. Action in accord with reality, willingness to become guilty, and acting in freedom, are part of Bonhoeffer's Christologically informed understanding of what constitutes appropriate responsible action. Scholars tend to see Bonhoeffer as expressing these characteristics in his own decision for conspiracy. Joel Lawrence describes *Stellvertretung* or vicarious responsible action as the 'key reason for his [Bonhoeffer's] willingness to act in the conspiracy against Hitler' (2010: 30). Clifford Green argues that Bonhoeffer saw his own involvement in conspiracy as an act of repentance and a willingness to take the guilt of his action upon himself (2009: 13). This guilt was both Bonhoeffer's own guilt and a willingness to bear the guilt of others: his nation and his church. Larry Rasmussen likewise argues that Bonhoeffer's decision to join the conspiracy was essentially Christological:

> If Jesus did not seek first of all to be good or to preserve his innocence, if he instead refused to shun the fellowship of guilt and took upon himself the guilt of others, if he stood in solidarity with those enmeshed in inescapable responsibilities that could not but incur guilt in an evil order – if he, true man, did this, then responsible men should do the same. (2005: 62–63)[12]

Peter Frick gives four steps similar to the key criteria of responsible action just described, in order to 'make intelligible perhaps the most complex aspect' of Bonhoeffer's life: his involvement in the conspiracy to kill Hitler (2012: 318–319; 2017: 18–19).[13]

Highlighting the theme of redemption, Michael DeJonge argues that Bonhoeffer's thinking in struggle and resistance grew out of 'Christ's personal presence spoken in the church's word and sacrament' and an outworking of 'God's work in the temporal kingdom in terms of preservation toward redemption' (2017: 259). The concept of responsibility as it emerges in *Ethics* is also linked to Bonhoeffer's active political protest: 'Bonhoeffer's decision to take part in the conspiracy to assassinate Hitler was embedded in his concept of *Verantwortung*, a judgment that this course of action would lead to the end of his rule, an action for which he accepted the responsibility and the personal guilt' (Blackburn 2004: 232).

Yet, simply interpreting Bonhoeffer's conspiracy involvement as Christlike is fraught with difficulty. Consider for example the following discussion of 'reality' that emerges in the History and Good manuscript. In the explicitly political passage tied to Machiavelli's *necessitá*, Bonhoeffer describes the ultimate necessities of life *as* acting in accordance with reality [*wirklichkeitsgemäßes Handeln*]. Moreover, he describes such action as impossible to regulate by law or human reasoning, which may require the political necessity of war or deception for the sake of the preservation of life. He argues that such scenarios speak directly to the free responsibility of the one who acts, and that such responsibility cannot be bound by any law. Bonhoeffer therefore appears to discuss reality as an existential event or encounter in which life itself is threatened, and which requires the suspension of ethical norms and existing laws in order to preserve life itself. Yet, Bonhoeffer also grounds responsible action in a Christology that repeatedly and unerringly describes Christ as reality [*Christus-Wirklichkeit*] and as the model of action in the extraordinary situation. Thus, a twofold meaning to reality seems to be in play. There is the existential appearance of reality in connection with the extraordinary situation, and the explicit understanding of a Christ-reconciled reality that is the broader theme in *Ethics*. Which is the 'real reality' for the Christian actor in an extraordinary situation? Is it the reality of *neccesitá*? Or is it the redemptive work of Christ? Bonhoeffer perhaps wants to show that Christ is the foundation of the 'primordial facts of life', or to put it in an ontologically correct ordering, that the primordial facts of life are also reconciled in Christ. Responsible action in an extraordinary situation is therefore to be understood as an act of faith in the enduring reality of Christ's sovereignty in a morally corrupt world. Yet, in his description of the extraordinary situation analogous to Machiavelli's *neccesita*, Bonhoeffer doesn't simply pose Christ as the answer, nor does he turn to Christology to justify his own actions. Indeed, only sentences before he introduces the 'structure of responsible life', Bonhoeffer explicitly states that simply repeating 'biblical terminology' in ethics can be dangerous (2009b: 256).

Christ remains important in the History and Good manuscripts, including in Bonhoeffer's discussion on the extraordinary situation. In Bonhoeffer's discussion of 'responsible action' in the two versions of the History and Good manuscript, there is a clear link between Christ as saviour and redeemer and therefore the ontological basis of vicarious representative action, and the ethical expression of this by Christians who demonstrate responsible action in an extraordinary situation. In Christ, who 'is the responsible human being par excellence', the theological and ethical are joined, writes Bonhoeffer (2009b: 258–259). It is clearly important for Bonhoeffer that he maintains unity between action that is in accordance with the nature and character of Christ and action that is also simultaneously required in an 'extraordinary situation'. Yet, I think a tension emerges in viewing responsible action from above, or theologically/conceptually, and from below, which reflects far more the experiential nature of that action, including how one encounters or understands the concrete, historical and political reality of the 'extraordinary situation'.

Rather than proposing Christology as an answer to explain Bonhoeffer's own actions, and with this provide a normative model for Christian action in a boundary scenario, a more helpful way to view the passage of the extraordinary situation is to see it as the world confronting Bonhoeffer's understanding of faith itself. The idea itself is already inherent in *Discipleship*, where the confrontation with the world is itself considered an important marker of discipleship. But it also emerges in *Ethics*, where responsible action is explored in a worldly context in the midst of Bonhoeffer's own conspiracy involvement. The world as it appears in the 'extraordinary situation' passage challenges Bonhoeffer to rethink key ideas of Christology and to consider how these fit with a new form of action that cannot be easily reconciled with his understanding of Christian ethics/norms for moral action, such as those outlined in his Sermon on the Mount interpretation in *Discipleship*.

THE EXTRAORDINARY SITUATION: THE CHALLENGE OF JUST WAR THEORY

For some scholars, the discussion on the 'extraordinary situation' raised by Bonhoeffer in *Ethics* belongs to the broader context of just war theory. Beginning with Augustine, following the rise of Christianity as the official faith of the Roman Empire, the 'just war tradition' appeals to historical rules and agreements that have aimed at circumscribing rationalisations for going to war (*jus ad bellum*), actions in war (*jus in bello*) and most recently, accountability of actions after war (*jus post bellum*).[14] Just war theory is therefore concerned with the *justification* of why and how wars are fought. To what extent can Bonhoeffer's actions and writings be made intelligible within the context of an existing tradition of just war theory?

Larry Rasmussen believes that Bonhoeffer, in the context of his wider writings and testimony from friends and co-conspirators, gives five 'operative guidelines' for the case of tyrannicide, understood as the assassination of a tyrant, or unjust ruler. These are the requirements: (1) there must be clear evidence of gross misrule; (2) active resistance must respect the scale or hierarchy of political responsibility; (3) there must be reasonable assurance that tyrannicide can be successfully executed, and, following the execution, there must be a plan to restore order as quickly as possible; (4) only such force and violence that is necessary to abolish the abuse of misrule is permissible; and (5) active resistance 'can be turned to only as the very last resort, after nonviolent and legal means have been exhausted' (Rasmussen 2005: 145). Thus, Rasmussen envisages a possible scenario, after all other means have failed, where tyrannicide may be permissible, as long as it observes boundaries, such as an established hierarchy and an existing plan.

Commenting on the 'extraordinary situation' passage in *Ethics*, and referring to Rasmussen, David Gides in *Pacifism, Just War, and Tyrannicide* (2011) argues that, in addition to legitimising the taking of life in the context of a defensive war, Bonhoeffer himself develops principles that resemble a just war position. Gides notes a passage from a paper written by Bonhoeffer possibly in the period after April 1941, where Bonhoeffer states that if the government oversteps its task at some point, for example by claiming lordship or divinity over the church-community, 'then at this point it is to be disobeyed for the sake of conscience and for the sake of the Lord' (Bonhoeffer 2006: 517).[15]

Also worth noting is respected Bonhoeffer scholar Clifford Green, who refers to Bonhoeffer's conspiracy involvement as 'tyrannicide', which takes place in the moral framework of 'killing a tyrant' (2005: 41). According to Green, Bonhoeffer regarded the planned coup 'as an absolute last resort' and participated in the coup 'against the background of an established moral tradition that allowed tyrannicide under certain strictly defined criteria' (2005: 41). Green places Bonhoeffer in a specific ethical tradition that includes Aquinas, Calvin, Beza, Knox and Barth who all allow for tyrannicide in the form of God's command in conditions of 'extreme public emergencies' (2005: 41). For Rasmussen, Gides and Green, Bonhoeffer's act of tyrannicide belongs in a just war tradition that considered tyrannicide morally legitimate under certain conditions.

These justifications of Bonhoeffer's actions suggest that Bonhoeffer's action can be considered morally legitimate, and that the actions of others who claim to follow Bonhoeffer's example can likewise be measured within the just war tradition, and found to be legitimate or illegitimate.[16] I think Bonhoeffer's discussion around the 'extraordinary situation', and his invocation of Machiavelli at this point, can be seen as a significant challenge to the idea that there may be nascent elements of a just war theory in his writings. At the very least, any suggestion of a set of guidelines that can be applied to other scenarios must be approached with great care, given Bonhoeffer's own emphasis of the singularity of the extraordinary situation, or the isolated nature of these experiences, and the lack of coherence within existing structural frameworks of law and order of such instances.[17] Contradicting those who would seek to find a just war theory in Bonhoeffer, Jeffrey Lenowitz argues that Bonhoeffer actually does not present a formal system regarding just war at all: 'Bonhoeffer never departs from a deeply Lutheran position, one that digs in and firmly denies man's ability to truly understand the world in its totality, something that any developed ethical system implicitly implies' (2008: 45). Protestant theology has struggled with the idea of a just war theory because of the historical suspicion of the natural law tradition, and the idea that human reason can develop principles that justify war.[18] Because of his deep Lutheran character and commitment, Bonhoeffer's view of ethics and politics is built on the premise of humanity's own ignorance and lack of knowledge about the whole, in particular in terms of a system of ethics that can be applied to a wide range of situations—such as that invoked by those who wish to apply Bonhoeffer's decision for conspiracy into a Christian justification for a war on terror. Bonhoeffer believes natural law principles are not reliable because, while they are formal, they are filled with content determined by fallible human beings, declaring that 'Natural law can establish the tyrannical state as well as the state governed by law, the people's state as well as imperialism, democracy as well as dictatorship' (2006: 510).[19]

Rasmussen acknowledges this problem. He notes that while the guidelines *he* lists mirror that of a just war tradition, Bonhoeffer himself eschews any attempt to develop a theory of just war.[20] Rasmussen argues that, for Bonhoeffer, tyrannicide 'is an act justified by *no* law, even when the purpose is to hallow the law by doing what is necessary to retune to the Rule of Law' (2005: 144). Similar to Rasmussen, Heinz Tödt argues that this passage does not offer a rational legitimisation for a revolutionary overthrow or violent struggle for liberty; there is no possibility for a just war theory on this account (2007: 67). The only authorisation possible is from the clash with primordial necessities of life themselves, such as when the state itself destroys law and order, and this can only be determined in a particular situation: '[t]he certainty that this is an emergency is the prerequisite of extraordinary illegal action' (Tödt 2007: 68). For Tödt, such action cannot become the foundation of a new type of ethics. In the same paper quoted by Gides in support of *his* argument that Bonhoeffer develops principles that resemble a just war position, Bonhoeffer, after extensive reflections on the various levels of responsibility of government, the church and individuals, concludes that:

> The various connections between government and church do not allow for the regulation of the relationship on the basis of a principle; neither the separation of state and church nor the state church form is in itself a solution of the problem. Nothing is more dangerous than drawing generalized theoretical conclusions from isolated experiences. (Bonhoeffer 2006: 525)

The isolated experiences to which Bonhoeffer refers can be understood in the context of the extraordinary situation as those acts that escape regulation by law. Bonhoeffer has already noted that extraordinary situations cannot be regulated. That is also why we should be cautious about attributing even emerging just war guidelines to Bonhoeffer's reflections and seeming justifications for his conspiracy involvement. Just war theory seeks to regulate precisely the kind of extraordinary situations that Bonhoeffer believes cannot be regulated.

THE EXTRAORDINARY SITUATION: *NECESSITÀ*

In this chapter, I have emphasised the connection between Bonhoeffer's concept of the 'extraordinary situation' and Machiavelli's concept of *necessità*, which required that the prince is capable of behaving beastly, as well as virtuously, and to enter on the path of wrongdoing, if required. Bonhoeffer's use of Machiavelli in relation to his concept of the extraordinary situation is significant, as it helps us to see more clearly Bonhoeffer's divergence with just war theory. But importantly, it also highlights emerging issues as Bonhoeffer attempts to articulate what constitutes responsible action in an extraordinary situation.

The concept of necessity has a long history, grounded in the political maxim, *Necessitas legem non habet* (necessity has no law), which from its earliest expression was considered a principle of natural law that could be applied 'during extreme situations that could not be pre-identified' (Desierto 2012: 63). The religious beginning of the maxim in the twelfth century found later expression in the political discourse of emerging nation states, which displaced the church as the focus of political authority, and necessity became understood as the right of sovereigns to protect the state from perceived dangers that threatened its self-preservation.[21] The early architect of this was arguably Machiavelli. Machiavelli prescribed 'a near absolute discretionary space for the sovereign's actions at home or abroad' (Desierto 2012: 70–71). For Machiavelli, *necessità* was understood primarily as a 'self-judging doctrine unilaterally available to sovereign rulers at all times' (Desierto 2012: 92). Consequently, there was little accountability to those who would invoke the doctrine as a justification for immoral acts. It is worth noting that Machiavelli's view received strong critique from contemporaries such as Hugo Grotius, who is considered one of the founding figures of modern international law. For Grotius, necessity should be invoked only on the basis of temporary restrictions on property ownership and use of force in self-defence, that should be 'purposely conditional, restrictive and temporary in its application' (Desierto 2012: 85–86). Machiavelli and Grotius presented two different understandings of necessity, with important consequences. For Grotius, claimed acts of necessity are measured against external international obligations, building in accountability to those who would invoke necessity. The German historian, Friedrich Meinecke in his book, *Die Idee der Staatsräson in der neueren Geschichte* (1924),[22] described Grotius as an idealist, oblivious to the demands of 'raison d'etat': 'as if it were possible to altogether to confine the behaviour of States to one another within legal and moral bounds' (cited in Desierto 2012: 85). It is worth noting here that Bonhoeffer encountered Machiavelli through reading Meinecke (Zerner 1999: 194).[23]

The contemporary political philosopher, Michael Walzer explores at length the implication of Machiavelli's concept of necessità in the modern political context. Walzer uses the term 'dirty hands', which he defines as 'a particular act of government [...] may be exactly the right thing to do in utilitarian terms and yet leave the man who does it guilty of a moral wrong' (1973: 161). In both Machiavelli's and Walzer's accounts, the problem of 'dirty hands' actions is one for politicians who may be required to act with brutality when needed to protect the greater good, the people whom they serve. This is based on the understanding that politicians bear a greater responsibility than ordinary citizens. However, Tony Coady argues that Walzer's discussion on the surpeme emergency in terms of political community could be more broadly extended to 'the moral community', a term that is at times used by Walzer himself (Coady 2008: 85–86). Thus, the discussion around dirty hands actions can be extended from politicians to include non-state actors. For Coady, Bonhoeffer presents such an example[24]:

> The relevance of the philosophical discussions of dirty hands (and moral dilemmas) to Bonhoeffer is that some of his critique of ethics may be connected to his sense of the tragic choices that emergency situations can provide to an agent. This has particular salience in the context of resistance to the horrors of the Nazi regime in Germany [...]. (2012: 465)

Leslie Griffin likewise invokes Bonhoeffer in her writing on the problem of dirty hands. Unlike Coady, for Griffin Bonhoeffer does not 'strictly speaking' present a problem of 'dirty hands, since he is concerned with the actions of those plotting to overthrow a government rather than with the actions of politicians themselves' (1989: 39). Yet, I would suggest that Bonhoeffer provides an interesting case study *precisely* because the question of dirty hands is in his account extended from the beastly acts required only by politicians. Bonhoeffer's example shows that ordinary citizens may also be required to act beastly when faced with human atrocities or the suffering of others. Indeed, Bonhoeffer is a particularly salutary example because his theological and philosophical reflections are written during his own involvement in political conspiracy.

Bonhoeffer's concept of action in an extraordinary situation belongs to a broader tradition of thinkers that include his contemporaries, Carl Schmitt, Karl Jaspers, and the later Karl Barth. Puffer identifies Bonhoeffer's unique contribution to this context as the conflict between ethical norms. For Puffer, Bonhoeffer's understanding of *Grenzfall* as conflict of ethical norms distinguishes his use of the term from those of Carl Schmitt's political state of emergency, and Karl Jasper's existential understanding where the term describes the condition of human existence more generally.[25] Yet, I suggest Bonhoeffer doesn't simply experience or describe a conflict between 'ethical norms'. He is immersed in a politically volatile and existentially anxious situation; indeed, the passage that is most relevant to Bonhoeffer's own conspiracy involvement, is a politically explicit passage in its invocation of Machiavelli. There are significant implications to Bonhoeffer's turn to Machiavelli. Bonhoeffer's concept of the 'extraordinary situation' is the context of a thinker who provided near absolute discretion to a sovereign power to act beastly, if the situation was judged to require this. In such a scenario, there are few moral limitations imposed from outside. As a result, the application of the state of *necessità* is not necessarily conditional, restrictive or temporary, as advocated by early developers of international law. Indeed, the political consequences of 'unlawful' action based on necessity in an extraordinary situation can be disastrous, as it involves the risk of compounding the lawlessness that required the extraordinary action in the first place. It is here that the political thinker 'par excellence' on the *Grenzfall* can articulate the dangers of political action in an extraordinary situation more clearly. While Bonhoeffer's concept of the 'extraordinary situation' is not identical to Carl Schmitt's political *Grenzfall* scenario, engaging with Schmitt and his critics enables us to more fully explore the dangers to which Bonhoeffer's own concept of 'responsible action' might lead, if the latter is seen as a Christian (Christlike) model for last resort violence in an 'extraordinary situation'.

NOTES

1. 'The man who acts out of free responsibility is justified before others by dire necessity; before himself he is acquitted by his conscience, but before God he hopes only for grace' (Bonhoeffer 2009b: 282–283). That this is autobiographical is noted by Clifford Green, who argues that this is evident through Bonhoeffer's use of *der Mann* or 'the man', rather than his normal use of *der Mensch* or 'the human being' and 'given the pertinence of these sentences to his personal involvement in the conspiracy against Hitler, this usage suggests an autobiographical interpretation of these sentences' (Green 2009: 283, fn. 138)

2. That *Ethics* remained unfinished was a regret Bonhoeffer expressed to Eberhard Bethge while in prison; 'Personally, I reproach myself for not having finished the *Ethics* … and it comforts me somewhat that I have told you the most important things' (Bonhoeffer 2010: 181); '[I] sometimes think my life is more or less behind me and all I have left to do is to complete my *Ethics*' (Bonhoeffer 2010: 222).

3. Both the latest German and English editions refer to the sections of *Ethics* as 'manuscripts' rather than 'chapters', since this is faithful to the origins of the book *Ethics*.

4. The most important event for Bonhoeffer during this period was a meeting at Sigtuna, in which he provided to Bishop Bell details of those ready to cooperate in the overthrow of Hitler (Bethge 1977: 666). Bell's notes of that conversation included references to Bonhoeffer's writing of this time: 'In 1941–1942 [Bonhoeffer] had worked on a Book of *Ethics*, and memos for the Brethren's Council, and in evening political activity' (cited in Bonhoeffer 2006: 304).

5. Both the latest German and English editions have included both drafts of 'History and Good'. As Green indicates, a 'close analysis and comparison of the two versions would be a valuable study', however, to date such an analysis, to my knowledge, has not been undertaken (2009: 311, fn. 40).

6. Amongst others, Bonhoeffer sought help from Karl Barth for this manuscript. During his visit to Switzerland, in May 1942 Bonhoeffer was able to read proofs of a volume on Barth's ethics in *Church Dogmatics*.

7. Recent critical editions of Bonhoeffer's works, in both the English and German editions, support such a reading, as these have organised the collected manuscripts chronologically, according to the phases in which they were composed. As Green points out, by ordering the manuscripts chronologically, an interpretive element is already applied (2009: 303).

8. Puffer points to a range of other ethical conflicts that arise in various manuscripts throughout *Ethics*, including rights to life, suicide and sterilisation, and the divine mandates that Bonhoeffer envisions as a way to order society. Puffer thus contextualises the *Grenzfall* example in the redrafted History and Good manuscript is the focus of this chapter, in the context of the other conflicts between ethical norms that Bonhoeffer explores throughout *Ethics*.

9. In the manuscript HG2, the phrase 'is a deed that can no longer be decided by the laws of reason' is deleted and replaced with 'it is irrational action' (Bonhoeffer 2009a, p. 273, fn. 102).

10. By changing the focus of individual salvation, and its development into the forms private faith that have become emblematic of modern notions of faith, Bonhoeffer prioritises the individual's responsibility in the context of community; living in relationship with other human beings becomes the proper expression of faith. The implications of this in terms of understanding Christian action in an extraordinary situation will be critically considered in further chapters.

11. Heinz Tödt points out that 'vicarious representative action' should not be confused with the idea of solidarity between equals. Yet, even the practice of modern democracy cannot do without this idea of representation on

behalf of another, for example, where 'the mother or father step in for children, the free for the imprisoned, the gifted for the ungifted' (Tödt 2007: 5).

12. 'Through his own personal *Schuldübernahme* on behalf of these, Bonhoeffer moves away from his momentary fascination with saintliness into the deeper dimensions of deputyship where guilt is not merely accepted through sympathetic understanding, but rather is born through assertive and often agonizing action' (Rasmussen 2005: 51).

13. These four steps are the one reality of Jesus Christ, ethical responsibility, ethical borderline situations and leaving judgement in God's hand.

14. Its contemporary forms are grounded in Aquinas' *Summa Theologicae*, and Hugo Grotius, who did much to secularise just war theory in the seventeenth century. See Evans, Mark. 2005. 'Introduction: Moral Theory and the Idea of a Just War'. In *Just War Theory: A Reappraisal*, edited by Mark Evans. Edinburgh: Edinburgh University Press.

15. The paper is called 'A theological position paper on state and church'.

16. This is the basis on which Clifford Green rejects the appropriation of Bonhoeffer by violent anti-abortion protestors. Green views Paul Hill as an individual acting on a self-appointed mission; Bonhoeffer acted in a resistance group within a shared judgement, argues Green (2003).

17. This would exclude those who seek to develop just war principles from Bonhoeffer's writings, but also those who see Bonhoeffer as an example of Christian 'last resort' violence.

18. There is an obvious absence of a chapter on just war in the Protestant tradition in Robinson, Paul. 2003. *Just War in Comparative Perspective*. Aldershot: Ashgate.

19. Jordan Ballor argues that Bonhoeffer should be understood as 'as advocating a kind of Christological natural-law approach, an ethic of normative moral orders', challenging the prevailing view that Bonhoeffer belongs to the 'Barthian tradition of rejecting natural law' (Ballor 2012: 66). Perhaps a 'natural-law approach' is not quite the same as fully fledged natural law theory. Yet for reasons that will become clearer later, I would hesitate to see Bonhoeffer's attempt to ground an ethical framework on Christology as something that is analogous to natural law.

20. Rasmussen notes that because of his Lutheran and Prussian heritage, Bonhoeffer cannot conceive of a doctrine that might develop a *right* of resistance. He can only appeal to duty and the responsibility of the individual in such a situation. It is, argues Rasmussen, similar to the German notion of the *Ausnahmezustand*, and it is premised on the idea that such a situation is always framed in terms of the 'must' of duty, rather than the 'may' of rights (Rasmussen 2005: 146).

21. Agamben notes that this was originally formulated in a religious context, to do with the celebration of mass, which was required to be offered in a consecrated place. The transgression of the sacred through a single, specific case of exception could happen in a supreme necessity. Applied by Aquinas to the sovereign's power to grant dispensations from the law, the term became increasingly used to apply to describe a political context that describes the limit of the juridical law (Agamben 2005: 24).
22. Translated into English as *Machiavellism: The Doctrine of Raison d'Etat and Its Place in Modern History* (1957).
23. It is not clear why Bonhoeffer turn to Machiavelli rather than Grotius. It is interesting to note that Bonhoeffer mentioned Grotius in one of his letters written in prison, on 16 July 1944, where Bonhoeffer advocates for the world's autonomy (Frick 2008: 169).
24. Provocatively, Coady suggests that the supreme emergency/dirty hands qualification may apply if terrorists aim to save a communal way of life. Walzer rejects this, suggesting that the terrorist argument that they have no alternative in the face of oppression is only 'the pretense of a last resort' (Walzer 2004). No such scepticism is expressed about last resort justifications offered by governments who might use similar actions and justify these in terms of the supreme emergency.
25. Puffer further challenges the way Bonhoeffer's concept of *Grenzfall* has been taken up in subsequent theological ethics, including the work of Karl Barth, Yoder, and Rasmussen.

References

Agamben, Giorgio. 2005. *State of Exception*, trans. Kevin Attell. Chicago and London: University of Chicago Press.

Ballor, Jordan J. 2012. Dietrich Bonhoeffer, the Two Kingdoms, and Protestant Social Thought Today. *La Revue Farel* 6 (7): 62–75. https://doi.org/10.2139/ssrn.2145346.

Bethge, Eberhard. 1977. *Dietrich Bonhoeffer: Theologian, Christian, Contemporary*, trans. Eric Mosbacher, Peter and Betty Ross, Frank Clarke, and William Glen-Doepel. London: Fountain Books.

Blackburn, Vivienne. 2004. *Dietrich Bonhoeffer and Simone Weil: A Study in Christian Responsiveness*. Religions and Discourse. Bern, Switzerland: Peter Lang.

Bonhoeffer. 2003. *Discipleship*, trans. Barbara Green, and Reinhard Krauss. Dietrich Bonhoeffer Works English. Minneapolis: Fortress Press.

Bonhoeffer. 2006. *Conspiracy and Imprisonment, 1940–1945*, trans. Lisa E. Dahill. Dietrich Bonhoeffer Works English. Minneapolis: Fortress Press.

Bonhoeffer. 2010. *Letters and Papers from Prison*, trans. Isabel Best, Lisa E. Dahill, Reinhard Krauss, and Nancy Lukens. Dietrich Bonhoeffer Works English. Minneapolis: Fortress Press.

Bonhoeffer, Dietrich. 2009a. *Act and Being*, trans. Martin Rumscheidt. Dietrich Bonhoeffer Works English. Minneapolis: Fortress Press.

Bonhoeffer, Dietrich. 2009b. *Ethics*, trans. Reinhard Krauss, Charles C. West, and Douglass W. Stott. Dietrich Bonhoeffer Works English. Minneapolis: Fortress Press.

Coady, C.A.J. 2008. *Messy Morality : The Challenge of Politics*. Uehiro Series in Practical Ethics. Oxford and New York: Oxford University Press.

Coady, C.A.J. 2012. Moralism and Anti-moralism: Aspects of Bonhoeffer's Christian Ethic. *Sophia* 51 (4): 449–464. https://doi.org/10.1007/s11841-012-0340-2.

DeJonge, Michael. 2017. *Bonhoeffer's Reception of Luther*. Oxford: Oxford University Press.

Desierto, Diane A. 2012. *Necessity and National Emergency Clauses: Sovereignty in Modern Treaty Interpretation*. International Litigation in Practice: v. 3. Leiden. The Netherlands: Martinus Nijhoff Publishers.

Frick, P. 2008. Bonhoeffer's Intellectual Formation: Theology and Philosophy in His Thought. In *Religion in Philosophy and Theology*. Tübingen: Mohr Siebeck.

Frick, Peter. 2012. Dietrich Bonhoeffer: Engaging Intellect—Legendary Life. *Religion Compass* 6 (6): 309–322. https://doi.org/10.1111/j.1749-8171. 2012.00357.x.

Frick, Peter. 2017. *Understanding Bonhoeffer*. Tubingen: Mohr Siebeck.

Gides, David M. 2011. *Pacifism, Just War, and Tyrannicide: Bonhoeffer's Church-World Theology and His Changing Forms of Political Thinking and Involvement*. Eugene, OR: Pickwick Publications.

Green, Clifford J. 2003. Bonhoeffer: No! To Paul Hill. *International Bonhoeffer Society Newsletter* 83: 10.

Green, Clifford J. 2005. Pacifism and Tyrannicide: Bonhoeffer's Christian Peace Ethic. *Studies in Christian Ethics* 18: 31–47.

Green, Clifford J. 2009. Editor's Introduction to the English Edition. In *Ethics*, ed. Clifford J. Green. Minneapolis: Fortress Press.

Griffin, Leslie. 1989. The Problem of Dirty Hands. *Journal of Religious Ethics* 17 (1): 31–61.

Krauss, Reinhard, and Nancy Lukens. 2009. Translation Notes. In *Sanctorum Communio*, ed. Clifford J. Green. Dietrich Bonhoeffer Works English, vol. 1, Minneapolis: Fortress Press.

Lawrence, Joel. 2010. *Guides for the Perplexed: Bonhoeffer*. London, GBR: Continuum International Publishing.

Lenowitz, Jeffrey. 2008. Obedience at the Time of Necessitá: Dietrich Bonhoeffer's Theory of Resistance. Paper presented at the Annual Meeting of Western Political Science Association, San Diego.

Machiavelli. 1988. *The Prince*, trans. Russell Price. Cambridge: Cambridge University Press.

Muller, Denis G. 1997. Bonhoeffer's Ethic of Responsibility and Its Meaning for Today. *Theology* 794: 108.

Palmisano, Trey, and Reinhard Krauss. 2016. *Peace and Violence in the Ethics of Dietrich Bonhoeffer: An Analysis of Method*. Eugene, OR: Wipf & Stock.

Puffer, Matthew. 2014. The Borderline Case in Bonhoeffer's Political Theology. In *A Spoke in the Wheel: The Political in the Theology of Dietrich Bonhoeffer*, ed. Kirsten Bush Nielsen, Ralf Wüstenberg, and Jens Zimmermann, 257–269. Gütersloher, Germany: Gütersloher Verlagshaus.

Rasmussen, Larry. 2005. *Dietrich Bonhoeffer: Reality and Resistance*. Louisville: Kentucky Westminster John Knox Press.

Tödt, Heinz Eduard. 2007. *Authentic Faith: Bonhoeffer's Theological Ethics in Context*, trans. David Stassen, and Ilse Tödt. Grand Rapids, MI: Eerdmans.

Walzer, Michael. 1973. Political Action: The Problem of Dirty Hands. *Philosophy & Public Affairs* 2 (2): 160–180.

Walzer, Michael. 2004. *Arguing About War*. New Haven: Yale University Press.

Zerner, Ruth. 1999. Church, State and the 'Jewish Question'. In *The Cambridge Companion to Dietrich Bonhoeffer*, ed. John de Gruchy, 190–205. Cambridge: Cambridge University Press.

CHAPTER 5

Political Theology and the State of Exception

In order to draw out the political and social implications of Bonhoeffer's 'extraordinary situation' for those who wish to appeal to this as a legitimate option in a situation of 'last resort', it is useful to investigate this concept more critically using the work of the pre-eminent theorist of the exception of the twentieth century, Carl Schmitt, known as the state lawyer for Hitler's newly established Reich, and as such 'the most controversial German legal and political thinker of the twentieth century' (Schwab 2005: xxxvii).[1] His political concept of exception was developed in *Political Theology*, a slim book originally published in 1922. Republished with some minor changes twelve years later, it also included an updated preface that sought to consider the new political environment: the emergence of the one-party state under National Socialism.[2]

Schmitt uses a range of terms to describe the concept of exception, including *Ausnahmezustand* (state of emergency), *Ausnahmefall* (crisis or state of urgency), *Notstand* and *Notfall* (the more general emergency or state of need) (Schlegel cited in Strong 2005: xiii). The concepts of *Ausnahmezustand* and *Notstand* seem similar to Anglo-Saxon terms such as 'martial law' and 'emergency powers'. It is therefore easy to approach the problem of the exception from the Anglo-Saxon perspective as a matter of definition that, if correctly understood, solves the problem itself. However, as the philosopher Giorgio Agamben points out, the idea of martial law implies a special form of law that applies to the state of war (2005: 4). For Schmitt, the exception is not to be understood as another form of law, but an instance in which the rule of law has failed,

© The Author(s) 2019
P. Brown, *Bonhoeffer*,
https://doi.org/10.1007/978-3-030-05698-8_5

or it is no longer operative. It is therefore highly relevant to our read-ing of Bonhoeffer's concept of the extraordinary situation, which like-wise applies precisely when the law has failed to protect the individuals, and society, from preserving the basic conditions that make life possi-ble. Bonhoeffer acts in defiance of the law, in order to preserve the law. Schmitt's concept of exception is similar in that it also breaks with the rule of law (and therefore cannot be understood as another type of law), and for Schmitt is also necessary in order to guarantee the effectiveness of the law.

EXCEPTIONS

While Bonhoeffer seems to use the term in a fairly straightforward way, based on Machiavelli's concept of *necessità*, in Schmitt's investigation of the political basis for the concept of exception, there is no single defini-tion. The most famous definition of the exception given by Schmitt is introduced in the well-known opening sentence of *Political Theology*—'Sovereign is he who decides on the exception [*Ausnahmezustand*]' (2005: 5). The exception seems to be defined as the decisive sovereign, the individual who proclaims a state of exception, and who through that proclamation is the one who can be identified as the sovereign ruler. For Schmitt, the sovereign is the one who has the power of decision, or alter-natively, the individual who through decisive action can be identified as the sovereign. The exception understood as the sovereign decision is the most widely known part of Schmitt's theory of the exception.

Yet, this is not the full account of Schmitt's concept of the state of exception. Schmitt in fact appears to give a variety of definitions through his attempts to describe the exception in distinctive ways. The second definition of exception in *Political Theology* is as follows: 'The exception (*Ausnahmefall*), which is not codified in the existing legal order, can at best be characterised as a case of extreme peril (*äußerster Not*), a dan-ger to the existence of the state, or the like' (Schmitt 2005: 6). Here, Schmitt defines the exception as an event that threatens the state itself. The third definition of exception in *Political Theology* is given when Schmitt quotes the Danish philosopher Søren Kierkegaard (not by name) at the end of Chapter 1:

> The exception [*Ausnahme*] explains the general [*Allgemeine*] and itself. And if one wants to study the general correctly, one only needs to look

around for a true exception. It reveals everything more clearly than does the general. Endless talk about the general becomes boring; there are exceptions. If they cannot be explained, then the general also cannot be explained. The difficulty is usually not noticed because the general is not thought about with passion but with a comfortable superficiality. The exception, on the other hand, thinks the general with intense passion. (Kierkegaard cited in Schmitt 2005: 15)

It suggests that only the concept of exception is able to apprehend or understand the general appropriately. That is, the general is correctly understood in light of the exception.[3] Yet, it is more than a statement about the logical relationship between the exception, or the singular, and the general, or the universal. By drawing on this quote, Schmitt also introduces an existential element into his concept of the exception. And this existential element approvingly describes the exception as 'intense passion'. Just prior to the Kierkegaard quote, Schmitt states that, '[i]n the exception the power of real life [*Kraft der wicklichen Lebens*] breaks through the crust of a mechanism that has become torpid by repetition' (2005: 15). As such, the exception appears as a power that returns life, vitality and energy in a civilisation that has become stagnant. The fourth definition of exception in *Political Theology* is found in the third chapter where Schmitt appears to begin a discussion on the theological origins of modern sovereignty. Here, he states that the 'exception [*Ausnahmezustand*] in jurisprudence is analogous to the miracle [*Wunder*] in theology' Schmitt (2005: 36). Little more is said about this in this passage, Schmitt declaring that '[a] detailed presentation of the meaning of the concept of the miracle in this context will have to be left to another time' (2005: 37). Bonnie Honig in *Emergency Politics: Paradox, Law, Democracy* devotes a chapter to the place of miracle in the state of exception. She provides a definition when she argues that for Schmitt, 'the miracle on which the exception is modelled is an interruptive force that suspends the ordinary lawfulness of the world and thereby exhibits divine power and sovereignty' (2009: 94). This suggests that, for Schmitt, a central feature of the miracle is the interruption of the everyday, of the suspension of normal lawfulness.[4]

We have found that Schmitt conceptualises the exception in a number of ways. The most famous and central definition appears to make the decision key to the concept of exception. In this first definition, the exception has some unique features. First, it cannot be approached as an abstract theory. For Schmitt, it is always a question of concrete application undertaken by the decision maker, the individual sovereign. Second, the prioritisation of the concrete decision puts the sovereign in a special relationship to the law. Because the question of exception is based on the sovereign who decides, the exception cannot be anticipated, predicted or contained within the existing juridical order. The sovereign makes the decision *independent* of law. As a result, suggests Schmitt, the constitutive, specific element of a decision appear as 'new and alien' in the eyes of the law (2005: 31). Indeed, according to Schmitt, the normative content of the law and the state constitution *depends* on the sovereign's decision for its stability. Because the decision is prior to law, all law is in fact 'situational law', guaranteed by the decision of the sovereign (Schmitt 2005: 13). Within this understanding of the expectation, the decision is given precedence over the law.

Yet, while the first and most famous definition of the exception highlights the role of the decision in relation to the exception, the other three definitions seem to conceptualise the exception as an event that is *independent* from human decision-making. In the second definition of the exception as *Ausnahmefall*, the exception is understood as a threat to the stability of the state, a stability made possible through the rule of law. The appearance of the exception is now understood as *requiring* or necessitating a sovereign, an individual not bound by the law in order to restore the stability of the rule of law and the state. Furthermore, within his discussion of the exception as event, Schmitt describes it as both a threat to the state, and as an existential event and power that restores vitality and energy to a stagnant civilisation. This positive view of exception does not agree with Schmitt's claim that the appearance of the exception as event is necessarily dangerous or a threat. Thus, an ambiguity arises as to how we are to understand the exceptional event.[5]

Within his various treatments of the concept, it appears that the exception can be theorised in two different ways: either as grounded in the decision of the sovereign and therefore *initiated* by human decision and action (the first definition) or as *independent* from human decision-making processes in its appearance. On the one hand, Schmitt seems to want to argue that the essence of sovereignty is the independent decision that proclaims the state of exception. Yet, in his subsequent description of the exception as an event that requires the sovereign decision, Schmitt establishes an ambiguous relationship between the exceptional event that precedes and therefore *requires* the sovereign decision and the idea of sovereignty as characterised by the power to decide independently of outside influences.[6] Thus, there is a curious dialectic at play between the 'exceptional event' that requires the absolute sovereign, and the sovereign who *decides* or *proclaims* the 'exceptional event' into existence. This ambiguity is itself inherent within the language of the first definition of exception found in *Political Theology*. The phrase, 'Sovereign is he who decides on the exception' [*Soverän ist, wer über den Ausnahmezustand entscheidet*] can actually be rendered into English either as 'he who decides what the exceptional case is' or 'he who decides what to do about the exceptional case' (Strong 2005: xi–xii). The former links the exception to the decision, the latter prioritises the exception as event. Schwab's translation uses 'decides on the exception', argues Strong, thereby 'retaining the seeming ambiguity [that] is central to grasping what Schmitt wants to say'. It therefore appears that Schmitt is not only aware of the ambiguity of his various characterisations of the exception, but understands this ambiguity as key to the concept of exception itself. Yet this ambiguity has consequences that are perhaps not foreseen by Schmitt. As a result of the conflation between the two forms of exception, the individual or sovereign who declares the exception also has the power to initiate the exception as an event or to proclaim the event into being. This power I will now suggest lies first and foremost in Schmitt's use of theology to support his political concept of exception.

The Political Theology of the State of Exception

Schmitt has been described as 'the twentieth-century godfather of political theology' (Hollerich 2004: 107). Yet, in terms of Schmitt as a political theologian, a number of qualifications need to be made. The first qualification is regarding the 'theological' status of Schmitt's *Political Theology*. There is much debate as to what extent Schmitt can actually be said to provide a consistent 'political theology'. While Schmitt has been read as a political and legal theorist, in more recent years, his own claim to be engaging in political theology has gained the attention of Anglo-American scholars. Arguably, this interest was stimulated by the publication of Heinrich Meier's *Carl Schmitt, Leo Strauss und 'Der Begriff des Politischen'* (1988), translated into the English-speaking world in 1995 as *Carl Schmitt & Leo Strauss: The Hidden Dialogues*.[7] According to Meier, the centre of Schmitt's thought 'is his faith in revelation' and this is what makes Schmitt a political theologian (1995: xiv). Indeed,

Meier's Schmitt can be seen as the political theologian par excellence, as for Meier political theology is located in the framework of revelation: 'Political theology presupposes faith in the truth of revelation. It subordinates everything to revelation and traces everything back to it' (Meier 2011: 20).[8] Jan-Werner Müller notes that 'Meier mixed the personal and the academic', drawing on 'Schmitt's often highly personal theories in his interpretive strategy' (2003: 204). Yet, Müller also notes that for Schmitt, 'political theology was always nothing less than a matter of life and death [...] it was in theology that the personal and the political met for Schmitt', thus seeming to suggest that Schmitt himself did not have a clear separation between his political philosophy and his own views (2003: 156).

Schmitt himself in *Political Theology* appears to be ambivalent about the relationship between the theological and the political and seems to be interested in the former only in order to better understand the origins of the modern state:

> All significant concepts of the modern theory of the state are secularized theological concepts not only because of their historical development ... but also because of their systematic structure, the recognition of which is necessary for a sociological consideration of these concepts. (2005: 36)[9]

However, even with his interest in the theological origins of contemporary political concept, Schmitt's approach is hardly systematic. Indeed, in later correspondence, when reflecting on his 'method' or approach to political philosophy, Schmitt declared:

> I have a particular method: to let the phenomena approach me, to wait a little and think from the subject matter, so to speak, not from preconceived criteria. You could call this phenomenological, but I do not like to engage in such general methodological preliminary questions. (cited in Muller 2003: 8)

Schmitt's broad-stroke reference to phenomenology suggests he attempts to borrow from phenomenology (via Husserl and Heidegger) the idea that phenomena are things that show themselves, and it is the task of the phenomenologist to describe these things in their appearance, not on the basis of pre-established categories of understanding.[10] This shows it is best not to approach Schmitt's 'political theology' as a systematic exercise in theological ideas applied to the sphere of the ordering of human society, but rather through considering the theological imagery that emerges in Schmitt's own concepts of sovereignty.

The second qualification acknowledges that Schmitt (like Heidegger) was a German Catholic who explicitly claimed to speak from a Catholic position.[11] This may therefore impact any attempt to compare the political theology of Schmitt with the emerging ideas of Bonhoeffer. However, scholars suggest that Schmitt developed a highly idiosyncratic Catholic political stance, that was neither neoscholastic, nor Romantic as German Catholicism tended to be at this time (Balakrishan 2000: 43). His relationship both to the Catholic Church and to its theological traditions was deeply politically mediated. Furthermore, Schmitt's own reading of the New Testament departed significantly from an orthodox Catholic position and 'Schmitt's theology owed some of its most significant elements to the Protestant side, especially to Luther and Calvin' (Hohendahl 2008).[12] This increases the relevance of Schmitt's concept of the exception as a lens through which to critically examine Bonhoeffer' concept of the extraordinary situation.

Having addressed the qualifications of Schmitt as a theologian, particularly noting his lack of systematic approach to theology, it is time now to consider Schmitt's use of theology to support his political concept of exception. Already noted was a brief reference to the exception as analogous to the miracle. This, however, is not the key theological idea to emerge. Rather, it is his description of the sovereign decision that is shot through with theological imagery. The following references to the 'decision' in *Political Theology* demonstrate the extent to which Schmitt injects his political concepts with theological authority: Schmitt refers to the exception as that which 'reveals [*offenbart*] ... the decision in absolute purity'; he states that the moment [*Augenblick*] the decision is made, the decision becomes independent of its argumentative base; he also declares that, considered 'normatively, the decision emanates from nothingness' [*aus dem Nichts geboren*] (2005: 13, 30, 31–32). It seems that despite the conflation between different concepts of the exception and the lack of theological explication in terms of the concept of the miracle, Schmitt's central concept of decision is itself actually thoroughly theological: it has the character of *revelation*. Marc De Wilde notes that 'Schmitt implicitly aims at an analogy between the legal concept of the decision and the theological concept of *creatio ex nihilo*' (2006: 195).

The Christian doctrine of 'creation out of nothing' emphasises that creation is unconditioned. Furthermore, it denotes a radically free and sovereign act on the part of God (Gunton 2004: 91). The Protestant theologian Jürgen Moltmann emphasises that such creation is 'without any preconditions. There is no external necessity which occasions … creativity, and no inner compulsion which could determine it' (1991: 74). The doctrine of 'creatio ex nihilo' is a distinctive Judeo-Christian metaphysical doctrine that accounts for the existence of things and sees such existence as being a 'non-reciprocal relation of dependence […] between temporality of the world and the eternality of God' (Cogliati 2010: 8).[13] It has also been described as an 'apocalyptic' account of creation that affirms the absolute distinction between God and the world, and the freedom of the Creator (Adams 2015: 160). A defining character of God's nature is the ability to begin anew, spontaneously, and the world is the specific outcome of God's decision of will. Goldstone describes the doctrine of *creatio ex nihilo* as one of Christianity's key ideas that has influenced modernity's distinctive logic of sovereign power, and furthermore, that today's discussions around sovereignty and power bears the 'unmistakable imprint of Carl Schmitt's recasting of the Western political and philosophical tradition through the figure of decision and exception' (2014: 100). Thus, Schmitt's political exception mirrors the divine nature of God's creation, as bringing life *ex nihilo* that is without preconditions, and through the irruptive event of the miracle, continues to reinvigorate or renew existing life.

It is finally the doctrine of *creatio ex nihilo* that informs Schmitt's concept of sovereignty as the power to proclaim the exception as the authority over law. What are the political consequences of this? The political philosopher Hannah Arendt is highly critical of the modern concept of sovereignty as it is grounded on the Judeo-Christian doctrine of *creatio ex nihilo*. For Arendt, this has led to a view of sovereignty that treats other human beings as material objects and shapes them as clay in the potter's hands. It encourages the delusion that:

[…] we can 'make' something in the realm of human affairs, - 'make' institutions or laws, for instance, as we make tables and chairs, or make men 'better' or 'worse' – or it is conscious despair of all action, political and non-political, coupled with the utopian hope that it may be possible to treat men as one treats other 'material'. (Arendt 1998: 188)

For Arendt the concept of sovereignty itself views the world, including its social institutions and laws, as open to a radical new beginning where other human beings do not constitute a limit to the self-realisation of the project. Far from the omnipotent state that unifies institutions and people, Arendt argues that claims to sovereignty represent nothing more than 'a shapeless, hectic, maelstrom of permanent revolution and endless expansion' (Canovan 2000: 9). It leads to totalitarianism that is obedient only to the 'law of movement', a restless and dynamic force of destruction that wipes away all human cultural institutions it holds the belief that 'everything is possible' (Arendt 1962: 459, 463). In Protestant theology, the phrase 'everything is possible' belongs only to God, and its primary meaning is in the theological concepts of grace understood as the forgiveness of sins. But for Arendt, when assigned to the concept of sovereignty, the phrase 'all things are [or everything is] possible' becomes fertile ground for a totalitarianism which nullifies even the category of criminality itself (Sitze 2005: 283).[14] This nullification of criminality appears indirectly in Schmitt's description of the exception and decision. What characterises the exception *as* exception is 'principally unlimited authority, which means the suspension of the entire existing order' (Schmitt 2005: 12). This means that the sovereign who decides on the state of exception has unlimited authority and must be seen as 'infallible' in his decision-making (Schmitt 2005: 55).[15]

This is a significant departure from either Niccolo Machiavelli or Thomas Hobbes' early modern notions of sovereignty. As Andrew Neal points out, Schmitt's political theology goes further than Machiavelli, whose prince lacks power over *fortuna*; when *fortuna* turns against the prince, it marks the end of his power and reign, signalling that the reign of the prince is temporary. Neal suggests that this does not apply to Schmitt's sovereign (Neal 2010: 71). Schmitt's departure from sovereignty as an early modern idea is also evident in Schmitt's reading of Hobbes' *Leviathan*. It was from Hobbes' *auctoritas, non veritas facit legem* (the one who has authority can demand obedience) that Schmitt developed his concept of the sovereign. But Schmitt here extends the concept of sovereignty beyond the question of authority to include the existential decision.[16] For Schmitt, it is not always the *legitimate* sovereign who possesses this authority. Rather, as Neil points out, sovereignty is revealed through the proclamation of authority; 'it is the *capacity* for this kind of authority that actually reveals who is *truly sovereign*' (2010: 58, italics original). For Schmitt, sovereignty is revealed through proclamation or decision, separated from the authority of law and office that would normally be considered to give the proclamation its legitimacy, and instead is injected with quasi-divine authority that draws on the theological concept of *creatio ex nihilo*.

This too fits with Meier's reading of Schmitt's political theology, with revelation as the foundation that is linked to obedience on the part of the subject: 'Insofar as political theology champions the binding force of revelation, it places itself in the service of obedience' (Meier 2011: 20). Linking together the ethical, the theological and the martial, Meier addresses the existential person addressed by the revelatory divine proclamation:

> Whoever persists in contemplation does not hear the call that confronts him with the decision between either God or Satan, friend or enemy, good or evil. He does not orient his existence towards the command that is given him from outside. (Meier 2011: 16)

Note the either/or reverberated: God or Satan, friend or enemy, good or evil. There is no place for contemplation or critical reflection, only for obedience to the revelatory or divine command that establishes the categories that confront the believer, or citizen, and requires obedience. There is little doubt that Schmitt stands on the side of authority, revelation and obedience: of political theology proper, according to Meier. My interest here is not in whether Schmitt can be read to endorse this political theology wholeheartedly. Rather, it is the division itself, which lies latent in Schmitt's own thinking around the concept of exception. It is the primacy of revelation over reason that is the troublesome aspect that Arendt identified as located in the Judeo-Christian concept of sovereignty. Müller argues that Schmitt's concept of the exception signifies 'the moment of the existential choice between God and Satan', according to Meier's view (Müller 2003: 204). If this is so, then Schmitt's political concept of exception is saturated with a political theology that is grounded on the revelatory event that prioritises the existential crisis and links this directly to a demand for obedience to the sovereign ruler who is able to act without checks and balances to their power.

CONSEQUENCES OF THE EXCEPTION: LOSS OF THE WORLD

The outcome of Schmitt's concept of exception as the basis of political life and as grounded in political theology leads directly to the loss of the world, by which I mean the loss of the communal or shared world,

and it does so in three ways: through the loss of mediating institutions; through the loss of democracy; and through encouraging a space
of force outside the bounds of law. The first 'world' that disappears is
that of mediating institutions, which vanish along with the norms that
are secured by custom and law. Schmitt's concept of the exception prioritises the existential decision made 'ex nihilo' and thereby abandons
traditional and existing rationales and reflections that have informed
actions. Established institutions that mediate complex situations, whether
in political forms such as processes and policies, or social forms, such
as customs and traditions, appear to be simply dismissed by Schmitt as
impotent in the exceptional situation. What is meant by mediating institutions, and why are they significant? Alisdair Macintyre in *After Virtue*
argues that moral actions are intelligible within a social or communal setting, which may be an institution or practice, or 'a milieu of some other
human kind' that has a history which makes the action intelligible (1984:
206–207). On this account, inherited traditions constitute the starting
point of a moral life. Bourdieu understood this as *habitus*, the structural
framework or 'community of dispositions' that enables agency and action
(1977: 35).[17] Hannah Arendt placed similar value on the role of institutions, particularly the capacity for language to establish a human world in
which human beings could discuss and dissent ideas in a way that could
mediate more biological and primal functions of the human condition.

Such accounts are dismissed by Schmitt as an effective way to respond
to the state of exception. The tone of crisis invoked during the state of
exception suggests that a quick response without due consideration is the
most desirable answer. In Schmitt's account of the exception as authoritative over custom, norm and law, there is no process that can question
or test the claim to exception. Schmitt's claim that unlimited authority is
the proper response to the exceptional event suggests an absence of the
usual forms of mediation made possible by co-ordinated responses from
a variety of sources, and the deliberation, discussion and planning that
accompanies such responses. But the loss of mediating institutions is not
only the demise of government as good governance or administration, it
entails a wider loss of the world, through a demise of tradition, culture,
history. These are the processes that establish the complex social world
which profoundly shape our identity and enable a myriad of relationships
to take place through public offices, professions, familial responsibilities
and civic life.

The demise of this complex and diverse social world leads to the
second consequence of Schmitt's exception: the loss of democracy.

In keeping with the identification of the sovereign with a single individual, Schmitt refers to 'the decision', not to the plural 'decisions', which would suggest a social or democratic element. In his preface to the second (1933) edition of *Political Theology*, Schmitt emphasises the role of the individual who makes the decision by referring to the 'decisionist' who operates by means of a 'personal decision' that is to be understood as the 'genuine decision', not simply 'decisionism' (2005: 3). For Schmitt, *who* decides is more important than *how* the decision is made. While the former emphasises the subjective element of the decision, the latter frames the decision in relation to instituting objective formal and rational processes (Huysmans 2008: 168). It is the latter that Schmitt perceived as the failure of liberal democracy. In a lengthy tribute to the Spanish Catholic philosopher, Donoso Cortés,[18] Schmitt attacked liberal politics for its insistence on 'negotiation', which he declared is 'a cautious half measure, in the hope that the definitive dispute, the decisive bloody battle, can be transformed into a parliamentary debate and permit the decision to be suspended forever in an everlasting discussion' (2005: 63). Conversely, it is the decision that brings discussion to an end, and the sovereign is the person who demonstrates authority precisely by refusing to enter into further debate. It would appear that for Schmitt, true sovereignty demonstrates its authority by refusing to be persuaded by argument or reason. Political life on Schmitt's account is not to be understood as the association of equals in a democracy. Huysmans argues that, by employing a radical top-down interpretation of representation, Schmitt erases the concept of the people as a political multiplicity, preferring instead a vision of 'nationalist politics that amalgamates the people into a unity produced by leadership' (2008: 169, 180).

Schmitt's political theology undermines democratic ideas of cooperation and negotiation; indeed, for Schmitt the negotiation and compromise that is part of democratic life are antithetical to political life itself. Meier's observation that Schmitt's political theology prioritises the existential person is key to also understanding Schmitt's view of the political. Revelation (and the political exception) confronts the individual with the either/or decision, between God or Satan, friend or enemy, good or evil (Meier 2011: 16). The friend/enemy distinction is important for Schmitt, and in his later book, the *Concept of the Political*, it becomes the organising principle of the political itself. Here, it is described as an existential category of confrontation: the enemy appears as the other, the stranger and as 'something different and alien'; the friend–enemy relation is the 'utmost degree of intensity of union or separation, of an association or dissociation' that is expressed in conflict, not through existing norms or the judgement of a neutral third party (Schmitt 1996: 26, 27). Thus, the political is the total, and it is defined by 'existential and even violent conflict'; Schmitt reduces the political to a question of power 'based on an almost Manichean dualism of good and evil, resolvable only by brutal decision and command' (Hollerich 2004: 116–117).[19] For Schmitt, decision, command and violence are deeply entwined, and together form the basis of the political, which for Schmitt is a judgement about relationships between human beings. The political is not one domain amongst others, but the criterion to describe the condition of moral and existential relationality between human beings.

Thus, for Schmitt the possibility or appearance of violence is actually the basis of political life itself. Yet, such violence is not a force controlled by law. The loss of mediating institutions and practices in favour of the command of the leader places violence outside the regulative function of law. Agamben refers to this force as enabling 'a pure violence without *logos* [...] without any real reference' (2005: 40). In claiming that the state of exception enables a pure violence, Agamben suggests that the state of exception initiates a form of violence without justification, without reason, or *ratio*, to contain it. This has implications for the individual who acts in a state of exception, and the law that exists to prevent violence without *logos*. If the state of exception requires the suspension of the entire existing juridical order, then it is impossible to maintain a connection to the juridical order to ensure that the state of exception itself does not become a permanent state of affairs. Violence without reference will necessarily threaten to become its own form of justification. Furthermore, because of the lack of *ratio*, the individual who responds to the revelation of exception can pose the same danger to the state as the original situation of peril that required the exception in the first place. It is well-nigh impossible to measure the decision or action arising from that decision, since measurement requires a concept of *ratio*, of proportion, that is arrived at by measurement against a standard or a norm. If the state of exception is a suspension of the entire existing juridical order, it seems impossible to maintain a connection to juridical order to ensure that the state of exception does not later become the threat it was intended to prevent.

In his study on *Democracy and Political Violence*, John Schwarzmantel highlights the problem of legitimising violent action in a liberal-democratic society, as it involves the suspension of civil liberties that are foundational to the trust between the governed and the governing in a democracy. Any claims to emergency situations or emergency politics gives greater power to the executive elements of the state, overriding the foundations of liberal democracy:

> The state thus becomes itself a violent actor, employing violence in unrestricted ways which then call forth an equal and opposite reaction from those opposed to the liberal-democratic state. Examples from the US war against terror are obvious cases in point here, as witnessed by the abuses at Guantánamo and Abu Ghraib. (Schwarzmantel 2011: 68)

Schwarzmantel argues that traditional institutions that provide checks and controls over holders of state power are less effective in a 'surveillance society' in which the powers of the state are more concentrated, the latter being justifying itself on the grounds that there are security reasons for increased discretion and autonomy by executive powers (2011: 69). Thus, action in a state of exception is by its nature illiberal, anti-democratic and self-perpetuating in its own claims for necessity.

While he was deeply critical of liberal democracies, unchecked executive power may not have been Schmitt's intention. Agamben argues that the goal of *Political Theology* is 'the inscription of the state of exception within a juridical context'; it is an attempt to ascribe *within* the law the suspension of the juridical order itself (2005: 32–33). Agamben suggests that Schmitt tries to achieve a 'paradoxical articulation' through a distinction between two fundamental elements of law: norm and decision (*Entscheidung, Dezision*), each having its own sphere of autonomy. In the normal situation, the autonomous decision is minimalised; in the state of exception, the law recedes. This can be seen in *Political Theology* where Schmitt states that the sovereign both stands outside the normally valid legal system, yet belongs to it, 'for it is he who must decide whether the constitution needs to be suspended in its entirety' (2005: 7). A little later, Schmitt claims that the 'exception remains, nevertheless, accessible to jurisprudence because both elements, the norm as well as the decision, remain within the framework of justice' (2005: 12–13). As Jef Huysmans argues, Schmitt seems to want to rescue the essence of the law, which is actually the pronouncement of judgement and 'the certainty that a decision is being made' (2008: 168). Yet, Schmitt's claim that the exception is the point where the decision parts from the legal norm and authority proves itself as authority (over law) opens a space for force *outside* the bounds of law, a zone of *anomie*[20] in which all legal determinations are deactivated. For Agamben, the concept of exception 'defines law's threshold or limit concept' (2005: 1–2). It is a *Grenzbegriff* that 'presents a threshold, or a zone of indifference, where inside and outside do not exclude each other but rather blur with each other' (Agamben 2005: 23). The crucial problem is that all acts committed during the exception seem to escape all legal definition: they are neither transgressive, executive, nor legislative, rather, 'they seem to be situated in an absolute non-place with respect to the law' (Agamben 2005: 51). In Arendtian terms, this can lead to totalitarianism that has the capacity to nullify even the category of criminality itself.

This chapter has investigated the concept of exception in Carl Schmitt's political theology. Yet, rather than one concept of exception, I have suggested there are a range of concepts with differing characteristics that challenge a straightforward definition or understanding of the idea of exception. On one reading, Schmitt's concept of exception appears contradictory to the reader who looks for clear guidelines as to what constitutes an exception. However, Schmitt can also be read to articulate the challenges inherent in employing the concept of exception as a basis for political action. Schmitt attempted to maintain a connection between the sovereign and existing law, through the idea of a paradoxical articulation between norm and decision, where each has its own sphere of autonomy. Yet the danger in prioritising the decision, through elevating the sovereign decision to the status of divine infallibility, is the absence or disappearance of law and norm. While Schmitt sought to preserve the integrity of the law as the regulative structure that enables life together in the world, Schmitt's notion of sovereignty based on the exception threatens to nullify the authority of the law. It is finally the sovereign decision that must be implemented *ex nihilo* and therefore is required to create the political world anew. The divine sovereign decision decrees that the law, as the old shall pass away. But the promise of the new is not that which builds community or life for *peoples* on earth. No matter how much Schmitt's sovereign would *will* the creation of a better world, as Arendt noted, the unpredictability of human actions may well lead to violence where other human beings do not constitute the limit to one's own project. Schmitt's turn to exception, rather than law, as the basis for sovereignty has significant consequences for the stable structure of political society. Overriding mediating structures such as law and custom leads to a sense of existential crisis and ultimately unrestrained force, or violence without *ratio*, and the loss of the world as the world, in which individuals and people can individually and socially gather and create meaning.

Schmitt's articulation of the exception in *Political Theology* challenges us to be alert to the dangers of invoking exceptions in order to resolve difficult and trenchant political issues. Furthermore, Schmitt's articulating of the exception in terms of political theology, and Meier's interpretation of this, points to the danger of using theology to ground concepts of sovereignty, without also critically reflecting on the theological ideas themselves. Schmitt's uncritical references to theological ideas and his analogous application of these to sovereignty, potentially leads to a decisionism that is characterised as infallible. It is time now to return to Bonhoeffer's concept of the extraordinary situation, and consider the extent to which Schmitt's political concept of the exception, and the political theology in which it is grounded, can illumine some of the issues raised around the concept of the extraordinary situation as identified in the previous two chapters.

NOTES

1. It is difficult to evaluate Schmitt's political writings without recognising his Nazi past. Until his death in 1985, Schmitt was regarded by many in the Anglophone world as simply a Nazi theoretician. In the last 30 years, this image of Schmitt has undergone rehabilitation and his involvement in Nazism has been reinterpreted as typical of many fellow German conservatives for whom the choice was either Hitler or chaos. It is claimed that what led Schmitt to collaborate with the Nazis was not ethical nihilism but concern with order. Paul Hirst, for example, argued that Schmitt's 'political thought should not be evaluated on the basis of authors' personal political judgments...the value of Schmitt's work is not diminished by the choices he made' (1987: 16). In a similar vein, Schwab argues that Schmitt's involvement in Nazism was an attempt to form a 'distinctly Schmittian' theory of the state for the Third Reich that restored the 'personal element vital to the preservation of the modern constitutional state (2005: xl, xlii). On the other hand, Huysmans argues that this rehabilitation from Nazi theoretician to a morally neutral 'political theorist' is deeply disturbing because it 'decouples, implicitly or explicitly, Schmitt's choice for the Nazis from the substance of his political theory' (1999: 323). According to Huysmans, the question

of Schmitt's political choice is central to any interpretation of Schmitt's political ideas.

2. This occurred after 14 July 1933, the date on which the National Socialist party declared itself the only political party and outlawed all other parties. When Schmitt refers to 'movement' in the Preface, he had the National Socialist party and the SA (*Sturmabteilung*) in mind since neither, according to Schmitt, were subject to the control of ordinary courts, rather they were subject to their own systems of justice (Schwab 1989: 108–109, fn 26). Yet, despite this reference in the new preface, the focus of *Political Theology* itself remains on the individual sovereign.

3. Yet, while the quote from *Repetition* in Schmitt's *Political Theology* suggests a radically isolated concept of exception, this is not the case in the original passage. See Ryan, Bartholomew. 2014. *Kierkegaard's Indirect Politics: Interludes with Lukács, Schmitt, Benjamin and Adorno*. Amsterdam: Rodopi.

4. Here, Schmitt seems to follow Kant for whom the miracle names an event that is inexplicable or unintelligible on the basis of natural laws of cause and effect. For Kant, 'miracles' are 'events in the world that are operating laws of whose causes are, and must remain, absolutely unknown to us' (Kant 1960: 81).

5. It raises the question as to whether the event is a threat or a revitalising force. We will return to this in chapter nine, in the context of the intellectual milieu of the Weimar Republic.

6. See also Andrew Neal, who argues that Schmitt conflates three forms of exception: the exceptional *event* itself; the sovereign *decision* that the exceptional event exists; and the sovereign *response* to the exceptional event (2010: 72).

7. Until Heinrich Meier, the Anglo-American readership has tended to neglect the theological thought that undergirds Schmitt's political and legal discourse. Hohendahl has gone so far as to suggest that there is 'a divide' between Continental and European critics, who freely acknowledge and draw on the significance of Schmitt's political theology, and the Anglo-American scholars who have either played down or ignored this aspect altogether (2008). It is worth noting that the political theology of Schmitt has been studied since the 1960s by several 'left' leaning theologians, including the Catholic Johann Baptist Metz and the Protestant Lutheran Jürgen Moltmann, who both, inspired by the reforms of Vatican II, developed new political theologies in terms of a politically and socially committed church and looked to Schmitt to support their own revolutionary ideas. While Schmitt's right-wing conservatism doesn't seem to support the revolutionary ideals of the left, like the left, Schmitt pursues an active political theology based on concrete commitment.

8. See also (Meier 2011). For Meier, revelation is clearly key to how political theology should be understood. Yet, political theology is not concerned with revelation perse. Not emphasising revelation as such, William Cavanaugh in the *Blackwell Companion to Political Theology* defines political theology as 'the explicit attempt to relate discourse about God to the organisation of bodies in space and time' (Cavanaugh and Scott 2007: 3).

9. Schmitt, following Max Weber, understands 'secularized' as meaning the 'disenchantment' of the world. Schmitt attempts to restore to the concepts of sovereignty and political authority the 'transcendent' qualities that belonged to these categories as a matter of course in the sixteenth and seventeenth century. This fully secularised political sphere is referred to as 'the political' or *das Politische.*

10. Michael Marder contextualises Schmitt's political thought within the existential-phenomenological tradition, exploring the various connections between Schmitt and Husserlian phenomenology, Schmitt and Gadamer's hermeneutics, and Schmitt and Heidegger's concept of 'destruction' (2010).

11. A note on Schmitt's own Catholic heritage. Born in 1888 in a devout Catholic family in the predominantly Protestant town of Plettenberg in Westphalia, Schmitt was expected to join the priesthood, but studied law instead at the University of Berlin, in 1919 receiving his doctorate in jurisprudence from the University of Strasbourg in 1910. Schmitt remained emotionally and intellectually a Catholic until the First World War, where his experience of war and the subsequent instability of the Weimar Republic began to push him towards a 'starker political realism' (Schwab 2005: xxxviii).

12. It is worth noting that the concept of *nomos* (translated as order, law, rule or decision and key in Schmitt's book *Der Nomos der Erde*) appeared Schmitt's political vocabulary in 1933–1934, via German Protestant theology, replacing the more formal concept of *Gesetz* which Schmitt associated with the formal law of nineteenth-century jurisprudence, and which for Schmitt did not represent the act of the concrete political orders on which Europe was founded (Koskenniemi 2002: 415–416).

13. Scholars argue over the origins of the doctrine, with some suggesting it began with Hellenistic Judaism, and others in the early Christian period. There is a consensus that *creatio ex nihilo* was not a concept available to Greek philosophy. For Aristotle (and Plato) the world was considered eternal, *ex nihilo nihil fit* (from noting nothing comes) (Soskice 2010).

14. '[I]n their effort to prove that everything is possible, totalitarian regimes have discovered without knowing that there are crimes which men can neither punish nor forgive. When the impossible was made possible it became the unpunishable, unforgivable absolute evil which could no

longer be understood and explained by the evil motives of self-interest, greed, covetousness, resentment, lust for power, and cowardice; and which therefore anger could not revenge, love could not endure, friendship could not forgive' (Arendt 1962: 459).

15. Schmitt's exemplar here, who 'spoke with particular fondness of sovereignty', was Joseph de Maistre, the Catholic philosopher for whom infallibility was essential to decision-making; and for whom the infallibility of the spiritual order (the Roman Catholic Church) was equated with the sovereignty of the state order (2005: 55).

16. While Hobbes uses scientific argument as the basis of his thinking, for Schmitt there is only the 'abyss', an existential foundation (Ryan 2014: 93).

17. This evokes an older understanding of the concept of habit, one not reduced to a biophysiological phenomenon (such as a system of required reflexes or responses), but as designating a range of complex and intelligent behavioural dispositions, moral sentiments, acquired competences and forms of practical understanding and reasoning (Camic 1986).

18. Cortes is named by Schmitt as 'one of the foremost representatives of decisionist thinking' (2005: 51). Cortes radicalised the doctrine of Original Sin into 'a doctrine of the absolute sinfulness and depravity of human nature', which according to Schmitt was akin to 'the Lutheran understanding' of 'absolute worthlessness' (Schmitt 2005: 57). For Cortes, this found its political and historical expression in the battle between Catholicism and atheist socialism, the latter 'his deadly foe... endowed... with a diabolical nature' (Schmitt 2005: 63). Again, the connection with elements of Protestant theology emerges.

19. This is clearly an important qualification for Schmitt as a political *theologian* in that it argues against the Christian notion of divine love. Indeed, Schmitt's political theology was challenged by Catholic critics, who saw the church as being taken up into a conservative defence of power, rather than a 'sacrament of love' that defended un-represented parts of society: 'If the Church is as Carl Schmitt renders it, then ... the Grand Inquisitor is right and Christ is wrong' (Lönne cited in Hollerich 2004: 119).

20. Anomie is exception: 'the failure of the state to reign in undetermined life' (Huysmans 2008: 173).

REFERENCES

Adams, Samuel V. 2015. *The Reality of God and Historical Method: Apocalyptic Theology in Conversation with N.T. Wright*. New Explorations in Theology. Downers Grove: InterVarsity Press.

Agamben, Giorgio. 2005. *State of Exception*, trans. Kevin Attell. Chicago and London: University of Chicago Press.

Arendt, Hannah. 1962. *The Origins of Totalitarianism*, 2nd English edition Aufl. New York: Meridian Books.

Arendt, Hannah. 1998. *The Human Condition*. Chicago: University of Chicago Press.

Balakrishnan, Gopal. 2000. *The Enemy: An Intellectual Portait of Carl Schmitt*. London and New York: Verso.

Bourdieu, Pierre. 1977. *Outline of a Theory of Practice*. Cambridge Studies in Social Anthropology. Cambridge, UK: Cambridge University Press.

Camic, Charles. 1986. The Matter of Habit. *American Journal of Sociology* 91 (5): 1039–1087.

Canovan, Margaret. 2000. Arendt's Theory of Totalitarianism: A Reassessment. In *The Cambridge Companion to Hannah Arendt*, ed. Dana Villa, 25–43. Cambridge: Cambridge University Press.

Cavanaugh, William T., and Peter Scott. 2007. Introduction. In *The Blackwell Companion to Political Theology*, ed. William T. Cavanaugh and Peter Scott, 2–4. Malden: Blackwell.

Cogliati, Carlo. 2010. Introduction. In *Creation and the God of Abraham*, ed. David B. Burrell, Carlo Cogliati, Janet M. Soskice, and William R. Stoeger, 1–10. Cambridge, UK: Cambridge University Press.

De Wilde, Marc. 2006. Violence in the State of Exception: Reflections on Theologico-Political Motifs in Benjamin and Schmitt. In *Political Theologies: Public Religions in a Post-secular World*, eds. Hent De Vries and Lawrence E. Sullivan, 188–200. New York: Fordham University Press.

Goldstone, Brian. 2014. Life After Sovereignty. *History of the Present* 4 (1): 97–113. https://doi.org/10.5406/historypresent.4.1.0097.

Gunton, Colin E. 2004. Creatio ex nihilo and the spatio-temporal dimensions with special reference to Jürgen Moltmann and D.C. Williams. In *Doctrine of Creation: Essays in Dogmatics, History and Philosophy*, ed. Colin E. Gunton. London: Continuum International Publishing.

Hirst, Paul. 1987. Carl Schmitt's Decisionism. *Telos* 72: 15–26.

Hohendahl, P. 2008. Political Theology Revisited: Carl Schmitt's Postwar Reassessment. *Konturen* 1 (1): 1–28.

Hollerich, Michael. 2004. Carl Schmitt. In *The Blackwell Companion to Political Theology*, ed. Peter Scott and William T. Cavanaugh, 107–112. Malden: Blackwell.

Honig, Bonnie. 2009. *Emergency Politics: Paradox, Law, Democracy*. Princeton and Oxford: Princeton University Press.

Huysmans, Jef. 1999. Know Your Schmitt: A Godfather of Truth and the Spectre of Nazism. *Review of International Studies* 25 (2): 323–328.

Huysmans, Jef. 2008. The Jargon of Exception—On Schmitt, Agamben and the Absence of Political Society. *International Political Sociology* 2 (2): 165–183. https://doi.org/10.1111/j.1749-5687.2008.00042.x.

Kant, Immanuel. 1960. *Religion Within the Limits of Reason Alone*, trans. Theodore M. Greene and Hoyt T. Hudson. New York and London: Harper & Row.

Koskenniemi, Martti. 2002. *The Gentle Civilizer of Nations: The Rise and Fall of International Law, 1870–1960*. Hersch Lauterpacht Memorial Lectures. Cambridge, UK and New York: Cambridge University Press.

MacIntyre, Alasdair. 1984. *After Virtue*, 2nd ed. Notre Dame, IN: University of Notre Dame Pres.

Marder, Michael. 2010. *Groundless Existence: The Political Ontology of Carl Schmitt*. New York: Continuum.

Meier, Heinrich. 1995. *Carl Schmitt & Leo Strauss: The Hidden Dialogue*, trans. J. Harvey Lomax. Chicago: University of Chicago Press.

Meier, Heinrich. 2011. *The Lesson of Carl Schmitt: Four Chapters on the Distinction Between Political Theology and Political Philosophy*, trans. Marcus Brainard. Chicago: University of Chicago Press.

Moltmann, Jürgen. 1991. *God in Creation: A New Theology of Creation and the Spirit of God*, trans. Margaret Kohl. San Fransisco: Harper.

Müller, J.W. 2003. *A Dangerous Mind: Carl Schmitt in Post-war European Thought*. New Haven and London: Yale University Press.

Neal, Andrew W. 2010. *Exceptionalism and the Politics of Counter-Terrorism: Liberty, Security and the War on Terror*. Routledge Studies in Liberty and Security. New York: Routledge.

Ryan, Bartholomew. 2014. *Kierkegaard's Indirect Politics [Electronic Resource]: Interludes with Lukács, Schmitt, Benjamin and Adorno*. Amsterdam: Editions Rodopi.

Schmitt, Carl. 1996. *The Concept of the Political*, trans. George Schwab. Chicago and London: The University of Chicago Press.

Schmitt, Carl. 2005. *Political Theology: Four Chapters on the Concept of Sovereignty*, trans. George Schwab. Chicago and London: The University of Chicago Press.

Schwab, George. 1989. *The Challenge of the Exception: An Introduction to the Political Ideas of Carl Schmitt Between 1921 and 1936*. New York: Greenwood Press.

Schwab, George. 2005. Introduction. In *Political Theology: Four Chapters on the Concept of Sovereignty*, xxxvii–lii. Chicago: The University of Chicago Press.

Schwarzmantel, J.J. 2011. *Democracy and Political Violence*. Edinburgh: Edinburgh University Press.

Sitze, Adam. 2005. At the Mercy Of. In *The Limits of Law*, eds. Austin Sarat, Douglas Lawrence, and Martha Merrill Umphrey, 246–308. Stanford: Stanford University Press.

Soskice, Janet M. 2010. Creatio ex nihilo: Jewish and Christian Foundations. In *Creation and the God of Abraham*, eds. David B. Burrell, Carlo Cogliati, Janet M. Soskice, and William R. Stoeger, 24–39. Cambridge: Cambridge University Press.

Strong, Tracy B. 2005. The Sovereign and the Exception: Carl Schmitt, Politics, Theology, and Leadership. In *Political Theology: Four Chapters on the Concept of Sovereignty*, vii–xxxv. Chicago: The University of Chicago Press.

CHAPTER 6

The Extraordinary Situation and the State of Exception

Bonhoeffer's concept of the 'extraordinary situation' emerged in *Ethics*, the key text written during his conspiracy involvement, in connection with Machiavelli's concept of *necessitá*. Chapter 4 concluded by noting that there would be significant implications to Bonhoeffer's turn to Machiavelli. Bonhoeffer introduces the concept of the 'extraordinary situation' is the context of a thinker who provided near absolute discretion to a sovereign power to act beastly, if the situation was judged to require this. In such a scenario, there are few moral limitations imposed from outside. The political consequences of 'unlawful' action based on necessity in an extraordinary situation I suggested could be disastrous, as it involves the risk of compounding the lawlessness that required the extraordinary action in the first place. For this reason, the previous chapter provided an overview of the concept of the state of exception, developed by the *Grenzfall* political thinker par excellence, Carl Schmitt. Having considered key elements of Schmitt's concept of exception, it is time now to critically examine Bonhoeffer's concept of the extraordinary situation in light of the main findings of the previous chapter. While it will become clear that Bonhoeffer's concept of the 'extraordinary situation' is not identical to Schmitt's political *Grenzfall* scenario, nevertheless a critical examination through the critique of Schmitt developed in the previous chapter will be helpful. It enables us to more fully explore the dangers to which Bonhoeffer's own concept of 'responsible action' might lead, if the latter is seen as a Christian (Christ-like) model for last resort violence in an 'extraordinary situation'.

© The Author(s) 2019
P. Brown, *Bonhoeffer*,
https://doi.org/10.1007/978-3-030-05698-8_6

BONHOEFFER AND SCHMITT

At first appearance, it might seem that Bonhoeffer and Schmitt have little in common, given their responses and actions during the war. As a jurist, Schmitt was politically influential throughout the declining years of the Weimar Republic and the rise of National Socialism. Schmitt's own position, as conservative and anti-democratic led him to argue in favour of strong sovereignty, and he could not finally support tyrannicide, even though one of his closest friends played a leading role in the July 20 assassination plot for which he paid with his life.[1] Like many of his fellow theologians, Bonhoeffer protested against National Socialism initially on theological grounds until he became a double-agent in the Abwehr as an act of 'free responsibility' in an 'extraordinary situation'. While Schmitt argued for and supported (at least initially) the political leader who acted decisively to initiate a state of exception, Bonhoeffer acted against the same leader. Yet, while the two responded to National Socialism in radically different ways, nevertheless Schmitt's concept of the exception bears important similarities to Bonhoeffer's concept of the extraordinary situation. Giorgio Agamben notes that the problem of the state of exception presents clear analogies to the right of resistance. In both instances, Agamben argues, what is ultimately at issue is the 'question of the judicial significance of the sphere of action that is in itself extrajuridical' (2005: 11). Both the state of exception and the right of resistance present borderlines cases.[2] It is for this reason that Schmitt and Bonhoeffer can be read together as exploring the implications of the concept of the exception, even if, or perhaps especially because, they appear to belong to diametrically opposed camps.

To date, little scholarship has been done on an intellectual connection between Bonhoeffer and Schmitt. One important connection between the two has been discovered by Karola Radler, in her MA thesis (Radler 2011). Schmitt and Bonhoeffer never met,[3] but Radler argued they shared a common interest and connection in the person of Gerhard Leibholz. Leibholz was a professor of constitutional law who in the mid to late 1920s had both written correspondence and personal meetings with Schmitt. Leibholz was also Bonhoeffer's brother in law.[4] Radler has suggested that Bonhoeffer carries on a 'hidden dialogue' with Schmitt on the concept of representation, aware of Schmitt's work due to his close contact with Leibholz. Radler describes Leibholz as facilitating 'the jurisprudential link on one side to Schmitt and on the other to

Bonhoeffer' (2011: 12).[5] Leibholz exposed Bonhoeffer to jurisprudence that would inform Bonhoeffer's theological reflections, particularly through Leibholz's own opposition to Schmitt. Radler's investigation is the single most systematic attempt to discover an intellectual history between Schmitt and Bonhoeffer.[6]

To begin to see connecting ideas on the concept of exception between Schmitt and Bonhoeffer, it is worth placing the two passages discussed at length in previous chapters alongside each other. Here are, respectively, an extract from Schmitt's opening chapter of *Political Theology* and Bonhoeffer's description of the extraordinary situation in *Ethics*.

> Sovereign is he who decides on the exception [*Ausnahme*]. Only this definition can do justice to a borderline concept. Contrary to the imprecise terminology that is found in popular literature, a borderline concept is not a vague concept, but one pertaining to the outermost sphere [...] The decision on the exception is a decision in the true sense of the word [...] The exception, which is not codified in the existing legal order, can at best be characterized as a case of extreme peril, a danger to the existence of the state, or the like. But it cannot be circumscribed factually and made to conform to a preformed law. It is precisely the exception that makes relevant the subject of sovereignty, that is, the whole question of sovereignty. The precise details of an emergency cannot be anticipated, nor can one spell out what may take place in such a case [...] Precisely a philosophy of concrete life must not withdraw from the exception and the extreme case, but must be interested in it to the highest degree. (Schmitt 2005: 5–15)
>
> There are occasions when in the course of historical life, the strict observance of the explicit law of a state, a corporation, a family [...] entails a clash with the basic necessities of human life. In such cases, appropriate responsible action departs from the domain governed by laws and principles, from the normal and regular, and instead is confronted with the extraordinary situation [*Außerordentliche Situation*] of ultimate necessities that are beyond any possible regulation by law [...] There can be no doubt that such necessities actually exist. To deny them would mean ceasing to act in accordance with reality. It is equally certain, however, that these necessities, as primordial facts of life itself, cannot be captured by any law and can never become laws themselves. They appeal directly to the free responsibility of the one who acts, a responsibility not bound by any law. They create an extraordinary situation, and are in essence borderline cases [...] The *ultima ratio* lies beyond the laws of reason; it is irrational action. (Bonhoeffer 2009: 272–273)

From these passages, it is clear that both Schmitt and Bonhoeffer refer to the exception or extraordinary situation, in which the laws that govern the regular state of affairs are suspended. Both claim such scenarios are part of the reality of concrete life. Both refer to the borderline situation or case where a form of action is required that begins with the individual, Schmitt through the decisive sovereign, Bonhoeffer through the person who engages in responsible action. Both Schmitt and Bonhoeffer view the law as possessing limited authority, and the decision is central to their respective concepts of exception. For both, the action is personal, made by an individual; for Bonhoeffer, this is the person who follows Christ in *Discipleship* and who undertakes responsible action in *Ethics*, for Schmitt this is the sovereign who decides the exception in *Political Theology*.[7]

The previous chapter on Schmitt's concept of exception identified some issues around Schmitt's description of the term. It suggested that Schmitt's concept of exception was ambivalent from the beginning as *Political Theology* seems to argue that the exception encompasses both the autonomous decision of the sovereign and the unpredictable event. By conflating these two definitions, Schmitt establishes an ambiguous relationship between the exceptional event that precedes and therefore requires the sovereign decision, and the idea of sovereignty as the power to decide independently of outside influences. As a result of the conflation between the two forms of exception, the individual or sovereign who declares the exception also has the power to initiate the exception as an event or to proclaim the event into being.

A similarly ambiguity appears in Bonhoeffer's concept of the extraordinary. Bonhoeffer's concept of the 'extraordinary situation' in *Ethics* is described as analogous to Machiavelli's concept of *necessità* and bears some resemblance to Schmitt's concept of exception as event, and as a situation where the norms no longer apply. Yet, Bonhoeffer's concept of the 'extraordinary' as explicated in *Discipleship* is grounded in the figure or person of Christ. The first appearance of the concept of the extraordinary was the declaration of the person as righteous through Christ, through which she in turn became marked as extraordinary, or the disciple. Subsequently, the disciple is required to live an extraordinary life in the world, demonstrating this by obedience to Christ's command in the Sermon on the Mount: the extraordinary command to love her enemies. Such love, concluded Bonhoeffer, is only possible with the help of Christ, who is the exemplar of the extraordinary. Because of its theological orientation, *Discipleship* gives a more fully developed exposition on what it means to be extraordinary than the single reference to the 'extraordinary situation' in *Ethics*. *Discipleship* actually suggests far more clearly that the concept of the extraordinary belongs to the person (the disciple through Christ), yet the introduction of the 'extraordinary situation' as *event* complicates such an understanding. This is further evidenced by the curious double meaning tied to the use of the world 'reality' in *Ethics*, which I noted in Chapter 4. On the one hand, Christ was here referred to as the 'real one'. On the other hand, in the passage associated with Machiavelli's *necessità*, Bonhoeffer described the ultimate necessities of life *as* reality beyond any possible regulation by law or human reasoning, an external event that requires a decisive (and extra-legal) response, including the political necessity of war or deception for the sake of one's own life. Thus, as with Schmitt, there is an ambiguity in Bonhoeffer's writing between the extraordinary understood as situation or event and, as person, modelled on Christ the Extraordinary.

Bonhoeffer's Emerging Political Theology

Earlier I argued that the ambiguity of Schmitt's two forms of exception leads to a situation in which the individual or sovereign has the power initiate the event through their proclamation. I pointed to the theological origins of this idea in Schmitt's concept of the decision: the doctrine of *creatio ex nihilo*. I suggested that Schmitt makes the strongest possible case for absolute sovereignty by imbuing the concept of decision with quasi-divine authority based on elements of the doctrine of creation. As I noted, Schmitt's use of the doctrine to shore up state power is not unique in the political history of the West, and Schmitt stands in a broader history where rule and governance on earth is based on a divine model. Sovereignty based on the doctrine of *creatio ex nihilo* has been criticised by political philosophers, such as Hannah Arendt, who have perceived it as anti-democratic in nature.

Bonhoeffer's own link between Christology and the extraordinary situation may seem to have little to do with Schmitt's use of theology to support his concept of the political exception. And there's no evidence to suggest that Bonhoeffer explicitly or implicitly seeks to use theology to prop up political power. Indeed, Bonhoeffer's Christology emerges as a direct challenge to National Socialist attempts to appropriate Christian theology for imperial ends. Thus, one would not expect Bonhoeffer's nascent political theology to map onto Schmitt's engagement with political theology. Furthermore, while Schmitt is acknowledged as reintroducing the term 'political theology' to twentieth-century debates, the term is not one generally associated with Bonhoeffer's writing or thinking.[8]

Yet, some valuable comparison can be made between Bonhoeffer's turn to Christology as he explores the political action in which he engages, and Schmitt's sovereign decision based on the creation doctrine. This can be done through Bonhoeffer's own exposition of the doctrine of creation, found in *Creation and Fall*. This book is based on a series of lectures Bonhoeffer gave in the winter semester of 1932–1933 at the University of Berlin, during the waning days of the Weimar Republic. For Bonhoeffer as with most theologians, the doctrine of *creatio ex nihilo* posits unconditioned divine freedom: 'Between Creator and creature there is simply nothing [*das Nichts*]' (2004: 32). The doctrine of *creatio ex nihilo* challenges any doctrine that views creation as an emanation or divine self-unfolding; there is no inner divine necessity behind creation, according to Bonhoeffer. The significance of the doctrine is not about the origins of the natural world as a challenge to scientific, evolutionary biology.[9] Rather, Bonhoeffer's interest in the doctrine of creation is first and foremost as it relates to the reality and salvation history of Jesus Christ. For Bonhoeffer, the doctrine of creation is to be understood Christologically; it is a testimony or witness to the messianic work of Christ. Indeed, in order to understand the doctrine of creation correctly, Christian theology should look to the resurrected Christ for knowledge of creation and the created order; creation and resurrection mutually inform each other (Adams 2015: 160). In this vein, Bonhoeffer writes: '[T]he God of creation, of the utter beginning, is the God of resurrection. The world exists from the beginning in the sign of the resurrection of Christ from the dead' (2004: 34).

Bonhoeffer makes a claim about the need to read Genesis exegetically in light of the later resurrection narrative of Christ. But he does more than this. He seems to suggest that the creation doctrine has no meaning apart from the resurrection of Christ: 'Indeed, it is because we know of the resurrection that we know of God's creation in the beginning, of God's creating out of nothing' (Bonhoeffer 2004: 35). The resurrection of Christ is not only equivalent in mystery to the original creation doctrine, but in Bonhoeffer's account it provides the meaning of the doctrine of creation. As Neils Gregersen notes, Bonhoeffer seems to suggest that 'the theology of creation stands and falls with the event of resurrection' (2007: 141). Given Bonhoeffer's context, there are good reasons why he subordinates the doctrine of creation to the Christ event. Luther's idea of 'orders of creation' had tried to specify shared realms of human life for Christians and non-Christians by virtue of their common nature as human beings.[10] During the Nazi period, these 'orders of creation' were reframed to justify so-called natural conditions of nation and race.[11] Bonhoeffer sought to challenge such a view of 'natural society', emphasising Christ as the principle of normative order for social arrangements in the world. Yet, by making Christology the only correct interpretive lens through which to understand the doctrine of creation, Bonhoeffer dismisses not only Jewish and other religious traditions, but also different but equally important Christian theological interpretive lenses, such as the doctrine of the Trinity. Indeed, Gregersen perceives a danger in Bonhoeffer's 'over-use of Christological concepts' in that there is an 'under-use of Trinitarian resources' in his exposition of the Genesis 1-3 (2007: 139). As a result, more relational forms of understanding the doctrine of creation are excluded.[12]

The exclusion of relational forms of understanding is further seen in Bonhoeffer's separation between the created world and the new creation. By viewing the creation doctrine through the lens of the resurrected Christ, Bonhoeffer introduces a division between the 'old' existing and fallen world, and the 'new' creation:

> The dead Jesus Christ of Good Friday and the resurrection *kýrios* of Easter Sunday – that is creation out of nothing, creation from the beginning [...] There is absolutely no continuum between the dead Christ and the resurrected Christ, but the freedom of God that in the beginning created God's work out of nothing. (Bonhoeffer 2004: 35)

The dead Christ, here part of the fallen, existing creation, has passed away. The Messianic, salvific, resurrected Christ heralds the new creation. From this, argues Gregersen, we are to understand that the new creation 'happens through an annihilation of the world, in order that the new world may shine forth' (2007: 140). Just as there is no continuity between the dead Christ and the resurrected Christ, so there is no continuity between the fallen world and the new creation.

The lack of continuity has implications for how we are to understand the relationship between God and the world. In Bonhoeffer's Christological interpretation, the world is not only to be understood as metaphysically distinct from divine nature, but as 'fallen' and as he states, judged (2004: 22). To use theological parlance, the world is in sin and only Christ can redeem this world, not by recreating the old world but by creating a new world that has 'no continuum' with the dead world. The metaphysical nature of Christ's resurrection as *ex nihilo* means that there can be no continuation with the existing world. Through emphasising the redemptive nature of Christ's work in the world, Bonhoeffer is in danger of separating God's creative act and the world itself. That is, *creatio ex nihilo* as the doctrine of creation of the natural world recedes but at the cost of the natural world disappearing altogether. What re-emerges is a theological doctrine about the sinfulness and redemption narrative of humanity, but one that seems quite separate from anything to do with the origins and fate of the existing world.

This is not to say that there is a lack of relation between nature and God. Nature itself operates according to natural laws, states Bonhoeffer (2004: 52). The mathematical and regulative structure of the world remains unaffected by the fallen world of sinful humanity. But in Bonhoeffer's account, nature seems irrelevant in the redemptive work of Christ, the latter predestined even before the creation of the world.[13] Indeed, while laws of nature remain unaffected by the fall, how humanity views these regulative structures post-fall *is* affected. Post-fall, humanity desires to be autonomous, and to perceive the world autonomously, without the Creator: 'human beings no longer know that numbers too are upheld by God's word and command alone. Numbers are not the truth of God itself' (Bonhoeffer 2004: 53). For this reason, Bonhoeffer is wary of the concept of 'natural law', as the latter would deny the importance of the resurrection event. An account of morality based on natural law in Bonhoeffer's view is an invention of post-fall humanity, an attempt to deny its own sinfulness and need for redemption.[14] The limit of post-fall humanity is further emphasised as Bonhoeffer imposes restrictions on what we can know about the creation of the world. We cannot ask 'why the world was created, what God's plan for the world was, or whether the creation was necessary. These questions are exposed as godless questions' (Bonhoeffer 2004: 31).

Philip Ziegler asks in 'Dietrich Bonhoeffer—An Ethics of God's Apocalypse' whether Bonhoeffer's theological ethics can be characterised as an ethics intended to conform to 'the contours of Paul's apocalyptic gospel' (2007: 580).[15] Revelation (*apocalypsis*) here 'denotes God's redemptive invasion of the fallen order of things such that reality itself is decisively re-made in the event' (Ziegler 2007: 580). Christ's entry into the world is considered a disruptive event: '[u]nexpected and unbidden, God's sovereign entry onto the field of human affairs questions – nay, *assails* – the putative rule of human reasoning, ways and means', writes Ziegler (2007: 584). Revelation in this context is not simply unveiling previously hidden secrets or revealing something about future events. Rather, it is to be understood as an event that initiates a new state of affairs. Furthermore, this event is not only a possibility but an actuality that does not depend on acceptance for its realisation. It is a reality that God has already decided and enacted, so that all that remains is our living out the revelational event in the world. Such are the contours of Paul's apocalyptic gospel as recounted by Ziegler.

This seems to link well with Bonhoeffer's creation doctrine, which highlights the irruptive event of Christ in the world that does not permit access to the plans of God.[16] The freedom of God in this context can appear to be 'indistinguishable from arbitrariness' as without any further explanation, the reader is left with a divine fiat that is explained by 'reference to the unique event of the resurrection of Jesus' (Gregersen 2007: 142). In Bonhoeffer's account, the doctrine of creation, viewed through the Resurrection event, is a matter of faith and obedience to the revelation of Christ, not of knowledge about the world and humanity's place in this.

Bonhoeffer's focus on Christ as the meaning of the creation doctrine comes at the expense of deeper hermeneutical understanding of the doctrine that considers relationality between persons, between persons and the existing world, and between humanity and nature. The revelational event of Christ appears as free and unfettered from how humanity experiences and understand the world. Peter Scott, in the entry on 'Creation' in the *Blackwell Companion to Political Theology*, writes that creation is one of the least discussed themes of political theology, usually subsumed to 'the theme of redemption': 'a lack of attention paid to the theme of creation leads to a political theology that is insufficiently *materialist* as it cuts off the natural or physical world in favour of a narrative of redemption that saves from creation (2004: 333). This separation is a danger in Bonhoeffer's Christological account of the creation doctrine, in which the salvation event of Christ is prioritised, and the materiality of the world, which can also be understood as concrete, existing life, is separated from the divine ordering of salvation history.

Recall now that Heinrich Meier enthusiastically described Carl Schmitt as the political theologian par excellence because of his faith in revelation. For Meier revelation is linked to obedience, which confronts the individual with an either/or choice between God and Satan. In light of the previous analysis, we can reframe this as a choice between Christ and the fallen world. Revelation offers an existential confrontation to which the individual responds with acceptance and obedience (becoming the disciple), or which the individual rejects and thereby remains in the fallen world. The former decision places the individual in relationship to Christ, overcoming the 'putative nature of human reasoning', to borrow Ziegler's phrase (2007: 584). Rejecting Christ means that the individual continues to exist in the fallen world, subject to human reasoning and judgement. Humanity is subjected to ethics; the disciple is freed from ethical discourse to be obedient to Christ's sovereign command as this emerges through the revelational event.

CONSEQUENCES OF THE EXTRAORDINARY SITUATION: THE LOSS OF THE WORLD

In the previous chapter, I argued that the outcome of Schmitt's concept of exception leads directly to the loss of the world, by which I meant the loss of the communal or shared world. While Bonhoeffer's Christology is not simply equivalent to Schmitt's concept of political sovereignty, in light of Bonhoeffer's exposition of the creation doctrine, is his emerging political theology at risk of negating or forgetting the communal or shared world of a diverse humanity? In the previous chapter, I identified three ways in which Schmitt's political theology leads to the loss of the world. I want to test the consequences of Bonhoeffer's concept of the extraordinary situation in view of these three ways.

The first consequence identified was the diminishing of norms, customs and laws that lead to a loss of mediating institutions in Schmitt's account. Based on the foregoing discussion, it would seem clear that the norms, customs and laws of the world, or natural life, are discarded in Bonhoeffer's interpretation of the creation doctrine. But a similar move also appears in *Discipleship*, where following Christ is characterised as transgressive. Any visible agreement between Christian values and those of the world implies that the Christian is no longer obedient to the higher law of Christ. In this way, Christian identity is established through opposition to the world. Through a sharp division between the natural and the extraordinary, Bonhoeffer effectively places the disciple, and what it is to be a Christian, outside any notion of a natural or regulative world. Likewise in *Ethics*, the 'extraordinary situation' is described as beyond the laws of reason. Here, too, the category of the extraordinary places the Christian in a space that is not subject to the natural or the regulative space of worldly or secular affairs.

In the previous chapter, I suggested that the demise of democratic political society is the second of the consequences of Schmitt's emphasis on the exception as the basis of sovereignty. There is an often-quoted event that occurred two days after Hitler came to power. Bonhoeffer was scheduled give a radio address, and he spoke on the concept of leadership, analysing and critiquing the idea of the *Führer*, particularly as it had emerged in the post-war youth movement. He argued that leadership on the *Führer* principle was no longer viewed as tied to a particular office, but exhibited a messianic aspect which in turn freed the leader from the limits of the control of law. If the leader should acquiesce to this concept of leadership, 'then the image of the leader shifts to one of a misleader, then the leader is acting improperly toward the led as well as toward himself' said Bonhoeffer (Bonhoeffer cited in Schlingensiepen 2010: 117). Bonhoeffer's critique of messianic leadership suggests that he was attuned to the dangers of dictatorship, inherent in Carl Schmitt's concept of leadership.

However, Bonhoeffer's critique of the leadership principle is not based on a defence of liberal political values associated with democracies. Bethge comments that Bonhoeffer's critique of leadership was 'derived rather from a conservative notion of order [...] Bonhoeffer was concerned with the correct structuring of authority' (1977: 193–194). Stephen Plant similarly observes that 'It was not the loss of democracy that troubled Bonhoeffer in the collapse of the Weimar constitution, but the loss of the law, the loss of the limits that constrain office holders in the exercise of their authority' (2004: 22–23). Indeed, John Moses notes that Bonhoeffer had reservations about the possibility of a successful liberal democracy in Germany (1999: 20). Thus, Bonhoeffer's attack on the leadership principle should not be understood as a defence of democracy, but as grounded on his understanding of Christ as the true Messianic leader.

I suggest that Bonhoeffer's own conservative political views may share important elements with Schmitt's argument for sovereignty, and this is to be found precisely in Bonhoeffer's Christology. For Schmitt, sovereignty is identified with the single individual who is capable of making the decision on the exception. For Schmitt, who decides is more important than how the decision is made, the latter being the failure of liberal democracy. Political life on Schmitt's account is not to be understood as an association of equals in democracy who come to agreement or consensus on action. For Bonhoeffer, the political organisation of human life on earth is subservient to the lordship of Christ, who is the exemplar of the extraordinary situation, and whose command directs the disciple. The requirement of Christ's command or direction is not discussion but obedience.

Instead of an association of equals, the basis of Schmitt's concept of the political is the revelational event that confronts the individual with the either/or decision, between God or Satan, friend or enemy, good or evil (Meier 2011: 16). This is the friend/enemy distinction that is key to Schmitt's understanding of political life. For Schmitt, the political is not one domain amongst others, but the criterion to describe the condition of moral and existential relationality between human beings. Bonhoeffer's emphasis on the revelational nature of Christ and the relationship with the disciple shares similar themes. Chapter 3 briefly explored the concept of the enemy as it emerged in relation to the category of the extraordinary. The enemy was described as the 'extraordinary' (*das Außerordentliche*) and as 'the one who hates me' (Bonhoeffer 2003: 139). The use of this term shows that for Bonhoeffer, the concept of the enemy is theologically grounded. The enemy serves as the visible expression of Christ's love, and because of this, there is a connection between the enemy and Christ as manifestations of the concept of the extraordinary. In accordance with Bonhoeffer's vision of what it is to be a Christian community, the enemy should be seen as a gift, an opportunity to demonstrate the depth of Christ's love to the world.[17] Bonhoeffer interprets this in terms of the disciple who now has the opportunity to demonstrate love, for in the confrontation with the enemy, 'the more animosity the enemy has, the more my love is required' (2003: 139). The enemy does the work of Christ in teaching the disciple to love as Christ loves the world, enabling the Christian to love her enemy as though the enemy is already part of that filial love shown between Christians.[18] As a theological idea, this is a challenging demand.

But there is perhaps an unintended consequence to this. The theological and spiritual framing of the enemy removes 'natural' distinctions such as civilians and combatants, or degrees of enmity that may require different responses. Effectively, by defining the enemy as 'the person who hates me', the enemy is understood primarily as an existential encounter; the enemy is the person who confronts me, who opposes me, who wishes my annihilation or my end, pace Schmitt. Bonhoeffer's insistent separation between what is natural and what is uniquely Christian could also lead to the claim that the enemy can *only* be understood through theological categories and through existential confrontation with another person. As noted in Chapter 3, the question that confronts the reader: what happens when, in the face of concrete reality, a different kind of 'extraordinary situation' arises? One that challenges the filial love understood as Christian sisterhood that *includes* one's enemies and places the Christian squarely into the concrete situation in which the concrete enemy threatens the lives of concrete loved ones? It is here that Bonhoeffer lack of mediating categories places the resistor in the same existential framework of Schmitt's friend–enemy relation. The political becomes the total to the extent that the enemy is understood only existentially, as opposition and threat to one's own life and that of loved ones. As Schmitt describes this relationship, it is the utmost degree of separation that can only be expressed in conflict.

In the previous chapter, force outside the bounds of law was identified as the final way that Schmitt's concept of exception destroys the communal or shared world. Schmitt's claim that the exception is the point where the decision parts from the legal norm and authority proves itself as authority (over law) opens up a space for force *outside* the bounds of law. It involves the possibility of a type of violence, defined by Agamben as being 'without *logos* ... without any real reference' (2005: 40). The state of exception initiates a form of violence without justification, without reason or *ratio*, to contain it. This has implications for both the individual who acts in a state of exception and cannot measure their action, and the law that exists to prevent violence, which is nullified precisely through the willingness of the individual to enact violence on the basis of exception. This problem can also be found in Bonhoeffer's thinking around action in the extraordinary situation.

In *Ethics*, Bonhoeffer's claim that 'free responsibility' results in 'a deed which can no longer be decided by the laws of reason' suggests that such action is beyond *ratio* and beyond measurement (2009: 273). In a similar pronouncement, Bonhoeffer argues that 'killing' on the 'basis of unconditional necessity' must be carried out despite 'any number of other reasons', even good reasons (2009: 190). The question of appropriate or measured action becomes clearly impossible if the killing must be done despite 'good reasons' to refrain from killing and the only reason is necessity itself. As with Schmitt, in this account, too, violence threatens to become its own justification, in the extraordinary situation.

Schmitt attempted to maintain a connection between the exception and law, as for Schmitt the law remains the norm and the space of everyday life and organisation of society. Similar to Schmitt, Bonhoeffer too tried to keep a connection between necessity and law, arguing that when the law is 'broken, violated … out of dire necessity' it is in that very act affirmed as legitimate precisely through the violation (2009: 274). Yet, while the individual may intend to break the law in order to affirm the validity of the law, without the boundary of law itself as a guide to appropriate action, it is difficult to measure violence as appropriate to the situation or circumstances in which it is required. The individual who suspends the law in order to kill (even with the intention of preserving life) is at risk of becoming part of the extraordinary situation she seeks to end. Here, the same critique directed at Schmitt must be directed at Bonhoeffer. If the extraordinary situation requires that the disciple acts by suspending the ethical law, how does the resistor ensure her action does not pose the same danger to the law as the peril that necessitates the exception?

As I noted in the previous chapter, regulative norms and laws of a society are founded on reason, or rational principles that can be tested, measured, discussed, amended and applied across different contexts and scenarios. Once the state of exception is invoked, it is difficult to test the claim that the moment of exception has indeed arrived. Similarly, once the extraordinary situation is invoked to justify a form of action previously judged forbidden to Christians, it is difficult to question or test the claim that the situation is, indeed, extraordinary. As with the decision of Schmitt's sovereign, there is no process that can question Christ's revelation to the disciple in an extraordinary situation, or indeed, the belief that the extraordinary situation is at hand. Bonhoeffer ascribes sovereignty to Christ in a way that diminishes the authority of law, the one element that might check claims to power, whether such claims are intended for good or ill. That is, the one check that circumvents good intent in this instance, the impartiality of law, is nullified in a notion of sovereignty that is primarily understood as a personal in both Schmitt and Bonhoeffer. In both contexts, when the personal is emphasised, the important objective measures of norms and laws becomes ineffective in testing the exceptional decision.

In this chapter, I have identified key ideas shared by Schmitt and Bonhoeffer as they think through their respective *Grenzfall* scenarios. Yet even though there are important connections between the ideas of the exception and the extraordinary situation, there are also notable differences. Karola Radler suggests that the term 'sovereign' means different things for the two thinkers: for Bonhoeffer it is grounded in the concrete moment of obedience to Christ's commandment in responsible discipleship, for Schmitt, sovereignty refers to the decision of the sovereign around the state of exception (2011: 120).

Following my analysis of their respective political theologies, I also see as significant Schmitt's language of divine power as applied to the exceptional individual, the sovereign. Bonhoeffer, on the other hand, does not assign quasi-divine authority to any human individual. While both Bonhoeffer's Christ and Schmitt's sovereign can be characterised as 'uncommanded commanders' (Hirst 1987: 21), Schmitt attributes divine power to a fallible human being in order to secure stability against the unprecedented or exceptional event; Bonhoeffer does not at any point assign divine power to a human individual, not even in response to the appearance of the extraordinary situation.

The second significant difference lies in the power of the actor. Although both Bonhoeffer and Schmitt prioritise exceptional action over law, the greatest difference between the two initially seems to lie precisely in the power invested in the one who acts; a power accorded by Schmitt to the sovereign, by Bonhoeffer to the resistor. This difference is significant because it points to the primary motivator or concern in the respective thinkers' attempts to grapple with *Grenzfall* scenarios. Schmitt in developing the concept of exception is primarily concerned with affirming or strengthening authority to face the chaotic exception. This is evident in his comprehensive definition of the exception as the decision of the sovereign. In developing his concept of the extraordinary situation, Bonhoeffer is primarily concerned with resisting the Nazi abuse of authority in situ, through his participating in resistance activities. This is shown by the fact that Bonhoeffer's first engagement with the politically charged idea of the exception is through a description of the extraordinary situation *as* event, which he encounters as part of the resistance. The different departure points would suggest that Schmitt's exception, in according greater power to sovereignty, is more likely to lead to a totalitarian state, as was noted in the previous chapter. Since Bonhoeffer's resistor responds to the appearance of the extraordinary situation, she lacks the power to initiate the extraordinary situation in the way that Schmitt's sovereign can. Yet, could Bonhoeffer's resistor be as existentially radical as Schmitt's sovereign?

Bonhoeffer's emphasis on the messianic nature of the doctrine of creation echoes Schmitt's vision of messianic leadership, where the sovereign leader is able to act apart from the existing order and stands apart from fellow human beings. Furthermore, following Christ is characterised as transgressive in *Discipleship*. Obedience to Christ transgresses society's moral standards and laws; it is described as an 'offense'. Any apparent agreement between Christian values and those of the world can be seen as evidence that the Christian is no longer obedient to the higher law of Christ. In defining discipleship by the extraordinary and transgressive command, Bonhoeffer is in danger of radically devaluing the ordinary world where people conduct their daily businesses and affairs. For the disciple, there is no continuity, no world to provide guidance and direction. I suggest that Bonhoeffer, in his emphasis on Christ's sovereignty over the law, develops a notion of discipleship that prioritises the existential moment of obedience to a sovereign Christ, who is free to break his own command as given in the Sermon on the Mount. It is now time to consider how this affects the Christian's relation to the world.

NOTES

1. 'In my conversations with Professor Schmitt I asked whether he supported the July 20, 1944, attempt on Hitler. He replied negatively, despite the fact that one of his closest friends—Johannes Popitz—played a leading role in the events leading up to it and for which he paid with his life. Schmitt feared a complete breakdown inside Germany, because the Germans could not negotiate a settlement with the Allies as a result of the Allied demand for unconditional surrender' (Schwab 1989: 147, fn. 11).

2. Agamben draws attention to the Constitution of the German Federal Republic (1949) in which Article 20 unequivocally legalises the *right* of resistance, stating that 'against anyone who attempts to abolish that order [the democratic constitution], all Germans have a right of resistance, if no other remedies are possible' (cited in Agamben 2005: 11). While no references to a 'state of emergency' existed in the Constitution established in 1949, an amendment was passed in 1968 that reintroduced the

state of exception, now defined as the 'state of internal necessity', *innere Notstand* (Agamben 2005: 15–16).
3. As a curious fact of history, both Schmitt and Bonhoeffer were in Barcelona in 1929—the young 23-year-old Bonhoeffer as a curate, who gave the lecture on ethics discussed in the previous chapter to his German ex patriot congregation, the 41-year-old Schmitt gave a lecture on 'The Age of Neutralizations and Depoliticizations', later added to the 1932 edition of *Political Theology*.
4. He had married Bonhoeffer's twin sister Sabine in 1926.
5. Radler describes a 'triangular connection' emerging in the early 1930s between Schmitt, Leibholz and Bonhoeffer. Bonhoeffer opposes Hitler's ascent to power in a radio address on 1 February 1933, Leibholz publishes a booklet on the authoritarian theory of state early in 1933, while Schmitt became a member of the NSDAP on 1 May 1933 and was subsequently appointed to the faculty of law at the University of Berlin (2011: 45–47).
6. See also Brown (2013). Apart from my 2013 contribution, little research has been done comparing Carl Schmitt's 'state of exception' to Bonhoeffer's 'extraordinary situation'. In a 2008 draft paper Jeffrey Lenowitz inserts the following footnote—'Barth and Kierkegaard's conception of the teleological suspension of the ethical, which occurs at the exception, also influenced Carl Schmitt, a very different thinker than Bonhoeffer, but one who wrote around the same time and addressed similar sorts of problems' (2008: fn. 68). In a separate footnote, Lenowitz also mentions the problem of Bonhoeffer's mandates in relation to Schmitt's analysis of the relationship between judgement and the universal legal principle (2008: 23, fn. 60; 38: fn. 103). My thanks to Jeffrey Lenowitz for granting permission to cite his draft paper in my work. Matthias Eichhorn undertook a book length comparison between Barth and Schmitt, suggesting both were intellectually shaped by the failure of the first world war, both passionately argued against the liberalism and rationalism of the Enlightenment and its faith in progress. Intriguingly, Eichhorn argues the closest conceptual ground shared by Schmitt and Barth is the irreducible relation between Schmitt's 'friend and enemy', which for Barth is conceptualised theologically as 'truth and heresy'. Eichhorn argues that Schmitt's political distinction of friend/enemy requires Barth's theological distinction of truth/heresy; however, Schmitt's choice for National Socialism rendered him theologically incapable of distinguishing friend from enemy (Eichhorn 1994). The *Blackwell Companion to Political Theology* (2004) includes chapters on Schmitt and Bonhoeffer, as it happens separated by a chapter on Karl Barth. Bonhoeffer and Schmitt are emerging as a locus of study for contemporary political-theological contexts. See for example,

Jason T.S. Lam. 2017. Engaging Dietrich Bonhoeffer and Carl Schmitt in the Contemporary Chinese Context. *Logos & Pneuma-Chinese Journal of Theology* 46: 339–374.

7. Beyond these similarities on the concept of exception, Schmitt and Bonhoeffer shared a broader agenda. Both thinkers criticized their particular intellectual climate, arguing that the prevailing neo-Kantian attempts to understand the world were unable to account for the decision and action required of the individual in a state of chaos. For Schmitt, it was political liberalism that could not cope with the exception; for Bonhoeffer, it was theological and philosophical liberalism that failed in an extraordinary situation. And both shared a belief in the primary place of the concrete situation and the importance of distinctive national characteristics and attitudes shaped by a cultural worldview. See also Chapter 9.

8. The *Blackwell Companion to Political Theology* (2004) includes a chapter on Bonhoeffer, contributed by Stanley Hauerwas. In his contribution, Hauerwas sees Bonhoeffer's contribution to political theology primarily in terms of retrieving the political significance of the church: 'As Christ was in the world, so the church is in the world. These [...] claims [...] are at the very heart of Bonhoeffer's theological politics' (2004: 141). Also of interest here is Phillip Ziegler's claim that 'from beginning to end, Bonhoeffer had a quite specifically theological interest in politics' and that for Bonhoeffer the political was important only in so far as the world was the place in which Christians acted in 'public witness to the gracious and saving dominion of God in Christ Jesus in the midst of the world' (2013: 324).

9. Bonhoeffer does not see the doctrine of *creatio ex nihilo* as a defence of 'creationism', he agrees with Darwin that human beings are derived from the earth and that our bond to the earth is essential to our being (Bonhoeffer 2004: 76). Adams likewise notes that the doctrine of *creatio ex nihilo* is not a doctrine about temporal origins, but it describes the ontological and metaphysical relationship of God to creation, and from the perspective of soteriology, this is Jesus the Messiah (Adams 2015: 162).

10. Luther's three estates of government, household/family and church, were intended to organize society. Yet, these concepts were taken up Nazi ideology of Volk (sometimes regarded as a fourth estate), race, class, fatherland, kingdom and Reich.

11. Even moderate conservative Lutherans such as Werner Elert and Paul Althaus signed the *Ansbach Memorandum* 1934, which included the following statement: 'The law, "the unchangeable will of God"...obligates us to the natural orders to which we are subject, such as family, people

[*Volk*], race (that is, blood relationship)' (cited in Bonhoeffer 2009: 56, fn. 36).

12. Gregersen finds this troubling as it appears to bypass the relationality of God's freedom as it emerges in the doctrine of the Trinity. This is the eternal divine love between Father, Son and Spirit that finds its expression in the created order as making possible a community of love: 'Divine freedom and divine love cannot and should not be pitted against one another', concludes Gregersen (2007: 142). Emphasising the relational aspect of the doctrine of *creatio ex nihilo*, Peter Scott describes the doctrine as 'the free decision of the social God: a gratuitous action. God has no "need" of creation; creating is rather an action of God's love […] When God wills to be not-God, creation comes to be' (Scott 2004: 336). The importance of a Trinitarian understanding of the doctrine of creation is also noted by Scott, who suggests the *ex nihilo* tradition needs to be reframed through the 'triune God'. Because of the triune nature of God, creatures are 'oriented on one another in receiving and giving' (2004: 345).

13. As Gregersen notes, there is 'no reflection on the inner relationship between the numbers or *logoi* of creation, and the Logos of God in Jesus Christ' (2007: 145). However, Gregersen further points out that this is not the only theme that emerges in *Creation and Fall*. It runs as a thread alongside a fuller account of the relation of Christ to the world that will emerge more fully in Bonhoeffer's later writings, particularly his prison writings (Gregersen 2007: 145).

14. Bonhoeffer's views on natural law follows that of the Reformers who argued natural law failed to take seriously the condition of human sin, placing misguided trust in the powers of a debilitated human reason (Charles 2008: 113).

15. Ziegler bases this interpretation on recent interpretative accounts of Paul via J. Louis Martyn.

16. Ziegler identifies key aspects of an apocalyptic ethics in Bonhoeffer's writing, particularly in *Discipleship*, which Bonhoeffer himself described in a letter to Karl Barth as 'an exposition of …. the Pauline doctrine of justification and sanctification' (cited in Ziegler 2007: 583). But Ziegler also suggests that in *Ethics*, there is 'a whole way of thinking whose organising logic is very closely aligned with that of Paul's apocalyptic gospel' (2007: 588). Thus, according to Ziegler, Paul's apocalyptic gospel reverberates through key texts of Bonhoeffer, including his key 'pacifist' text and his later key 'conspiracy text'.

17. Paul's exhortation that Christ loved us while we were still his enemies comes to mind.

18. It is interesting that Bonhoeffer's describes the love of enemies in *Discipleship* as modelled on the love shown between brothers and sisters. Bonhoeffer relies on 'natural' metaphors such as brother and sisterhood, but applies this to the existential enemy. The enemy is therefore included in the natural love of one's own. Ultimately, it would seem that he appears to find this demand unrealistic in the face of the concrete enemy.

REFERENCES

Adams, Samuel V. 2015. *The Reality of God and Historical Method: Apocalyptic Theology in Conversation with N.T. Wright*. New Explorations in Theology. Downers Grove: InterVarsity Press.
Agamben, Giorgio. 2005. *State of Exception*, trans. Kevin Attell. Chicago and London: University of Chicago Press.
Bethge, Eberhard. 1977. *Dietrich Bonhoeffer: Theologian, Christian, Contemporary*, trans. Eric Mosbacher, Peter and Betty Ross, Frank Clarke, and William Glen-Doepel. London: Fountain Books.
Bonhoeffer. 2003. *Discipleship*, trans. Barbara Green and Reinhard Krauss. Dietrich Bonhoeffer Works English. Minneapolis: Fortress Press.
Bonhoeffer, Dietrich. 2004. *Creation and Fall*. Dietrich Bonhoeffer Works English. Minneapolis: Fortress Press.
Bonhoeffer, Dietrich. 2009. *Ethics*, trans. Reinhard Krauss, Charles C. West, and Douglass W. Stott. Dietrich Bonhoeffer Works English. Minneapolis: Fortress Press.
Brown, Petra. 2013. Bonhoeffer, Schmitt, and the State of Exception. *Pacifica: Australasian Theological Studies* 26 (3): 246–264.
Charles, J.D. 2008. *Retrieving the Natural Law: A Return to Moral First Things*. Grand Rapids, MI: Eerdmans.
Eichhorn, Mathias. 1994. *Es wird regiert!* Berlin: Duncker & Humblot.
Gregersen, Niels Henrik. 2007. The Mysteries of Christ and Creation. In *Mysteries in the Theology of Dietrich Bonhoeffer*, ed. Kirsten Busch Nielsen, Ulrik Nissen, and Christiane Tietz, 135–158. Göttingen: Vandenhoeck & Ruprecht.
Hauerwas, Stanley. 2004. Dietrich Bonhoeffer. In *The Blackwell Companion to Political Theology*, ed. Peter Scott and William T. Cavenaugh, 136–149. Malden and Oxford: Blackwell.
Hirst, Paul. 1987. Carl Schmitt's Decisionism. *Telos* 72: 15–26.
Lenowitz, Jeffrey. 2008. Obedience at the Time of Necessitá: Dietrich Bonhoeffer's Theory of Resistance. Paper presented at the Annual Meeting of Western Political Science Association, 2008 Annual Meeting, San Diego.

Meier, Heinrich. 2011. *The Lesson of Carl Schmitt: Four Chapters on the Distinction Between Political Theology and Political Philosophy*, trans. Marcus Brainard. Chicago: University of Chicago Press.

Moses, John A. 1999. Bonhoeffer's Germany: The Political Context. In *The Cambridge Companion to Dietrich Bonhoeffer*, ed. John de Gruchy, 3–21. Cambridge and New York: Cambridge University Press.

Plant, Stephen. 2004. *Bonhoeffer*. London and New York: Continuum.

Radler, Karola. 2011. "…*Whereas I Am Trying to Think Theologically*": Dietrich Bonhoeffer's Hidden Dialogue with Carl Schmitt on Representation: A Theological Response to a Jurisprudential Challenge During a Political Crisis. Edmonton, Alberta: St Stephen's College.

Schlingensiepen, Ferdinand. 2010. *Dietrich Bonhoeffer 1906–1945: Martyr, Thinker, Man of Resistance*, trans. Isabel Best. London and New York: T & T Clark International.

Schmitt, Carl. 2005. *Political Theology: Four Chapters on the Concept of Sovereignty*, trans. George Schwab. Chicago and London: The University of Chicago Press.

Schwab, George. 1989. *The Challenge of the Exception: An Introduction to the Political Ideas of Carl Schmitt Between 1921 and 1936*. New York: Greenwood Press.

Scott, Peter. 2004. Creation. In *The Blackwell Companion to Political Theology*, ed. Peter Scott and William T Cavanaugh, 333–347. Malden and Oxford: Blackwell.

Ziegler, Philip G. 2007. Dietrich Bonhoeffer—An Ethics of God's Apocalypse? *Modern Theology* 23 (4): 579.

Ziegler, Philip G. 2013. Witness to Christ's Dominion: The Political Service of the Church. *Theology* 116 (5): 323–331. https://doi.org/10.1177/00405 71x13493582.

CHAPTER 7

The Obedient Existential Disciple

The previous chapter concluded by drawing attention to Bonhoeffer's emerging vision of discipleship as shaped by the extraordinary and transgressive command of Christ. This chapter draws out the 'existential' aspects of Bonhoeffer's concept of discipleship more explicitly, particularly as it appears in the pacifist text, *Discipleship*. Here, Christ issues a call that comes to each person alone, and each has to decide alone in obedience to Christ. The challenge of Christ's command requires a response, a decision from the hearer that is heard and understood in isolation. Important themes emerge from *Discipleship* that include obedience, isolation and the anxiety of the existential decision.

Critical to a discussion of the existential disciple as it emerges from *Discipleship* is Sören Kierkegaard, the nineteenth-century Danish philosopher, often referred to (somewhat archaically) as the 'father of existentialism'. Both Bonhoeffer and Carl Schmitt belonged to a generation of Germans deeply influenced by the writing of Kierkegaard.[1] Kierkegaard is also important in drawing attention to existential motifs as these emerge in Bonhoeffer's writing. This chapter therefore considers Kierkegaard's influence on Bonhoeffer's concept of discipleship and finds that for both thinkers, the individual is key to understanding discipleship as a response in obedience to Christ's call, and the 'extraordinary' is a mark of distinction for Christ's followers.

In the final section of this chapter, ethical implications of Bonhoeffer's isolated disciple are explored through examining a text that significantly predates both *Discipleship* and *Ethics*. This is a 1929 Sermon, in which

© The Author(s) 2019   123
P. Brown, *Bonhoeffer*,
https://doi.org/10.1007/978-3-030-05698-8_7

Bonhoeffer interprets discipleship not in terms of obedience to the Sermon on the Mount, but as a 'decisive moment' of obedience to the free will of God revealed to the disciple.

THE DISCIPLE WHO IS OBEDIENT TO CHRIST'S CALL

In *Discipleship*, Bonhoeffer devotes an entire chapter to the question of the individual disciple. The image of the isolated disciple in relationship to Christ emerges clearly:

> Jesus' call to discipleship makes the disciple into a single individual. Whether disciples want to or not, they have to make a decision; each has to decide alone. It is not their own choice to desire to be single individuals. Instead, Christ makes everyone he calls into an individual. Each is called alone. Each must follow alone. (Bonhoeffer 2003: 92)

In order to demonstrate what discipleship involves, Bonhoeffer describes how Abraham was called by Christ, not just once, but twice. Bonhoeffer argues that in the first call, Christ commanded Abraham to leave his family (Gen 12:1). Here, Christ came between Abraham and his relatives, visibly breaking all 'natural immediate relationships' (Bonhoeffer 2003: 92). In the second call, Christ commanded Abraham to sacrifice his son (Gen 2:22). Here, Christ came 'between the father of faith and the son of the promise', breaking all 'unmediated spiritual relationships' (Bonhoeffer 2003: 97). Thus, the second call instigates an *invisible* break. The invisible or secret break is made visible only in the moment of obedience, when Abraham brings his son to be sacrificed. In that moment of obedience, everything that he has given up is restored to Abraham. Because Abraham 'was prepared to obey God's command literally, he is permitted to have Isaac as though he did not have him; he is permitted to have him through Jesus Christ', argues Bonhoeffer (2003: 97).[2]

Bonhoeffer's reading of the *Akedah* can hardly be considered faithful to a historical or Judaic interpretation of the narrative. Yet, it does not seek to be so. Bonhoeffer's interpretation echoes that of the nineteenth-century Danish philosopher, Sören Kierkegaard's retelling of the *Akedah* in *Fear and Trembling* (1843). This too should not be read as a historically accurate account of the Judaic narrative,[3] but a unique communication that is multi-layered.[4] It is worth noting the reasons for Kierkegaard's distinctive interpretation and communication of the *Akedah*, as this helps to understand how Bonhoeffer uses this in his own writing. In *Fear and Trembling*, Kierkegaard used Abraham's willingness to sacrifice Isaac as a tool to unsettle his Danish Lutheran contemporaries for whom the horror of Abraham's faith had disappeared in the complacency of Christendom found in the church pews. According to Kierkegaard, his respectable Danish bourgeoisie contemporaries praised Abraham as the father of their faith without understanding the cost such faith involves:

> We mount a winged horse, and in the same instant we are on Mount Moriah, in the same instant we see the ram [...] The whole thing is over in a moment; all you have to do is wait for a minute and you will see the ram, and the ordeal will be over. (Kierkegaard 1983: 52)

Kierkegaard wanted to draw attention to the concrete reality of Abraham's act. Kierkegaard argued that Abraham was not called to sacrifice the (abstract) 'best' to God, but his son Isaac (1983: 85). Kierkegaard makes Abraham appear to be monstrous in *Fear and Trembling*. For if God commands Abraham to sacrifice his beloved son, and Abraham is the 'father of faith' who demonstrates this precisely by his unquestioning obedience, what might God command those who wish to lay claim to the same faith as Abraham? It is precisely this question, what might God ask of *me*, that gives rise to Kierkegaard's anxiety, and in Kierkegaard's estimation ought to cause anxiety in all who would claim to belong to the Christian faith.

The problem that Kierkegaard raises is that of the 'teleological suspension of the ethical', a rather cumbersome term that Kierkegaard uses to ask whether God's command is a higher law than existing ethical duties (Kierkegaard 1983: 54–67). In this case, Kierkegaard argues that Abraham has an absolute duty to God and this command creates a crisis between his duty to protect his son and his duty to obey God's sovereign command. This crisis instigates the teleological suspension of the ethical, where the ethical is understood as the 'natural' duty of the father to love and protect his child.[5] If Abraham is declared an exception by Christians because he was willing to kill his son in obedience to God's command, then Abraham appears to be justified in committing heinous acts in the name of God.[6] Kierkegaard thought this was highly problematic, and *Fear and Trembling* is a wrestling with the question of how a loving God can command such acts that not only bring suffering to the obedient disciple, but deeply affects concrete familial expressions of love, such as being a father, a son or a husband. For Kierkegaard, the *Akedah* is a demonstration of how radically Christianity upsets what are generally considered to be 'natural orders' of human relations. Kierkegaard didn't directly address the question of Christian discipleship in *Fear and Trembling*.[7] Rather, he approaches the question of discipleship indirectly or *philosophically*, through the pseudonymous author, Johannes de Silentio.[8]

Bonhoeffer is far more overt and direct in addressing the issue of obedience to God's command. Bonhoeffer's exposition of Abraham confronts the reader with an either/or situation that demands an answer; it is an impetus to action. In Bonhoeffer's interpretation, the *Akedah* is framed Christologically in the context of *Discipleship*, a book that seeks to establish the sovereignty of Christ against other claims to loyalty in the disciple's life.[9] In Bonhoeffer's Christological interpretation, Christ is the mediator who stands between Abraham and Isaac and breaks the natural relationship between father and son, for a new relationship mediated through Christ who inverts the values of the world. Ernst Feil points out that nowhere else in his writing does Bonhoeffer's refer to Christ as mediator with such force as the Christology of *Discipleship* (1985: 79).[10] This was already noted in Chapter 3, in relation to the Sermon on the Mount. However, Bonhoeffer's application of Christology to the *Akedah* extends the hermeneutical interpretation from the New Testament to demonstrate Christ's lordship over *all* history, similar to his Christological framing of the creation doctrine in *Creation and Fall*.

But there is something further that is important in understanding what discipleship might mean. In Bonhoeffer's account, Abraham is described as experiencing not just one call, the more dramatic event of the *Akedah* itself, but two calls—where Christ's prior address to Abraham calls him on a journey away from his family of origin. And importantly, in Bonhoeffer's account, both the first and second call isolate Abraham from the world:

> No one hears about that call from God [...] Abraham remains completely alone. He is again completely the single individual, just as he was long ago, when he left his father's house. (Bonhoeffer 2003: 97)[11]

This motif of isolation in *both* calls is significant. For Bonhoeffer, it was not the dramatic command to sacrifice his child that established Abraham in relationship with Christ; it was the earlier command to leave the land of his forebears. While the drama of the *Akedah* dwarfs the perhaps more prosaic call to migrate, it is important to note that the second call was simply an intensification of the first.

The significance of the two calls can be further shown through Bonhoeffer's description of the Reformation theologian Martin Luther as a faithful disciple, also in *Discipleship*. Luther, like Abraham, received two calls: the original call to enter and the subsequent call to leave the monastery. According to Bonhoeffer, Luther left the world in order to devote himself to Christ. He followed Christ in a visibly costly way, abandoning the society which had formed him; following the call of Christ is seen in this instance as a form of separation from the world. Bonhoeffer argues that in the second call of Christ, Luther realised the doctrine of 'justification of sin' was in fact the 'secret of the justification of the sinner' (2003: 49). In the first call, Luther left the world in order to devote himself to God. In the second call, Luther came to realise the monastery too, was in the world, and Christ must be followed by living in the world. By placing Luther in the same context of a second call, Bonhoeffer shifts the focus from the dramatic act of the attempted child sacrifice. Here too, Bonhoeffer follows in Kierkegaard's footsteps, who also read Luther as a rejecting the heroic efforts of monastic life, which placed faith beyond the scope of ordinary Christians. Instead of the concept of the extraordinary as a category of monasticism that requires special effort, both believe the individual follower of Christ is called to be 'extraordinary' in their daily living in the world. Luther's apparent second call is quite ordinary, insofar as he receives a theological insight that leads him to abandon the monastery and return to the world.

Thus, for Bonhoeffer, it is not the observable facts that provide evidence of Christ's call. Christ's call must be understood in terms of the *existential meaning* of Luther's return to the world, the agony involved in leaving the monastery and the security of his faith. According to Bonhoeffer, it was not Luther's desire to leave the monastery. Luther's desire was to remain secluded in monastic life: 'Luther invested his whole life in his call to the monastery. It was God who caused Luther to fail on that path' (2003: 47). Because it was God who caused Luther to fail on that path and who commanded Luther back into the world, Bonhoeffer describes Luther's return to the world as a 'frontal assault' that demonstrated a complete obedience to Christ. Such obedience had previously been reserved for the monastic orders, but now it had to be carried out in daily life. Consequently:

> This deepened the conflict between the life of Christians and the life of the world in an unforeseeable way. The Christian had closed in on the world. It was hand-to-hand combat. (Bonhoeffer 2003: 48)

Hand-to-hand combat in this case should clearly be understood in terms of inner or spiritual battle. Bonhoeffer points towards the spiritual or inward struggle that may be experienced by the disciple in their return to the world. It is the fact that God commands the disciple that instigates the sense of combat, and it is the interiority of the heard command that is prioritised.

The prioritisation of the internal command is clear in the way Bonhoeffer views Abraham's two calls. Abraham leaving his father's house is connected to the more dramatic command to sacrifice his son. It is not the external drama that is important, but the internal battle within Abraham in both calls. Similarly, Luther's two calls, from separation of the world into the monastery and a subsequent return to the world, are both internal struggles. Here, it is significant that second call is the more difficult command to Luther: to abandon his separation from the world. Luther's second call seems less dramatic at first glance, but in Bonhoeffer's account, the existential anxiety is as God's command to Abraham to sacrifice his son. Indeed, the isolation that seemed most apparent in the drama of Abraham is more deeply present in Luther's existential or inward struggle, in secret, and following Bonhoeffer's own emphasis, the break that is born in hiddenness and faith is all the costlier because of its invisibility. Therefore, perhaps Luther, more than Abraham, demonstrates the qualities of Bonhoeffer's concept of the disciple as the isolated individual.

ISOLATION: THE EXISTENTIAL DISCIPLE

What does Bonhoeffer's interpretation of Abraham and Luther mean in terms of understanding discipleship? A key theme that emerges from this account is that of inward, or existential isolation. Again following Kierkegaard, Bonhoeffer frames discipleship in terms of Christ's command in Luke 14:26 that she who follows him must 'hate' her 'father and mother', her natural relationships even extending to the attachment to her own life.[12] Kierkegaard refers to this verse as 'a remarkable teaching on the absolute duty to God' (1983: 72); for Bonhoeffer, this verse indicates that Christ's call to discipleship makes the disciple into a single individual (2003: 92).[13] In discipleship, Christ steps between God and the individual; between person and person; and between person and reality. There is no part of the disciple's life that is not under the governance of Christ: Christ is the 'sole mediator of the world' (Bonhoeffer 2003: 94).

With Christ as mediator, the call to discipleship means nothing less than a separation or break what Bonhoeffer calls all 'natural, historical, or experiential unmediated relationships', which includes for Bonhoeffer the relationship 'between son and father, between husband and wife, between individual and nation' whether Christ is recognised or not (2003: 95). Bonhoeffer seems to argue that the disciple, called by Christ, is immediately removed from the life she knew, and all the relationships and obligations that constituted that life. Thus, the disciple is radically isolated from relationships that were previously considered natural and inviolable, such as familial and social bonds. These relationships are restored to her via Christ the mediator, but in a new way for it is now Christ who determines how she should live in her relationships and fulfil her duties and obligations. In this way, Bonhoeffer argues that Christ provides a new foundation for the disciple's life in the world. Reality is understood as established by Christ's call to the disciple through which they 'step out' of their previous existence and by which they 'exist' in the strict sense of the word (Bonhoeffer 2003: 58).[14] In calling the disciple, Christ makes the one he calls into an individual, through discipleship. That is, into an individual (disciple) that entails duties and responsibilities formed and shaped by relationship with Christ.

Yet, the relationship with Christ does not overcome separation from the world, in this account. The isolation persists, whether the break between disciple and world is external and visible, or hidden, known by the individual alone, who is nevertheless prepared to make it visible at any time. That is, the separation between disciple and the world can be exterior, or purely interior, but the isolation is present in both. Bonhoeffer's disciple finally exists in an exclusive, isolated relationship with a divine figure who communicates through the fear and trembling, or the anxiety experienced by the individual in situations that may seem remarkably prosaic to those around her.

Indeed, for Bonhoeffer, the external break remains easier for the Christian then the internal or secret break, which the solitary individual bears in 'hiddenness and faith' (2003: 98). The disciple begins with isolation from the world, and while she is returned to the world, as per Abraham and Luther, existential isolation may remain as each disciple is called alone, and must follow alone.

Before considering in more detail the relationship between the isolated disciple and the world, it is helpful to outline Kierkegaard's influence and relation to Bonhoeffer. The Danish philosopher, also considered the 'father of existentialism', has over the years been accused of promoting radical individualism as a form of 'exceptionalism', in which the solitary individual exists in a private relationship to God that is free from social responsibilities and ties.[15] The concept of the 'single individual' is indeed central to Kierkegaard's work.[16] While the role of the individual in relation to the social is far more complex in Kierkegaard's work than critics acknowledge, Kierkegaard did seek to resist the identification of Christians with the social faith of the Danish Lutheran church of his time. Bonhoeffer in *Discipleship* also sought to separate those who followed Christ from the growing influence of the national German Church. As Geoffrey Kelly points out:

> Both Kierkegaard and Bonhoeffer recognized that belonging to a large pack or sizeable group, where sacrifices in order to follow Christ to the cross were unthinkable, could provide the best places to hide from Jesus' embarrassing demands on individual Christians. (Kelly 2008)

In *Discipleship*, Bonhoeffer echoes Kierkegaard's attack on Christendom with his own indictment of the 'cheap grace' offered to bourgeois German Lutherans and promotes the 'costly grace' of incarnation and Christian discipleship. For both Kierkegaard and Bonhoeffer, the individual is key to understanding discipleship as a response in obedience to Christ's call that not only runs counter to the values of the world, but that also withstands the influence of a church that has abandoned Christ's call.

Scholars have widely acknowledged Kierkegaard's influence on Bonhoeffer.[17] Bonhoeffer greatly admired the Danish philosopher, naming Kierkegaard as one of a list of genuine Christian thinkers, alongside Paul, Augustine, Luther and Barth (Kelly 1974).[18] While referencing only three texts directly, like many of his contemporaries, Bonhoeffer read Kierkegaard with a feeling of personal affinity.[19] Matthew Kirkpatrick in *Attacks on Christendom in a World Come of Age* (2011) argues there are important links between Kierkegaard and Bonhoeffer's writings, particularly the influence of Kierkegaard's *Training in Christianity* on Bonhoeffer's concept of *Discipleship*, where both interpret disciple in terms of suffering and martyrdom.[20] According to Brian Gregor, Bonhoeffer and Kierkegaard were both troubled by the same persistent question: the ethical concreteness of discipleship. The Danish term *Efterfølgelse* and the German term *Nachfolge* are both translations of the Greek *akolouthein*, which means to go after or behind someone, where faith not about doctrinal belief, but 'the obedient response of following after Christ in concrete, everyday existence' (Gregor 2012: 152–153).[21]

For Bonhoeffer, Kierkegaard, like Luther, 'spoke like no other about the individuality of human beings' (cited in Kelly 2008: 159). Kierkegaard and Bonhoeffer shared the same reading of Luther, who rejected the monastic category as the heroic achievement of a few that was beyond the scope of ordinary Christians. Instead of the concept of the extraordinary as a category of monasticism that requires special effort, both believe the individual follower of Christ is called to be 'extraordinary' in their daily living in the world. While I have focussed on the emergence of the concept of the 'extraordinary' in Bonhoeffer's work, particularly as it appears from his analysis of the Sermon on the Mount, it was a term used frequently by Kierkegaard to mark the relationship between the Christian and God: the extraordinary (*Overordentlige*) could be made possible through the disciple's 'immediate God-relationship. Only in this sense can Christianity admit to extraordinary Christians' (Kierkegaard 1970: 356). 'The extraordinary is this: oneself humbled before God by the thought of his overwhelming grace and love'; 'to become a witness for truth, martyr and the like' (Kierkegaard 1967: 472–473, 475). For Kierkegaard, the 'extraordinary' belongs to the sphere of the religious, and it is the mark of being a disciple who follows Jesus. Thus, for both Kierkegaard and Bonhoeffer in *Discipleship*, the 'extraordinary' is a mark of distinction for Christ's followers.

In his study of Kierkegaard's influence on Bonhoeffer, Geoffrey Kelly argues that Bonhoeffer goes beyond Kierkegaard as he relates the extraordinary in *Discipleship* to acts that are highly *visible*, such as loving one's enemies (2008: 155).[22] If this is so, the concept of the

'extraordinary situation' could also be considered as a marker of discipleship, as it requires exceptional action. Thus, Bonhoeffer can be described
as instantiating Kierkegaard's 'teleological suspension of the ethical' in
his active resistance to the Nazi regime (Roberts 2005: 107). This, however, presents a new challenge. For how are we to understand the relationship between the disciple and the extraordinary situation in *Ethics*? In
the latter, the *visible* but pacifist resistance of the church in *Discipleship*
seems to be replaced by the *invisible* politically active resistor in *Ethics*:
the double agent in the *Abwehr* who is required to live in deceit. It
would seem that this is the resistor who, to use Kierkegaard's terms, is
considered a 'witness for truth, martyr and the like' for a contemporary
age, particularly amongst American evangelicals post 9/11.

As Bonhoeffer already realised in *Discipleship*, the external break with
the world would be easier than the internal or secrete break, which the
solitary individual bears in 'hiddenness and faith' (Bonhoeffer 2003:
98). Yet, for Bonhoeffer the disciple should be willing to make such
hidden obedience visible or public, if required. And to consider the
ethical implications of such obedience, it is important to make visible
or bring to light precisely the ethical framework that remains implicit
in Bonhoeffer's concept of the extraordinary, as it is explored in both
Discipleship and *Ethics*.

ETHICAL IMPLICATIONS OF THE ISOLATED DISCIPLE: THE 'DECISIVE MOMENT' AND OBEDIENCE

The ethical implications of obedience to Christ's call to the isolated disci-
ple can be drawn out through an investigation of the ideas of the young
Bonhoeffer. In a 1929 lecture to an expatriate German congregation
in Barcelona, Bonhoeffer introduces the themes of isolation, the decisive moment and obedience later so richly evident in *Discipleship*. But
Bonhoeffer also appears to anticipate his analysis of the Sermon on the
Mount in the first draft of the History and Good manuscript in *Ethics*.
Similar to his analysis of the Sermon in *Ethics*, Bonhoeffer argues that
the Sermon on the Mount should not be understood as a law providing
a Christian ethic, nor can it be a romantic ideal [*Schwarmertüm*] (2008:
302, 367–368). Yet, unlike his later argument for a separation between
what is Christian, or extraordinary, and what is natural, Bonhoeffer
now argues that the Sermon on the Mount is *not* uniquely Christian,

declaring that 'the proclamation of this particular commandment' was echoed by 'Jewish rabbis and pagan philosophers' (Bonhoeffer 2008: 364). Instead of a Christian law, ideal or particular commandment, the Sermon on the Mount has 'something completely different to offer', which is to place the individual in relationship to God's will (Bonhoeffer 2008: 365). Its function is to demonstrate to the individual the sovereignty of God and their complete dependence on God's will as revealed to the disciple.

For Bonhoeffer, God's will is revealed in each particular moment of that relationship in a way that makes a claim on the individual separately from ethical norms. The young Bonhoeffer describes the result of God's will and its relationship to morality as follows:

> There are no ethical principles enabling Christians, as it were, to make themselves moral. Instead, one has only the decisive moment at hand, that is, every moment is of potential ethical value. Never, however, can yesterday decisively influence my moral actions today. I must rather always establish anew my immediate relationship with God's will. (2008: 365)

Without principles to guide their actions, the Christian must rely on the decisive moment in which every moment has ethical weight, or *gravitas*, which cannot be determined by the disciple's actions yesterday, nor can it form a foundation for action tomorrow. The freedom of God's will requires that the disciple be established anew in an immediate relationship that cannot be predicated on existing moral frameworks, including Christian frameworks.

For the young Bonhoeffer, the Sermon on the Mount, like Christ's command to Abraham and Luther, instigates a crisis for the disciple. On the one hand, she can misunderstand the Sermon on the Mount as a 'Jesus ethic', a general law or principle; on the other hand, she can recognise the one who commands the Sermon on the Mount, and who in his freedom, commands the disciple anew each day, as long as the disciple establishes anew her immediate relationship with God's will in the 'decisive' moment. Contrasting the Christian message of 'grace' with the ethical attempt at 'righteousness', Bonhoeffer argues that there are innumerable ethical paths to righteousness, but only one incarnation that is God's message of grace. As a result, '[t]he question of Christianity is not a question of good and evil among people but the question of whether

God wishes to be gracious or not' (Bonhoeffer 2008: 363). Once the disciple is restored to relationship with God, through Christ, she is beyond moral categories or as Bonhoeffer puts this, 'beyond good and evil' (Bonhoeffer 2008: 363). For Bonhoeffer, this means that as belonging to the 'primal community', Christians become 'creative in their ethical actions': Christians create their own standards for good and evil; only Christians themselves provide the justification for their acts, just as they alone bear responsibility for them (Bonhoeffer 2008: 366). For the young Bonhoeffer, 'Christianity is basically amoral' because morality, or the categories of good and evil, arose after the fall (2008: 363). God's love for human beings is the original relationship; moral categories are a consequence of the entry of sin into the world. The implication is that this primal community between God and disciples predates the categories of good and evil that resulted from the fall. As such, Bonhoeffer argues, there can be no transition between the primal community and ethical law. Indeed, Bonhoeffer argues that Christ brings about 'the dismissal of principles, of fundamental rules — — in biblical terms, the law' (2008: 365). Action becomes creative, determined by Christians who take responsibility for action on the basis of their freedom in God.

In describing what constitutes creative action, Bonhoeffer draws on Nietzsche, arguing that the latter 'imbued the Overman [*Übermensch*] with many features of the free Christian as described and conceived by both Paul and Luther' (Bonhoeffer 2008: 366–367). According to Bonhoeffer, both Paul and Luther conceived of 'new decalogues' that reflect the new standards for measuring good and evil, laws based in creative freedom that is informed only by God's will. Subsequently, only 'Christians and God' can know whether they are acting rightly or wrongly (Bonhoeffer 2008: 367). This classic Lutheran position, echoed later in *Ethics*, argues that 'if we have Christ, we can easily establish laws and we can judge all things rightly' (Luther 1955–1968: 112–113). For the young Bonhoeffer, the ability of the Christian to judge their own actions leads to a view of Christian freedom in which there are 'no acts that are bad in and of themselves; even murder can be sanctified' (2008: 367).

Several pages following the pronouncement that murder can be sanctified, Bonhoeffer attacks those who read the Sermon on the Mount idealistically as a declaration against war. Now Bonhoeffer argues directly *against* the command of the Sermon on the Mount to love one's enemies. Bonhoeffer states that:

[W]hen my own people [*Volk*] are attacked [...] It would be an utter perversion of one's ethical sensibility to believe that my first duty is to love my enemy and precisely in so doing to surrender my neighbour to destruction, in the most concrete sense. (2008: 371)

Bonhoeffer argues that the concrete neighbour should be prioritised over the idealistic enemy of the Sermon on the Mount. For the young Bonhoeffer, the command to love one's enemies can only be understood in concrete terms of Christian decision, but such a decision needs to also be informed, at least in part, through recognising and affirming one's own concrete origin, heritage, history and culture. In one of the most provocative passages of the lecture, the young Bonhoeffer affirms his own heritage:

God gave me my mother, my people [*Volk*]. For what I have, I thank my people; for what I am, I am through my people, and so what I have should also belong to my people; that is in the divine order [*Ordnung*] of things, for God created the peoples. If for a single dangerous moment I do not act, then I am doing nothing other than surrendering my neighbours. (2008: 371)

The young Bonhoeffer apparently negates the command to love one's enemies in the Sermon on the Mount and then seems to justify war in the name of a concrete commitment that unites both Christ's divine or spiritual command with the natural love for one's own family and *Volk*. Unlike the spiritual 'hand to hand combat' in *Discipleship*, the Christian now acts decisively in the world. Indeed, the young, patriotic Bonhoeffer even seems to argue *for* defensive war, suggesting that Christian ethics may justifiably instigate a war if it is done to realise the call of God in each person to make history, to expand, to grow in strength. For the young Bonhoeffer, 'strength also comes from God, and power, and victory, for God creates youth in the individual as well as in nations, and God loves youth, for God himself is eternally young and strong and victorious' (2008: 373).

What are we, as readers, to make of these passages by the young Bonhoeffer, particularly in view of his pacifist commitment in *Discipleship*? Eberhard Bethge argues that this lecture demonstrates Bonhoeffer's 'conventionally Lutheran' attitude to the Sermon on the Mount 'spruced up with the titanic ethics of the immediate moment'

(2000: 119). Given the later attempts by Nazis to recruit Nietzsche's moral philosophy for National Socialist ideologies, we are justifiably alarmed by Bonhoeffer's reference to Nietzsche's Overman as a model of *Christian* creative action. Defending Bonhoeffer's lecture against claims that it is 'pre-fascistic', Heinz Tödt argues that it is best read as a modified form 'of the neo-Lutheran religious enhancement of the idea of the nation' that reflected the majority of German Protestantism at the time (2007: 118). This would suggest that Bonhoeffer's views in the lecture are an anomaly within the broader context of his theology.

However, I don't believe that the 1929 Barcelona lecture can be dismissed as an aberration. There are remarkable similarities between the isolated disciple who is called to be obedient to Christ in both the lecture and *Discipleship*, and both prioritise the decisive moment over the continued tradition of ethical law. Both also emphasise the lordship of Christ as revealed to the disciple in a crisis; in the lecture as the decisive moment, in *Discipleship* this is understood as a call. Furthermore, Bonhoeffer's exposition of the Sermon on the Mount in this early lecture is similar to the later account of the Sermon in *Ethics*. As I showed in Chapter 3, in *Ethics* the Sermon on the Mount is no longer understood as the specific command of Christ to love one's enemies, but reframed as a confrontation with 'the necessity of responsible historical action', which may include direct political action as the concrete neighbour is prioritised over the abstract enemy in a way that echoes his emphasis on the concrete neighbour in the 1929 lecture (Bonhoeffer 2009: 242, 245). The presence of the Barcelona sermon as a hermeneutical or interpretive lens makes clearer the continuity between the extraordinary requirement to love one's enemy in the Sermon on the Mount exposition and the extraordinary requirement to kill in *Ethics*.

Running as the *cantus firmus*[23] throughout these three very different texts and interpretations of the Sermon on the Mount is God's sovereign will. Bonhoeffer scholars such as Ernst Feil, readily connect Christology and the world as the link between the Sermon on the Mount in *Discipleship*, and Bonhoeffer's outline of responsible action in *Ethics*. The 'two sermons' in *Discipleship* and *Ethics* emphasise Christ as the mediator of the world and affirm that the world can only be approached and understood through the nature and example of Christ (Feil 1985). Both *Discipleship* and *Ethics* are considered to be thoroughly Christ-centred and both strongly emphasise 'God's will as revealed in Jesus Christ' (Stassen 2006: 59). Peter Frick even ties God's will as the basis of Christian ethics directly to Bonhoeffer's own decision to become a conspirator:

> Bonhoeffer's basic ethical premise – that Christians must create their own values and make responsible decisions – stems from his basic theological premise that there is only the one reality of God revealed in the world. Given further his philosophical premise – that the self is limited and incapable because of sin to come to itself – his prescription for ethical behaviour is simply the discernment of the will of God in a given situation. His own personal test case, so to speak, was the ethical dilemma of whether or not he should participate in the conspiracy on Hitler's life. (2012: 318)

Yet, few scholars acknowledge as constructive the role God's will plays in Bonhoeffer's 1929 sermon, where the command of Christ overrides existing laws in favour of acts of creative freedom based in God's will. Such creative freedom means even murder can be sanctified. As noted, mainstream Bonhoeffer scholars have considered this to be an aberration in Bonhoeffer's overall theology, and as Bonhoeffer being unduly influenced by an existentialist ethical framework that belonged to the majority German Protestant view of the time. But the themes of isolation and obedience to Christ's command in the moment emerge across the 1929 lecture, *Disciple* and *Ethics*, and therefore demonstrate significant continuity in Bonhoeffer's thought around the concept of existential discipleship and its relationship to moral norms.

This chapter began by drawing out the 'existential' aspects of Bonhoeffer's concept of discipleship as it emerges in the pacifist text, *Discipleship* in order to highlight the ethical implications of Christ's sovereignty, and how this affects the disciple relationship to the world, and its ethical norms. In *Discipleship*, Christ's call comes to each person alone; each has to decide alone in obedience to Christ. The existential anxiety that comes with such a decision is allayed for the disciple through faith in Christ's sovereign freedom over the law, or existing ethical norms. It would now appear that these themes of obedience and isolation from the world were not unique to Bonhoeffer's Finkenwalde monastic experiment. Years prior, Bonhoeffer highlighted the 'decisive moment' over the continued tradition of ethical law. As Christ is not bound by the law, neither is the disciple. The latter is able to act in 'creative freedom'. In both texts, Bonhoeffer emphasises the sovereignty of Christ, revealed to the disciple in a crisis or a confrontation that appears as an either/or situation. Thus, the sense of isolated discipleship, combined with the decisive moment of obedience to Christ's command revealed anew each day, means that the Christian herself exists in a 'state of exception' that is radically separated from the world governed through regulating law.

Without a mediator other than Christ, Bonhoeffer appears to have done away with ethics altogether, offering only a radical either/or between discipleship and ethics and therefore a radical *incompatibility* between ethics and Christianity. With the rejection of 'principles', Bonhoeffer effectively rejects human and social categories of mediation and problem-solving. Any account of discipleship that emphasises the call to discipleship, the decision and the actions that follow from obedience to the call cannot be evaluated, apart from the Christ-formed faculty that emphasises obedience. This obedience cannot be understood as a form of Christian ethics nor as a form of Christian witness. Both justification and confession are functions of language that mediate through reason. In terms of the individual who may believe herself commanded, she must ultimately, as with Abraham and Luther, act in silent obedience. The silence is significant because it demonstrates not only the limit of language in making herself understood to others, but also the limit of language in understanding her own actions in the moment of crisis.

For Bonhoeffer, the disciple is called into existence *as* Christ's disciple through Christ's command, a command that is addressed to, and heard by, the disciple alone. It is a command that is heard by the disciple in isolation, but it is also a command that is not bound by the written command of Christ (such as the Sermon on the Mount); indeed, it is a command that comes in the moment, so that Christ is free to command murder. The young Bonhoeffer's language of decision and the immediate relationship that reveals the will of Christ anew in each moment sits uncomfortably alongside the situation of war. By directly contradicting the command to love one's enemies in the Sermon on the Mount, claiming that Christ can sanctify murder, the young Bonhoeffer opens the door to divine justification of killing in the context of an extraordinary situation that may require war, deception or the breaking of a treaty. The two aspects of discipleship, recognition of Christ's sovereignty and separation from the world have important implications for how we are to understand Christian action in the world. If Christ's sovereignty means he is free to transcend the command of the Sermon on the Mount, then the disciple who is obedient to Christ is free to do likewise. And because of the underlying themes of separation and division from 'the world', obedience may even require action that runs counter to what has been considered historically and traditionally acceptable to Christians. When we view Bonhoeffer's concept of the 'extraordinary situation' through the lens of his 1929 sermon and *Discipleship*, his emerging political theology as it undergirds his own political involvement ought to warn us against too easily appropriating Bonhoeffer's decision for conspiracy as an example of legitimate Christian violence.

Kierkegaard was right to draw attention to Abraham's willingness to sacrifice Isaac, and the horror this should cause Christians. Kierkegaard confronted the Lutheran citizens of his day with the question: if Abraham is declared an 'exception' by Christians because he was willing to kill his son in obedience to God's command, then Abraham appears to be justified in committing heinous acts in the name of God. We should likewise ask those who would readily endorse Bonhoeffer's decision for conspiracy the same question: If Bonhoeffer is declared an exception because he is willing to commit violence as an act of obedience, what implications does this have for how we are to understand the Christian relationship to acts of violence?

NOTES

1. The influence of Kierkegaard on German intellectual life in the Weimar Republic will be further discussed in Chapter 9.
2. 1 Cor. 7: 29-31. In a reference to Karl Barth's *Epistle to the Romans*, Bonhoeffer writes, because of Christ, 'everything has changed' in 'a turnaround of 360 degrees' (2003: 97). Barth refers to the prophetic role of the church in the world, rather than individual discipleship: 'When such a Church embarks upon moral exhortation, its exhortation can be naught else but a criticism of all human behaviour, a criticism which moves through every one of the 360 degrees of the circle of our ambiguous life' (Barth 1968: 428).
3. Kierkegaard's interpretation of the *Akedah* has been described as 'highly eccentric' and even 'a distortion of Biblical faith itself' (Gordis 1976: 416).
4. As Thulstrup declares, Kierkegaard should not be read as a 'historian of philosophy', but a highly original thinker who 'worked most freely and best on his own' (1980: 287, 380). It is multi-layered because it is both a personal communication (directed towards Kierkegaard's former fiancée Regine) and a public communication (Hong and Hong 1983: xi).

5. According to Kierkegaard, the ethical understood *as* law 'fills the whole of existence'; it cannot be suspended, or is not 'capable of being surrendered... [and] preserved in the higher, which is its *telos*' or ultimate goal (Kierkegaard 1983: 54). The ethical law rests only on itself for its authority. The foundation and limit of the ethical law *is* its own authority. The ethical law entails obligations and duties for individuals who live under its governance. At times, duties may appear to clash. Kierkegaard gives three historical examples where duties under ethical law lead to a sense of 'crisis' for the individual concerned: Agamemnon, Jephthah and Brutus. Each of these individuals faces a similar crisis between their 'fatherly' duty to care for their child and their 'sovereign' duty to kill their child. The 'crisis' for each individual involved occurs because there are competing duties or obligations imposed by principles that command allegiance. Yet in each example, the laws and customs to which they belong justify these killings, and so they are 'tragic' figures, who sacrifice their own happiness (familial love) for a higher duty. In the hierarchical order, the individual resolves the crisis between duties and gains his 'tragic' element through resigning, or giving up one good in this life for a higher good in an act of will demonstrated by submission or obedience to the greatest good.

6. The philosopher, Immanuel Kant, was quite certain that the rational answer from Abraham would have been as follows: 'That I ought not to kill my good son is quite certain. But that you, this apparition, are God – of that I am not certain, and never can be, not even if this voice rings down to me from (visible) heaven' (Kant 1979: 115).

7. Kierkegaard approaches the question more directly through *Training in Christianity* (1850).

8. Kierkegaard approaches Abraham and discipleship indirectly, through adopting a 'what if?' posture. *Fear and Trembling* through its dialectical method remains essentially open-ended, leaving the reader free to accept or reject Abraham, the claims of the pseudonymous author, Johannes De Silentio, or Kierkegaard's own adaptation of the biblical narrative.

9. This contrasts with *Fear and Trembling*, which places Abraham's ordeal, rather than God, at the centre.

10. Similarly, Kelly and Godsey state that the 'Christocentrism of this book [*Discipleship*] is unmistakable' (2003: 20).

11. *Fear and Trembling* explores similar themes of isolation brought about by the 'silent' obedience of Abraham. Johannes de Silentio, whose name means 'the silent one', particularly grapples with Abraham's silence in the third *Problema* of *Fear and Trembling*. Abraham fails to explain his actions to those around him, unwilling or unable (in this case) to justify his actions in terms of existing moral norms.

12. 'If anyone comes to Me and does not hate his father and mother, wife and children, brothers and sisters, yes, and his own life also, he cannot be My disciple' Luke 14:26. See also the 1929 Barcelona Lecture in which Bonhoeffer uses this verse. Kierkegaard states in his journal, in reference to Luke 14:26—'Who are these words addressed to? According to the preacher, "they are for the extraordinary individuals", and not relevant to everyone. How does a person become the "extraordinary"? Not by virtue of natural qualifications, such as genius, but through the aid of God' (Kierkegaard 1967: 472).

13. This is perhaps the clearest link between *Fear and Trembling* and *Discipleship*, where 'absolute duty to God' and 'Christ's call', respectively, establish the disciple as an individual in relationship with God.

14. In his *Habilitation* thesis, *Act and Being*, Bonhoeffer uses Heidegger's concept of *Dasein* to distinguish the qualitative or existential mode of the being-there (*Da-Sein*) of human beings, in distinction from the being of all else (quantitative or historical mode of being). *Dasein* is unique in that human beings are disclosed to themselves as being in time, in which mode they 'exist' as different to all other things, aware of their finitude, of their own being as an issue and a responsibility.

15. As well as the early reception of Kierkegaard in Europe, this has been the majority view in the Anglophone world. Once scholars see Kierkegaard's individual as radically isolated, they read nihilism and irrationalism into *Fear and Trembling*. Robert Gordis argued that Kierkegaard's Abraham is a knight of faith because he 'disregards the accepted canons of ethics and humanity before the command of religion, and is ready to sacrifice his beloved son at God's behest, though the act is clearly immoral' (Gordis 1976). On Gordis' account, Kierkegaard advocates a warped faith in divine command theory over rational morality. This view of Kierkegaard's Abraham is shared by Levinas, Derrida and Mulhall. However, Merold Westphal (1996) argues that Kierkegaard's self is essentially relational. The isolation of the self from the crowd is not an end, but a means to restore the self in proper relationship, first to God, then to neighbour or to other human selves. Westphal interprets Kierkegaard's individual in a postmodern light, as a reaction to excesses perceived to be all too typical of modernity (1996: xi).

16. All of Kierkegaard's work, both the indirect and direct communications are addressed to *den Enkelte*, *Hinn Enkelte* or 'that individual'. Kierkegaard refers to *den Enkelte* or its variations 750 times, 450 times throughout his principle works (Otani 1955).

17. This includes Moltmann, Jürgen and Jürgen Weissbach. 1967. *Two Studies in the Theology of Bonhoeffer*. New York: Scribner; Kelly. 1974. The Influence of Kierkegaard on Bonhoeffer's Concept of Discipleship.

Irish Theological Quarterly 41 (2): 148–154; Green, Clifford J. 1999. *Bonhoeffer: A Theology of Sociality.* Grand Rapids: Eerdmans; Gouwens, David J. 1996. *Kierkegaard as a Religious Thinker.* Cambridge: Cambridge University Press; Plant, Stephen. 2004. *Bonhoeffer.* London and New York: Continuum; Walsh, Sylvia. 2009. *Kierkegaard—Thinking Christianly in an Existential Mode.* Christian Theology in Context. Oxford: Oxford University Press; Watkin, Julia. 2000. *Kierkegaard.* Outstanding Christian Thinkers. London: Continuum International Publishing Group.

18. Indeed, Kierkegaard is one of Bonhoeffer's intellectual influences that is actually named in *Discipleship* (Kuske and Tödt 2003: 301).

19. Bonhoeffer directly references *Fear and Trembling*, as well as *Works of Love* and *Sickness Unto Death*, in addition to extensive reading of Kierkegaard.

20. Though not the first to note Kierkegaard's influence on Bonhoeffer, Kirkpatrick is the first monograph-length study that provides an in-depth analysis of Bonhoeffer's reading and understanding of Kierkegaard.

21. Similar to themes explored in this chapter, Gregor identifies key features in *Discipleship* that are derived from Kierkegaard, including the connection between faith and obedience, where the call of Christ establishes the position of the disciple as a follower. Gregor notes that Bonhoeffer relies on Kierkegaard's journals in exploring the meaning of discipleship; according to Gregor, one can 'trace the influence of these journals almost point for point through the early chapters of Bonhoeffer's book' (Gregor 2012: 157).

22. It is interesting to note that Kierkegaard's description of Abraham's obedience to God as a mark of the extraordinary has received such wide attention, while Bonhoeffer's account of the extraordinary that links discipleship to the command to love one's enemies in the Sermon on the Mount has gone largely unnoticed.

23. The *cantus firmus* is 'a pre-existent melody that is used as a basis for a new polyphonic composition' (cited in Smith 2006: 200). For Bonhoeffer, the concept of *cantus firmus* was used to ground the counterpoint, as part of the 'polyphony of life' in which pain and joy exist alongside each other (Bonhoeffer 2010: 394–395, 396–397). 'The *cantus firmus* allows the Christian to live freely within the complexities of human existence', notes Smith (2006: 201).

References

Barth, Karl. 1968. Past and Future: Friedrich Naumann and Christoph Blumhardt. In *The Beginnings of Dialectic Theology*, ed. James M. Robinson. Richmond: John Knox Press.

Bethge, Eberhard. 2000. *Dietrich Bonhoeffer: A Biography*, trans. Victoria J. Barnett. Minneapolis: Fortress Press.

Bonhoeffer. 2003. *Discipleship*, trans. Barbara Green and Reinhard Krauss. Dietrich Bonhoeffer Works English. Minneapolis: Fortress Press.

Bonhoeffer. 2010. *Letters and Papers from Prison*, trans. Isabel Best, Lisa E. Dahill, Reinhard Krauss, and Nancy Lukens. Dietrich Bonhoeffer Works English. Minneapolis: Fortress Press.

Bonhoeffer, Dietrich. 2008. *Barcelona, Berlin, New York, 1928–1931*, trans. Douglass W. Stott. Dietrich Bonhoeffer Works English. Minneapolis: Fortress Press.

Bonhoeffer, Dietrich. 2009. *Ethics*, trans. Reinhard Krauss, Charles C. West, and Douglass W. Stott. Dietrich Bonhoeffer Works English. Minneapolis: Fortress Press.

Feil, Ernst. 1985. *The Theology of Dietrich Bonhoeffer*, trans. Martin Rumscheidt. Philadelphia: Fortress Press.

Frick, Peter. 2012. Dietrich Bonhoeffer: Engaging Intellect—Legendary Life. *Religion Compass* 6 (6): 309–322. doi:https://doi.org/10.1111/j.1749-8171.2012.00357.x.

Gordis, Robert. 1976. The Faith of Abraham: A Note on Kierkegaard's 'Teleological Suspension of the Ethical'. *Judaism* 25 (4): 414–419.

Gregor, Brian. 2012. Following-After and Becoming Human: A Study of Bonhoeffer and Kierkegaard. In *Being Human, Becoming Human: Dietrich Bonhoeffer and Social Thought*. Cambridge, UK: James Clarke Company.

Hong, Edna H., and Howard V. Hong. 1983. Historical Introduction. In *Fear and Trembling*, ed. Edna H. Hong and Howard V. Hong. Princeton: Princeton University Press.

Kant, Immanuel. 1979. *The Conflict of the Faculties*, trans. Mary J. Gregor. Norwalk: Abaris Books.

Kelly, Geffrey B. 1974. The Influence of Kierkegaard on Bonhoeffer's Concept of Discipleship. *Irish Theological Quarterly* 41 (2): 148–154.

Kelly, Geffrey B. 2008. Kierkegaard as 'Antidote' and the Impact on Dietrich Bonhoeffer's Concept of Christian Discipleship. In *Bonhoeffer's Intellectual Formation: Theology and Philosophy in His Thought*, ed. Peter Frick, 147–165. Tübingen: Mohr Siebeck.

Kelly, Geffrey B., and John D. Godsey. 2003. Editors' Introduction to the English Edition. In *Discipleship*, ed. Geffrey B. Kelly and John D. Godsey, 1–33. Minneapolis: Fortress Press.

Kierkegaard, Søren. 1967. *Journals and Papers*, trans. Edna H. Hong and Howard V. Hong. Bloomington: Indiana University Press.

Kierkegaard, Søren. 1970. *Journals and Papers*, trans. Edna H. Hong and Howard V. Hong. Bloomington: Indiana University Press.

Kierkegaard, Søren. 1983. *Fear and Trembling/Repetition*. Kierkegaard's Writings. Princeton, NJ: Princeton University Press.

Kuske, Martin, and Ilse Tödt. 2003. Editor's Afterword to the German Edition. In *Discipleship*, ed. Geffrey B. Kelly and John D. Godsey, 289–314. Minneapolis: Fortress Press.

Luther, Martin. 1955–1968. *Disputations*. Luther Works. Saint Louis: Concordia Publishing House.

Otani, M. 1955. Something about Kierkegaard's Inner History. *Orbis Litterarum* 10 (1–2): 191–195.

Roberts, J.Deotis. 2005. *Bonhoeffer and King: Speaking Truth to Power*. Louiseville, KY: Westminster John Knox Press.

Smith, Robert O. 2006. Bonhoeffer and Musical Metaphor. *Word & World* 26 (2): 195–206.

Stassen, Glen Harold. 2006. *Living the Sermon on the Mount: A Practical Hope for Grace and Deliverance*. San Francisco: Jossey-Bass.

Thulstrup, Niels. 1980. *Kierkegaard's Relation to Hegel*. Princeton, NJ: Princeton University Press.

Tödt, Heinz Eduard. 2007. *Authentic Faith: Bonhoeffer's Theological Ethics in Context*, trans. David Stassen and Ilse Tödt. Grand Rapids, MI: Eerdmans.

Westphal, Merold. 1996. *Becoming a Self*. West Lafayette, IN: Purdue University Press.

CHAPTER 8

The Limits of the Extraordinary Situation?

The previous chapter described the implications of the isolated disciple who acted outside social and regulating norms, and appeared justified in doing so, based on their immediate relationship to Christ. A troubling conclusion indeed. A view of discipleship that appears to sanctify murder is surely particularly objectionable in an age where acts of divinely justified killing saturate our television screens on a daily basis and perhaps all too ominously define the spirit of our own age, shaped as it is by terrorism. Bonhoeffer's theologically informed exhortation that the call to discipleship requires the travelling of a lonely road that puts one into conflict with the values of the world bears strange resonance to the 'lone wolf' characterisation with which we are familiar today. Yet, it is also this view of discipleship that encourages part of the evangelical readership, who also find themselves in a destabilised age, a heightened sense of crises, and for whom Bonhoeffer seems to be a model of the decisive and 'extraordinary' action of the kind that will increasingly be required of future generations.

This chapter considers the possible limits to action in the *Grenzfall* scenario of the extraordinary situation. This discussion began in Chapter 4, through exploring Bonhoeffer's concept of 'responsible action', which was based on the nature and model of Christ, according to Bonhoeffer. However, I also pointed to various issues that emerged from this. Thus, this chapter is not simply a reiteration of 'responsible action' as the solution to the problem of limit. Rather, it considers three other possible motifs in Bonhoeffer's writing that can function as limit. The first is the

P. Brown, *Bonhoeffer*,
https://doi.org/10.1007/978-3-030-05698-8_8

place of the church as the locus of discipleship, which puts a limit to the isolated, existential disciple. The role of church and community is widely recognised as an important counterpoint to Bonhoeffer's concept of discipleship, by both Bonhoeffer and broader scholarship. The second motif that explores the notion of limit is Bonhoeffer's ultimate/penultimate distinction, which is considered an important part of Bonhoeffer's political theology and locates existential action in a broader context. The final motif is the role of guilt as considering the limit of responsible action. This is the richest and most promising motif, as it was considered a key characteristic in Bonhoeffer's initial assessment of 'responsible action' as modelled on Christ, who bears the guilt of the world. But guilt is also an important idea in judging 'dirty hands' actions in political philosophy, thereby extending the discussion of guilt in responsible action from a theological framework, to political theology and political philosophy more broadly understood.

THE LIMITS OF ISOLATED DISCIPLESHIP: THE CHALLENGE OF CHURCH-COMMUNITY (*GEMEINDE*)

Those who have read *Discipleship* may well have exclaimed at various points in the previous chapter, 'but that's not the full picture of discipleship in *Discipleship!*', strongly disagreeing with my portrayal of the isolated disciple. And indeed, such an assessment is correct, to an extent. In *Discipleship*, the follower of Christ does not remain alone. Church-community (*Gemeinde*) is a key theme of *Discipleship*, and one that follows consistently from Bonhoeffer's doctoral dissertation, *Sanctorum Communio*, the latter considered to mark 'a milestone in Protestant ecclesiology of the early and mid twentieth century', as Bonhoeffer brought together theology with a sociology of the church (Nielsen 2012: 92). For Nielsen, it is in *Sanctorum Communio* that Bonhoeffer joins ecclesiology and Christology into one notion of vicarious representative action (*Stellvertretung*), something that was maintained in *Discipleship*, argues Nielsen (2012: 95, 100). Clifford Green similarly argues community is key to understanding what he terms Bonhoeffer's theology of sociality, which he defines as 'a set of clear, coherent, and interrelated theological convictions about the human person in both intersubjective encounters and in the corporate relations of human communities' (2012: 72).[1] Green first coined the term in his early research in 1971 and has consistently argued that this concept directed Bonhoeffer's whole theology, from his doctoral dissertation to his prison writings. Green points out that for Bonhoeffer, revelation through Christ is an 'inherently social event, which occurs in a human community of persons' (1999: 2).[2]

I do not disagree with either Green or Nielsen. In *Discipleship*, Bonhoeffer makes clear that following Christ involves participation in the church-community. Christ is the mediator who stands between persons to separate them, but also unites them: 'Everyone enters discipleship alone, but no one remains alone in discipleship' (Bonhoeffer 2003: 98–99). Indeed, Bonhoeffer explicitly argues that the Christian belongs to the church-community, which represents the body of Christ:

> Whoever seeks to become a new human being individually cannot succeed. To become a new human being means to come into the church, to become a member of Christ's body. The new human being is not the single individual who has been justified and sanctified; rather, the new human being is the church-community, the body of Christ, or Christ himself. (2003: 219)

Furthermore, as already noted in Chapter 3, *Discipleship* must first and foremost be understood as a text addressed to a church-community that struggled to remain true to what Bonhoeffer believed was the Christian call to peace in the face of an emerging totalitarian political regime. *Discipleship* functioned as a training manual for students of the underground seminary, Finkenwalde. Those who were tutored by Bonhoeffer were not isolated disciples, but were intended to be leaders within the Confessing Church. *Discipleship* takes place in a church-community and therefore must be understood communally, both in terms of the Confessing Church and the ecumenical or worldwide church.

Bonhoeffer was critical of what he considered Kierkegaard's emphasis on the individual. He quoted *Fear and Trembling* in a *Sanctorum Communio* footnote: 'As soon as the single one has entered the paradox, he does not arrive at the idea of the church', to which he added, 'Kierkegaard, who like few others knew how to speak of the burden of loneliness, comes to reject the concept of the church on that basis' (2009b: 162, fn. 20). Bonhoeffer therefore seems to reject the idea of isolated discipleship apart from the church-community. To some extent, Bonhoeffer was right in his critique of Kierkegaard. In *Fear and Trembling*, Kierkegaard *does* indeed state that there can be no 'knights of faith' (1983: 97). For Bonhoeffer, Kierkegaard's individual, isolated from the church, led to a view of the person as the 'self-establishing I', which Bonhoeffer argued entailed that Kierkegaard 'remained bound to the idealist position' (2009b: 57).[3] Bonhoeffer saw Kierkegaard as advocating an ethical philosophy that he believed simply could not work in a concrete situation of living and existing human beings. As Palmisano interprets this, 'For Kierkegaard, whether or not God speaks is not the point. This is because God's speaking is not an event deferred to the judgment of the community' (2016: 14). In Kierkegaard's account, it does seem that God addresses the individual, who must act against prevailing norms in ethical isolation.

Scholars see Bonhoeffer's concept of discipleship as church-community as an important point of difference from Kierkegaard. David Law notes that while there is much similarity between Bonhoeffer and Kierkegaard's respective concepts of discipleship, Bonhoeffer's concept has 'a communal basis lacking in Kierkegaard's thought' (2011: 25). For Law, this can be found in Bonhoeffer's concept of church-community in *Discipleship*, where the latter acts as Kierkegaard's 'paradoxical, offensive witness to the suffering, humiliated Christ' (2011: 25). Connecting discipleship with the concept of the extraordinary, Geoffrey Kelly suggests that Kierkegaard understood the extraordinary primarily in terms of the 'immediate God-relationship' while Bonhoeffer understood it in terms of the unconditional love of the suffering church-community in *Discipleship* (2008: 154–155). Togetherness is the goal of discipleship, rather than inwardness, argues Trey Palmisano in a similar fashion (2016: 34). My portrait of the isolated disciple therefore seems a caricature that does not take the church context adequately into account. I respond to this at two points: first addressing Bonhoeffer's reading of Kierkegaard and secondly by reconsidering the nature of the church.

For Bonhoeffer, discipleship cannot take place in abstract modes of thinking, but must be connected to concrete events, just as individuals do not exist as discrete atoms, but exist within communities. For this reason, Bonhoeffer initially corrected what he perceived was the individualism of Kierkegaard by forming his own theological and communitarian concept of the Christian person that replaces Kierkegaard's 'single individual' with the personhood of the church.[4] Yet, his interpretation of *Fear and Trembling* does not do justice to the text itself. As Kirkpatrick points out, Bonhoeffer's comment on this passage is curious as Kierkegaard makes no reference to the church in this passage, and the focus is rather on the responsibility of the individual before God (2011: 9). This misreading is significant because it is precisely on the individual's relation to the church that Bonhoeffer disagreed most strongly with what he believed was Kierkegaard's view. Yet, I would go further and say that this misreading points to a potential blind spot in Bonhoeffer's thinking around the nature of communal discipleship.

Bonhoeffer regards the church-community not as an institution, but as a collective person; the personhood of the church-community reflects its identity as the 'body of Christ' that is made of up 'actual, living human beings' who follow Christ (Bonhoeffer 2003: 226). The church-community is understood by Bonhoeffer to have 'personhood', and as such I suggest that it can suffer the same isolation experienced by Abraham or the isolated disciple in her obedience to Christ's call. The two calls explicated in terms of Abraham as the isolated disciple must also be understood as addressed to the church-community: the first call breaking with 'natural immediate relationships' in the world and the second call breaking with 'unmediated spiritual relationships'. The first call devotes the church-community to Christ; the second call intensifies that devotion. In this context, the church-community as Christ's disciple remains isolated from the world. Bonhoeffer himself makes this clear in his doctoral dissertation, *Sanctorum Communio*, 'the nature of the Church can only be understood from within, *cum ireat studio* (with passionate zeal), never by nonparticipants' (Bonhoeffer 2009b: 33). The Christian community is the only place where disciples are able to act together and be together, with and for each other. The love shown by Christ is accepted and practised with the church-community, and the expression of Christian love is not possible for those outside the Christian faith, whether understood in terms of an individual or a communal relationship to Christ. On this account, Bonhoeffer's model of a church is as cut off from the world as the medieval monastery he criticises.

In his own analysis of the concept of the extraordinary in Kierkegaard and Bonhoeffer, Kirkpatrick believes that Bonhoeffer himself moved away from an understanding of church as community to a model of discipleship more akin to Kierkegaard's individual who exists in an immediate God-relationship. Kirkpatrick extends this inversion of Bonhoeffer's concept of personhood to argue that the foundation for Bonhoeffer's theology is actually *not* the nature of the church and authority, as is often supposed, but 'the single individual, drawn away from direct relationship with others into the mediation of Christ, bound to undivided relationship with God' (2011: 220). Kirkpatrick concludes it is because of this undivided relationship with God that Bonhoeffer's ethics is best described as simple obedience to God's command that proceeds from His mouth anew every day. While we do not need to wholly agree with Kirkpatrick's conclusion, it is important to acknowledge his critique, particularly in light of Bonhoeffer's view of the church in *Discipleship* as separate from the world. The challenge of church-community cannot in itself function as a critical limit to the actions of the isolated disciple.

ULTIMATE/PENULTIMATE DISTINCTION

The second limit to responsible action is the ultimate/penultimate distinction, which is considered an important part of Bonhoeffer's political theology and locates existential action in a broader context. This discussion is found in *Ethics* in a manuscript titled 'The Ultimate and Penultimate Things'. The section and the articulation on ultimate and penultimate are considered to be the strongest part of Bonhoeffer's *Ethics*, and 'one of his most original and fertile concepts' (Kuhn cited in Law 2011: 18). It is also seen as Bonhoeffer's unique contribution to a political theology, which itself has long viewed Luther's two-kingdoms doctrine 'as an obstacle to politically engaged Christian life and thought' (DeJonge 2016). Luther's division between spiritual and temporal realms led to defined roles and distinct spheres of influence. Christians could seek spiritual freedom while being obedient citizens, and Luther's two-kingdoms doctrine became strongly associated with quietist obedience to authority (Whitford 2003: 181).

Bonhoeffer replaces the problematic separation between the two spheres in Luther's doctrine with 'a more dynamic and Christocentric framework', writes De Jonge (2016). Thus, Bonhoeffer envisions a two-fold understanding of the world that finds its completion in the figure of Christ as the 'one reality'. The ultimate (*Letztes*) is the event of justification of the sinner, and it is qualitatively the ultimate or God's final word: 'There is no word of God that goes beyond God's grace. There is nothing greater than a life that is justified before God' (Bonhoeffer 2009a: 149). For Bonhoeffer, this entails a 'complete break' with 'all that has gone before', which he calls here the penultimate a sphere associated with natural and necessary things (2009a: 149). Similar to his soteriological understanding of the doctrine of creation, where the resurrection event breaks with the natural order, so here Bonhoeffer's understanding of the ultimate views God's word of forgiveness as radically free in a way that 'excludes every method once and for all' (Bonhoeffer 2009a: 150). However, justification or forgiveness presumes that someone is guilty, and this is the purpose of the penultimate sphere. It is described as the time before grace, in which the sinner has to 'walk the full length of the way through penultimate things' such as Luther's time in the monastery (Bonhoeffer 2009a: 151). The penultimate is the pre-eschatological reality in which human beings living their lives, and 'prepares the ground for human beings' reception of the divine word, because it is through their existence in the penultimate that human beings become guilty' (Law 2011: 20). Thus, the penultimate functions as a preparation to lead persons to a realisation of their guilt, and the need for the salvation provided freely by God as the 'ultimate' meaning of existence. Once the ultimate appears, the penultimate remains in existence (for the forgiven sinner) 'even though it is completely superseded by the ultimate and no longer in force' (Bonhoeffer 2009a: 151). Similar themes seem to emerge that negate the existing world and its attendant cares, worries and responsibilities. Yet, it would also seem that the penultimate remains in existence, and that the Christian must continue to live in the world. How then should the disciple view their relationship to the world, while living in the penultimate sphere and all its attendant responsibilities?

Two mistakes are usually made here and should be avoided, suggests Bonhoeffer. These are the positions of radicalism and compromise. Radicalism views the ultimate and penultimate as mutually exclusive contraries. Christ is the destroyer and enemy of everything penultimate: 'Christ is the sign that the world is ripe to be consigned to the fire' (Bonhoeffer 2009a: 153). There are no distinctions for the radical. On the other hand, compromise sets the penultimate apart from the ultimate and treats it as though it had its own meaning—that is, treats the existing order as the ultimate. The divine ultimate is simply excluded. But in this, the status quo is justified as nothing judges the penultimate, nothing implies guilt. The dichotomy between radicalism and compromise cannot answer the question about Christian life and indeed point to the danger inherent in a concept of discipleship that views the world as completely lost.

For Bonhoeffer, the three elements of Christ's revelation in the world—incarnation, crucifixion and resurrection—are intended to hold the penultimate and ultimate together. Unlike the resurrection event in the earlier lectures on the creation doctrine, now 'eternal life' is described as 'new life, [that] breaks ever more powerfully into earthly life and creates space for itself within it' (Bonhoeffer 2009a: 158). John Manoussakis describes the connection between the penultimate and ultimate, not as a temporal relation, where one supersedes the other, but as an inner relation 'of interdependence and reciprocity – between God's creation and God's kingdom' (2009: 231).[5] This echoes the different parts of Bonhoeffer's understanding of revelation in Christ. In Manoussakis' view, the reciprocal relationship affirms the penultimate as the created world and its lived reality:

> The penultimate is indispensable for our effort of reaching for the ultimate; even more, the penultimate is indispensable in order for the ultimate itself to reach us. Indeed, through this reciprocal relationship we come to realize the indispensability of the created world for our salvation. We are not saved apart from this world or to the extent that we succeed in living by leaving the world behind us, by withdrawing from it or by denying it, but our salvation passes through and depends upon the world as well as our bodies with which we are bound to the world. (Manoussakis 2009: 239)

Aspects of Bonhoeffer's writing around the ultimate/penultimate distinction would reject the claim that a reciprocal relationship exists between the penultimate world and God's free decree. Yet, other parts affirm Manoussakis' statement that we are bound to the world. Bonhoeffer felt it was important to try to retrieve a sense of Christian engagement with the world that avoided either extreme of the radical, which fled the world, or that of compromise, which carried with it the danger of deification of existing orders, such as that of National Socialism.

In the manuscript following the discussion on the penultimate and ultimate distinction, Bonhoeffer sought to address an issue in Protestant faith that he believed led to a cleavage between the penultimate and ultimate understanding of Christian life and meaning. Protestantism, suggests Bonhoeffer, failed to address the question of the natural and subsequently:

> [P]rotestant thought no longer recognized the right relation of the ultimate to the penultimate. The results of this loss were far grievous and far-reaching. If there were no longer any relative differences within a fallen

creation, then the way was clear for any kind of arbitrariness and disorder. (Bonhoeffer 2009a: 172)

It is worth exploring Bonhoeffer's critique of Protestantism a little further.[6] The Reformers developed a pessimistic view of human nature and its capacity for reason. Sin meant that human reason was no longer able to participate in the eternal law. They rejected natural law, a tendency also noted in Bonhoeffer's exposition of the creation doctrine in Chapter 6.[7] As a result of the rejection of reason, moral law in Scripture was no longer considered an expression of natural law. At best, moral law was considered necessary to restrain the chaos and disorder brought into the world through sin, but it has no capacity to orient human beings to the eternal. When it tries to do so, moral law exhibits itself as a demonstration of human pride that should properly learn humility under the divine imperative. Protestantism has tended to overemphasise justification at the expense of justice, the latter functioning primarily as an indicator of guilt and the need for divine forgiveness.

Without the framework of moral law tied to reason, Protestantism developed an understanding of moral features that reflected the existential human condition of sin and the need for salvation. Moral action took on the characteristics of the salvation drama: the 'moment' that confronts the individual with an either/or situation, already determined by the sovereign God, whose will determines the content of moral behaviour. Gustafson describes the central moral features of the Protestant individual as one in which there is no sense of continuity between past and present; the person is in crisis and cannot be guided by general or universal principles, but only 'the subjective authenticity of a decision' makes an action valid (Gustafson 1978: 73).[8] Gustafson complains that God's power to proclaim 'forgiveness' and absolution from the judgement of law can lead to 'exceptions' that 'occur as a result of secret commandments of God, and the most rigorous counsels of Jesus apply to those with special vocations' (1978: 13). Gustafson's critique describes the danger of the 'teleological suspension of ethics', the subject of Kierkegaard's inquiry in *Fear and Trembling*. Every time Protestantism prioritises grace over law, the law recedes, subjected to a God who in freedom proclaims sinners are forgiven, and directs individuals and events according to his own (inscrutable) purposes.[9]

Through the lens of a critique of Protestantism, we can view the penultimate/ultimate distinction as another instantiation of Bonhoeffer's rejection of the world. Overemphasising the ultimate means that the penultimate has no value and has no meaning apart from its relation to the ultimate. As salvation is the goal, the experience of the penultimate has no purpose, apart from leading the individual to faith in Christ. The eschatological in this sense threatens to subsume the created, existing order. Yet, I do not think that Bonhoeffer fully supports this distinction. He recognises the danger of overemphasising the ultimate at the expense of the penultimate, as can be seen in his critique of radicalism.

In the manuscript 'Christ, reality and Good', Bonhoeffer seeks to overcome the natural/supernatural distinction, and affirms the existing world as a place in which the 'supernatural' can be found: arguing that the '"supernatural" is only in the natural, the holy only in the profane, and revelational only in the rational' (Bonhoeffer 2009a: 59). Christians bear responsibility for the world, as it is. They cannot simply defer this responsibility, nor seek to bring about the end of this penultimate world. Bonhoeffer asks whether it might be better sometimes to remain 'consciously in the penultimate' and through this point all the more genuinely to the ultimate, 'which God will speak in his own time' (2009a: 152–153). Political life in Bonhoeffer's view belongs to the sphere of the penultimate and is part of God's preserving activity. The penultimate is here linked with the preservation of the created world, while recognising that the created world should never be the totalising world, and the resurrection event, which should not itself become the focus at the expense of the created world. Fully affirming the created world as 'natural' would lead one to compromise or affirm the status quo; focusing on the resurrection event would lead to radicalism. In Bonhoeffer's account, preservation and redemption should not be collapsed.

There are no clear guidelines as to what constitutes limit to responsible action in this scenario. By the early 1940s, Bonhoeffer introduced the term 'mandates' to describe how life might be ordered within the penultimate and could be a stronger guide as to what constitutes limit to exceptional action.[10] The four mandates are work, marriage, government and church. However, the mandates in Bonhoeffer's account are envisioned to regulate behaviour and organise society for a post-war society, which does not answer the question of limits to responsible action in an extraordinary situation. I have therefore chosen to focus on the penultimate/ultimate distinction as providing an overarching framework that considers the relationship between the concrete, existing world and the eschatological world of the redemption narrative.[11] It provides context for action in that Bonhoeffer draws attention to the need to preserve a connection between the concrete world in which we exist, and the higher values that give meaning to our world.

THE ROLE OF GUILT IN THE EXTRAORDINARY SITUATION

This final section of the chapter considers the manifestation of guilt and conscience as it emerges in Bonhoeffer's writing during his conspiracy involvement, and asks how Bonhoeffer's reflection on this can provide a limit to action in an extraordinary situation. Bonhoeffer, more than Schmitt, attempts to qualify action in an extraordinary situation by referring to 'appropriate responsible action'. Chapter 4 described Bonhoeffer's idea of responsible action, which could be tested by the Christian's willingness to become guilty of intentional transgression of the law on behalf of others, without regard to their own interests. The question of guilt is not only a recurring theme in Bonhoeffer's concept of responsible action in a *Grenzfall* scenario, but it is also a rich theme in the broader debate 'dirty hands' actions.

Christine Schliesser in her doctoral thesis on the concept of guilt in Bonhoeffer asks towards the end of her study whether Bonhoeffer himself is guilty. She suggests that this question has two dimensions: that of Bonhoeffer's own view of himself as guilty, and whether 'we need to regard him as guilty for his participation in the coup d'état' (2006: 191). As noted earlier, some Bonhoeffer scholars justify his actions as a political necessity, as legitimate in order to protect the necessities of life. Bonhoeffer's actions can then be understood as requiring the breaking of the law in order to uphold the sanctity of the law in preserving life. In upholding a higher moral good, Bonhoeffer's dirty hands are justified. Yet, argues Schliesser, even if we agree that the action was necessary, 'this does not guarantee freedom from guilt' (2006: 195). The philosopher Thomas Nagel seems to argue something similar, when he suggests that even in situations that require beastly behaviour 'one cannot claim *justification* for the violation. It does not become *all right*' (1972: 137). Both Schliesser's reaction and Nagel's reaction to justifications of dirty hands point to the idea that perhaps there is some moral obligation on society that refuses to overlook the immorality of dirty hands actions, even if committed for the sake of society.

The political philosopher, Michael Walzer, believes guilt has a key role to play in determining 'dirty hands' actions undertaken in the political context. For Walzer, guilt indicates that the politician who is required to act immorally for utilitarian reasons nevertheless remains a good person, indeed that the 'moral politician' is known by their dirty hands: 'If he were a moral man and nothing else, his hands would not be dirty; if he were a politician and nothing else, he would pretend that they were clean' (1973: 168). The moral politician is moral precisely because she has and acknowledges the guilt of having dirty hands. Walzer suggests that 'to believe himself to be guilty. That is what it means to have dirty hands' (1973: 166). Yet, for Walzer there must be social implications for dirty hands actions. It is not enough to experience some kind of personal anguish. The person who engages in an act of dirty hands must be willing to pay the penalty imposed by society. The severity of the penalty would depend on the depth of the moral law transgressed in the first instance. Referring to both 'just assassination' and 'civil disobedience', Walzer argues that in both scenarios the actors 'violate a set of rules, go beyond a moral or legal limit, in order to do what they believe they should do. At the same time, they acknowledge their responsibility for the violation by accepting punishment or doing penance' (1973: 178–179). The example that Walzer invokes is Camus' play *The Just Assassins*. Walzer designates the heroes as 'innocent criminals, just assassins' who because they have killed 'are prepared to die – *and will die*'; their execution 'is not so much punishment as self-punishment and expiation. On the scaffold they wash their hands clean and [...] they die happy' (1973: 178). For Walzer, acknowledgement of guilt and acceptance of punishment seems to act as a kind of proof that the action is indeed dirty hands action—the actor remains morally good and demonstrates this through a willingness to be judged guilty.

Such a position seems to have also been supported by Bonhoeffer himself, who declared that 'the doer of the deed must remain open for the indictment' (Bonhoeffer cited in Rasmussen 2005: 144). As with Walzer, being willing to bear guilt appears to play an important role in determining objective guilt:

> Whether an action springs from responsibility or cynicism can become evident only in whether the objective guilt one incurs by breaking the law is recognized and borne, and whether by the very act of breaking it the law is truly sanctified. (Bonhoeffer 2009a: 297)

This echoes Bonhoeffer's own requirement that responsible action is recognised by its willingness to bear the consequences of breaking the law. Acknowledgement of guilt can play an important part in determining the limit to action on an 'extraordinary situation'.

Yet, Bonhoeffer's writing does not present a single coherent discussion on the role of guilt. As already noted in Chapter 4, some passages in *Ethics* speak of guilt in very general terms, but others seem to reference Bonhoeffer's own experience of guilt, which he describes in terms of the guilt of the church, that of the German nation, and his own 'upper bourgeois' social class (Rasmussen 2005: 54–58). As noted earlier, the German concept of guilt or *Schuld* carries with it an objective meaning grounded in a juridical context. Responsible action is therefore recognisable to the extent that it shows a readiness to become guilty under law. For Bonhoeffer, action undertaken on behalf of others in an extraordinary situation is undertaken by an innocent person willing to become guilty under law on behalf of others, accepting the guilt that comes with such action.

In his writings during conspiracy and his later prison letters, Bonhoeffer at times seems convinced of his own personal guilt, of actively having chosen to become a sinner through engaging in free responsible action. As Schliesser points out: '[Bonhoeffer] is surprisingly vague concerning a definition of guilt despite the fact that he refers to this topic repeatedly and extensively in his discussions' (2006: 189). Schliesser suggests that Bonhoeffer conflates two ways of discussing guilt: guilt that is actively or non-actively incurred. Non-actively incurred guilt is the example of Christians who carry one another's burden, just as Christ carried theirs. Essentially, this is pastoral guilt. Yet Bonhoeffer's concept of guilt also carries with it the objective judgment of being found guilty under law, in particular under divine law. This is actively incurred guilt, when acting on behalf of another. For Bonhoeffer, Christ is such an example:

> For the sake of God and human beings Jesus Christ became a breaker of the law: he broke the law of the Sabbath in order to sanctify it, out of love for God and human beings [...] he ended up being forsaken by God in his final hour. (Bonhoeffer 2009a: 278–279)

Christ appears to actively break the law on behalf of others (thereby respecting or sanctifying the law), but in so doing, he incurs the judgment of the law and is forsaken by God's forgiveness and grace in his final hour. For theologians, the breaking of the law signifies the fulfilment of the Old Covenant and the heralding of the New. Schliesser argues that Bonhoeffer fails to make this distinction; just as Christ broke the divine Mosaic law, his followers may be required to break the divine law of Christ such as that explicated in the Sermon on the Mount in the commandment to love one's enemies.[12] Schliesser's study concludes that there remain significant issues around Bonhoeffer's concept of guilt and his Christology, each of which carries different implications for what it means to accept guilt. It also means that it is not easy to determine the role guilt plays in Bonhoeffer's account of responsible action, or to what extent Bonhoeffer considered himself guilty. Or to put this differently, the question of whose judgment Bonhoeffer will finally accept depends on whether he believes he has broken divine or human laws, and/or whether his actions are justified in one framework, but not the other.

There is a further depth to the notion of guilt that appears in Bonhoeffer writing during his conspiracy involvement. In the first version of the History and Good manuscript (HG1), the question of guilt is viewed from a theological perspective. In this manuscript, God's redemptive plan is emphasised to the extent that even the actions of Judas Iscariot, guilty of betraying Jesus, find meaning and purpose: 'It is through Judas Iscariot that Christ becomes the redeemer of the world [...] Judas must act in order that the world receive the benefit of the reconciliation of God', and indeed, the disciples of Jesus 'cannot accomplish' what Judas Iscariot achieves (Bonhoeffer 2009a: 227). Thus, even those who would seem to be guilty find their actions taken up into God's plan. In the context of Bonhoeffer's own conspiracy involvement, the example of Judas' action expresses perhaps a hope or faith that even the most grievous evils play a part that cannot be foreseen by the actors in history.

In the second version of the manuscript, the perspective of guilt 'from below' appears more strongly. While HG1 considered the role of guilt primarily in terms of God's overarching redemptive plan, in HG2 the cost of responsible action appears intensified as guilt is no longer explained only in theological terms. Although not mentioned in the HG1 manuscript, in the HG2 manuscript, the role of conscience is key to Bonhoeffer's discussion of guilt. Bonhoeffer critiques what he calls 'legalistic and self-righteous conscience' that is bound by principles, such as that advocated by the philosopher, Immanuel Kant, for whom truth meant one would have to disclose a friend hiding from a would-be murderer (Bonhoeffer 2009a: 279–280). Out of love for one's neighbour, the responsible person is willing to forego a clean conscience, or is willing to act against one's own core values, to put this into more contemporary language. The model of this in HG2 is not Christ, but the 'profane' example of Iphigenia, who in Goethe's play, *Iphigenia in Taurus (Iphigenie auf Tauris)* is urged by her brother to act responsibly in violation of her inner law (Bonhoeffer 2009a: 280):

> You have remained untainted in this temple; life teach us, and you will learn it too, to be less rigorous with ourselves and others. This human breed is formed in such astounding fashion, so variously linked and interwoven, that keeping pure and disentangled within ourselves or with regards to others is far beyond a human being's grasp. Nor are we meant to judge ourselves: our first duty is to walk and watch our path, for we can seldom rightly judge what we have done, and still less judge what we are doing. (cited in Bonhoeffer 2009a: 280–281)

Goethe's play brings out the moral dilemma that Iphigenia faces, as she must lie to protect her brother, but believes in the necessity to tell the truth. Her concrete commitment to her family challenges her own deeply held values, yet her brother does not necessarily understand this. In Goethe's play, unlike Euripides original version, Pylades is cynical, and there is no recourse to a timely divine intervention; the drama takes place purely on the mortal plane (Lee 2003).

This lengthy reflection on Goethe's play is considered 'highly exceptional in [...] [Bonhoeffer's] published works' (Phillips 2018: 362). The mortal plane in this context can be seen to map onto Bonhoeffer's penultimate sphere, or his insistence on a concrete reality. There seems to be little recourse to a redemption narrative for those who engage in responsible action in an extraordinary situation in HG2:

> Those who in acting responsibly take on guilt – which is inescapable for any responsible person – place this guilt on themselves, not on someone else; they stand up for it and take responsibility for it. (Bonhoeffer 2009a: 282)

Whereas responsible action itself was described in HG1 as action in accordance with Christ, or Christ explicitly described as the model of such action, in HG2 the location, or where such action takes place, becomes the focus:

> Responsible action takes place in the sphere of relativity, completely sur-
> rounded in the twilight that the historical situation casts upon good and
> evil. It takes place in the midst of the countless perspectives from which
> every phenomenon is seen. Responsible action must not simply decide
> between right and wrong, good and evil, but between right and right,
> wrong and wrong [...] This very fact defines responsible action as a free
> venture [*Wagnis*], not justified by any law .... (Bonhoeffer 2009a: 284)[13]

There remains a hope for redemption, as Bonhoeffer notes the individual cannot justify their own action, but surrenders 'to God the deed
that has become necessary' (Bonhoeffer 2009a: 284). But far more than
HG1, the rewritten History and Good manuscript emphasises the lack of
knowledge and certainty for the actor.

In Bonhoeffer's analysis, Iphigenia appears to be at war between competing claims. Such a struggle is like 'suicidal action against one's own
life', suggests Bonhoeffer (2009a: 277). For Bonhoeffer, Christ has set
conscience free and enables the disciple to surrender the ego 'to God
and others' (2009a: 278). Nevertheless, even knowing that one acts for
the sake of others, there remains an 'irremovable tension' between the
now-freed conscience and the sense of guilt that accompanies responsible
action. Bonhoeffer phrases this in terms of 'taking on and bearing guilt',
of being able to 'bear the weight' [*Tragkraft*] of responsibility without
'being broken' (2009a: 281). The agent who acts on the basis of necessity acts 'without the support of people, conditions or principles', and
without 'defense or exoneration', other than their own action and person
(Bonhoeffer 2009a: 283). This suggests that even though Bonhoeffer
believes in and argues on the basis of the theological reality of the conscience freed in Christ, the *experience* of bearing guilt is not made any
easier. And this experience of guilt should be owned or acknowledged,
rather than escaped or deferred back to theology. In the sphere of rel-
ativity, or in concrete historical existence where everything appears as
'twilight', the responsible person acts in a free venture, willing to take
responsibility for the guilt incurred in such action, without recourse to
abstract principles or a divine plan unfolding in history. Now the person who engages in responsible action in an 'extraordinary situation' has
less recourse to redemption narratives, but must 'in the twilight of the
historical situation' or the political situation choose between 'wrong and
wrong'.

Bonhoeffer's account of guilt as it emerges in HG2 is closer to
Walzer's concept of 'dirty hands' actions, or as Tony Coady suggests,

this is the situation in which Bonhoeffer seeks to make sense of the tragic choices that face agents in emergency situations (2014: 465). Responsible action is now described in more phenomenological terms, as guilt that may be experienced. Here also emerges a wrestling with how responsible action can be understood from the *experience* of below. It suggests an irresolvable tension of the extraordinary situation that requires responsible action; such action takes place in 'twilight' where choices appear as 'wrong' and 'wrong'. In such a scenario, there is no good or evil, only the necessity of making a choice. In this scenario, actions, while they could never be considered Christlike in the traditionally understood sense, are nevertheless considered necessary.

This chapter has considered three possible ways to test the actions of the isolated disciple or agent in an extraordinary situation: the role of the church, the ultimate/penultimate distinction and the manifestation of conscience and guilt. The challenge of church-community I suggested cannot in itself function as a critical limit to the actions of the isolated disciple, particularly when the church views itself as radically different from the world, something that has appeared in aspects of Bonhoeffer's writing. There is no shared language between Bonhoeffer's church that can only be understood from within, and the external world. When the disciple or church withdraws from the world, they abandon the 'penultimate sphere'. When called by Christ, or impelled by the 'extraordinary situation' to return to act in the world, they can do so only on the basis of radicalism. And as Bonhoeffer notes in his critique of Protestantism, such action fails to recognise the relative differences within the created world and clears the way for 'any kind of arbitrariness and disorder'.

Bonhoeffer's reflections on the penultimate and ultimate distinction are intended to affirm political life as part of God's preserving activity of the created world. The distinction argues that the created world itself should never be the totalising world, and the redemptive or eschatological vision of Christian faith should not overwhelm the created world. In Bonhoeffer's account, both preservation and redemption need to be respected. And indeed, to avoid the danger of radicalism, Bonhoeffer counsels it would be better to remain in the penultimate, created world, to accept one's own limitations to time and place, and to leave redemption to God, who will 'speak in his own time'.

The final motif considered was the role of guilt. This is perhaps the most interesting and relevant in terms of contemporary issues in political philosophy, and also a rich theme in Bonhoeffer's own writing, particularly during his conspiracy involvement. Questions were asked around the meaning of guilt in Bonhoeffer's writing, how Bonhoeffer viewed his guilt, or what it might mean for Bonhoeffer to be described as guilty. Michael Walzer's account of 'dirty hands' actions and the role of guilt challenges attempts to justify immoral actions on the grounds of necessity. Indeed, Walzer views atonement as having important role in expiating the guilt one takes on oneself, even for the best of reasons. The actor remains morally good by demonstrating their own willingness to be judged guilty by those on whose behalf they claim to act. While certainly not wanting to suggest that Bonhoeffer somehow 'needed' to die, this view puts Bonhoeffer's own death in a new light, and it avoids the too-easily applied epithet of 'martyrdom'. Guilt is also the one motif that gives a very human insight into Bonhoeffer himself, as he chooses between 'wrong' and 'wrong'. In a scenario that clearly challenges Bonhoeffer's understanding of faith, the figure of Iphigenia emerges as a symbol of moral decisions made on the mortal plane, amongst flawed human beings in situations that are deeply and thoroughly compromised.

NOTES

1. Green has also described Bonhoeffer as developing a 'theological phenomenology of the human person in relation to other persons and to various types of corporate communities and institutions' (1999: 21).
2. Michal Valčo broadens the role of discipleship beyond church-community, as the latter is called to act in the world. He argues that the disciple is 'not placed in a spiritual vacuum and left dependent on esoteric-mystical inspirations' but acts within 'the given framework of his office as a specific place of responsibility in the world', where the latter is the official or public calling into which a person is legally called and appointed, thus extending discipleship from the church-community to the world (2017: 53).
3. For Bonhoeffer, Kierkegaard's idealist position was part of the negative heritage of the Enlightenment in terms of ethical action: 'Wherever the ethical is construed as apart from any determination by time and place, apart from the question of authorization, and apart from anything concrete, there life disintegrates into an infinite number of unrelated atoms of time, just as human community disintegrates into discrete atoms of reason' (Bonhoeffer 2009a: 373).
4. Bonhoeffer's basic concept of the relationship between God and individuals is different from Kierkegaard's insofar as Bonhoeffer's idea of God is based on the concept of a divine relation community that existed pre-fall. In his lectures on Genesis 1–3 in *Creation and Fall*, Bonhoeffer interprets

the image of God as '*imago relationis*'—human beings are created in the image of God and therefore also in relationship with others. For Bonhoeffer, the image of God is an intrinsically ethical concept (2004).

5. Manoussakis gives an account of how Christians might orient themselves towards the ultimate, while preserving the integrity of the penultimate through an interesting comparison between the ultimate and Immanuel Kant's analysis of aesthetic judgement: 'In the beautiful [...] we recognize a purpose – by means of purpose we see *now* an aspect that the thing will come to have only *at the end*'. As per Plato's form, what we encounter as beautiful is so by its participation in the form of the beautiful: 'This already implies that what makes something beautiful is not itself, that is, it is not to be found in the thing itself, but rather comes from beyond; it is other than the thing that one perceives as beautiful' (2009: 235–236).

6. I recognise that it is difficult to define 'Protestantism', given that the history of Protestant theology lacks the unified body and history of the Roman Catholic tradition. However, as J. Daryl Charles points out, despite its 'bewildering diversity', there exists in Protestantism a broad consensus that rejects natural law as 'a metaphysical notion rooted in divine revelation' (2008: 111).

7. I acknowledge that there is not one reformed rejection of natural law, and key figures such as John Calvin are noted for their use of natural law in ordering society. Stephen Grabill points to Karl Barth as being particularly influential in displacing natural law from contemporary Protestant theology (2006). See the next chapter for a brief discussion on Barth's influence on Bonhoeffer.

8. This moral 'occasionalism' would also become the key feature of existentialism, which no longer posits the divine, but instead emphasises radical human freedom as the ultimate meaning of life. Here also the need for subjective confirmation of moral choices and the uniqueness of each moment are grounded in the conviction that moral order of the universe is incomprehensible to human reason, and the individual's moral choices cannot be determined by appeals to principles of natural law.

9. Indeed, according to Gustafson, 'occasionalism' is correlated with a theological principal in which God acts and commands with sovereign direction for each person and event, and an accompanying anthropological principal of covenant partnership, which is described by relational metaphors, such as speaking-hearing, command-obedience, decision-action, response and responsibility (1978: 73). These are themes that have recurred throughout this book, particularly in my analysis of Bonhoeffer.

10. Bonhoeffer's thinking around political theology changes over time. In the 1930s, the concept of 'orders of preservation' replaced the more

Lutheran and established term, 'orders of creation', by the early 1940s Bonhoeffer begins to use the term 'mandates' rather than 'orders of preservation'.

11. When Bonhoeffer shifts to the concept of 'mandates', he more strongly emphasises the role of Christ who commands, or has the divine author- ity and thereby legitimises and sanctifies the mandates (DeJonge 2016). In addressing the question of the limit to extraordinary action, I want to avoid the sense of Christ's command as sanctioning the mandates, to a more phenomenological description of the penultimate world that receives its orientation from the ultimate, but avoids the philosophical problem of the divine command.

12. There are significant questions here about what it means to fulfil the divine law by breaking the law, and whether Christ can demand actions that contravene his divine law in a way that the Christian incurs active guilt in so doing. The question of what constitutes guilt in this account is further complicated by the fact that Bonhoeffer refers to Christ as the model for 'sinless-guilt'. This suggests not only that the divine law may be legitimately broken, in order to fulfil the law, but if done for the right reasons, such a breaking may even be the mark of true innocence: 'gen- uine guiltlessness is demonstrated precisely by entering to a community with the guilt of other human beings for their sake' (Bonhoeffer 2009a: 276). This suggests that the guilt incurred is not real guilt but actually innocence.

13. Note that HG1 also mentions the 'twilight' of the historical situation (Bonhoeffer 2009a: 221). In HG2, this reflection is developed and deepened.

References

Bonhoeffer. 2003. *Discipleship*, trans. Barbara Green and Reinhard Krauss. Dietrich Bonhoeffer Works English. Minneapolis: Fortress Press.

Bonhoeffer, Dietrich. 2004. *Creation and Fall*. Dietrich Bonhoeffer Works English. Minneapolis: Fortress Press.

Bonhoeffer, Dietrich. 2009a. *Ethics*, trans. Reinhard Krauss, Charles C. West, and Douglass W. Stott. Dietrich Bonhoeffer Works English. Minneapolis: Fortress Press.

Bonhoeffer, Dietrich. 2009b. *Sanctorum Communio*, trans. Reinhard Krauss and Nancy Lukens. Dietrich Bonhoeffer Works English. Minneapolis: Fortress Press.

Charles, J.D. 2008. *Retrieving the Natural Law: A Return to Moral First Things*. Grand Rapids, MI: Eerdmans.

Coady, C.A.J. 2014. The Problem of Dirty Hands. The Stanford Encyclopedia of Philosophy. https://plato.stanford.edu/cgi-bin/encyclopedia/archinfo. cgi?entry=dirty-hands. Accessed 14 August 2017.

DeJonge, Michael. 2016. Martin Luther, Dietrich Bonhoeffer, and Political Theologies. In *Oxford Research Encyclopedias*. Oxford: Oxford University Press.

Grabill, Stephen J. 2006. *Rediscovering the Natural Law in Reformed Theological Ethics*. Grandrapids, MI: Eerdsmans.

Green, Clifford J. 1999. *Bonhoeffer: A Theology of Sociality*. Grand Rapids: Eerdmans.

Green, Clifford J. 2012. Sociality, Discipleship, and Worldly Theology in Bonhoeffer's Christian Humanism. In *Being Human, Becoming Human: Dietrich Bonhoeffer and Social Thought*. Cambridge, UK: James Clarke Company.

Gustafson, James M. 1978. *Protestant and Roman Catholic Ethics*. Chicago and London: University of Chicago Press.

Kelly, Geffrey B. 2008. Kierkegaard as 'Antidote' and the Impact on Dietrich Bonhoeffer's Concept of Christian Discipleship. In *Bonhoeffer's Intellectual Formation: Theology and Philsoohpy in His Thought*, ed. Peter Frick, 147–165. Tübingen: Mohr Siebeck.

Kierkegaard, Søren. 1983. *Fear and Trembling/Repetition*. Kierkegaard's Writings. Princeton, NJ: Princeton University Press.

Kirkpatrick, Matthew D. 2011. *Attacks on Christendom in a World Come of Age: Kierkegaard, Bonhoeffer, and the Question of "Religionless Christianity"*. Princeton Theological Monograph Series 166. Eugene, OR: Pickwick Publications.

Law, David R. 2011. Redeeming the Penultimate: Discipleship and Church in the Thought of Søren Kierkegaard and Dietrich Bonhoeffer. *International Journal for the Study of the Christian Church* 11 (1): 14–26.

Lee, Kevin. 2003. Goethe's Iphigenie and Euripides' Iphigenia in Taurus. *Journal of the Australiasian Univerisities Modern Language Association*, Feb. 2003: 64–74.

Manoussakis, John Panteleimon. 2009. "At the Recurrent End of the Unending": Bonhoeffer's Eschatology of the Penultimate. In *Bonhoeffer and Contintal Thought: Cruciform Philosophy*, ed. Brian Gregor and Jens Zimmerman, 226–244. Bloomington: Indiana University Press.

Nagel, Thomas. 1972. War and Massacre. *Philosophy & Public Affairs* 1 (2): 123–144.

Nielsen, Kirsten Busch. 2012. Community Turned Inside Out. In *Being Human, Becoming Human: Dietrich Bonhoeffer and Social Thought*. Cambridge, UK: James Clarke Company.

Palmisano, Trey, and Reinhard Krauss. 2016. *Peace and Violence in the Ethics of Dietrich Bonhoeffer: An Analysis of Method*. Eugene, OR: Wipf & Stock.

Phillips, Jacob. 2018. 'Having-to-Be-Thus': On Bonhoeffer's Reading of Goethe's Iphegenia in Tauris. *Literature & Theology* 32 (3): 357–370. https://doi.org/10.1093/litthe/fry020.

Rasmussen, Larry. 2005. *Dietrich Bonhoeffer: Reality and Resistance.* Louisville, KY: Westminster John Knox Press.

Schliesser, Christine. 2006. *Everyone Who Acts Responsibly Becomes Guilty: The Concept of Accepting Guilt in Dietrich Bonhoeffer: Reconstruction and Critical Assessment.* Neukirchen-Vluyn: Neukirchener Verlag.

Schlingensiepen, Ferdinand. 2010. *Dietrich Bonhoeffer 1906–1945: Martyr, Thinker, Man of Resistance,* trans. Isabel Best. London and New York: T & T Clark International.

Valčo, Michal. 2017. The Value of Dietrich Bonhoeffer's Theological-Ethical Reading of Søren Kierkegaard. *European Journal of Science and Theology* 13 (1): 47–58.

Walzer, Michael. 1973. Political Action: The Problem of Dirty Hands. *Philosophy & Public Affairs* 2 (2): 160–180.

Whitford, David M. 2003. Luther's Political Encounters. In *The Cambridge Companion to Martin Luther,* ed. Donald K. McKim, 179–191. Cambridge: Cambridge University Press.

CHAPTER 9

Bonhoeffer in a Crisis-World

The early years of the twentieth century provided unprecedented challenges to Germany's identity, caused by political and social upheaval. Germany experienced no less than three radical constitutional changes in the space of 15 years.[1] Germany's defeat in 1918 in particular represented a crisis, separation or division from the continuity, order and security of the Bismarckian empire, a defeat that many thought pointed to the decline of Western culture (Bambach 1995: 257). During this period, there emerged a 'generational shift' between the classically trained German (and usually also Protestant) scholars, who found their civic and social identity as the *Bildungsbürgertum*, and the younger generation, who came of age in the tumultuous years following the start of the Great War. This generation lost faith with their classically educated forebears and sought new way of being human in a crisis-shaped and crisis-driven age. These younger intellectuals were also part of a wider cultural milieu that saw itself as engaged in generational conflict and with this brought destruction of tradition and loss of faith in progress and reason.

A significant amount of this chapter has been previously published in Brown, Petra. 2017. The sons destined to murder their fathers: crisis in interwar Germany. In *100 Years of European Philosophy Since the Great War: Crisis and Reconfigurations*, eds. Matthew Sharpe, Rory Jeffs, and Jack Reynolds, 67–82. Springer.

© The Author(s) 2019   167
P. Brown, *Bonhoeffer*,
https://doi.org/10.1007/978-3-030-05698-8_9

Fritz Ringer identifies three major groups of 'mandarin intellectuals' that developed through the eighteenth century, distinctions that he argues remained even into the early twentieth century: the Protestant pastor who derived his authority from his religious mission and shared the Pietists' faith in the value of the emerging soul; the bureaucrat who developed administrative skills and upheld the ideal of rationality in politics; and the humanist scholar and Idealist philosopher, who lived the honourable life of impractical learning and cultivation (Ringer 1969, 21). This chapter begins by examining the impact of a growing crisis culture on the academic landscape by considering three examples of 'mandarin intellectuals' broadly conceived: the Protestant theologian Adolf Harnack; the philosopher Ernst Cassirer; and the jurist Hans Kelsen. Each of these was challenged by a 'son', a younger intellectual who had come of age during the war. These were Karl Barth and Martin Heidegger, considered to be the greatest Protestant theologian and European philosopher of the twentieth century, respectively, and Carl Schmitt, whom we have already encountered in earlier chapters as one of the most important figures in political theology, and indeed political theory, in the twentieth century.

This is the time when Dietrich Bonhoeffer also came of age, and the final section of this chapter integrates Bonhoeffer with his contemporary peers, tracing key aspects of Bonhoeffer's own education and intellectual journey as a university and theology student, in the waning days of the Weimar Republic.[2] Victoria Barnett writes that scholars are increasingly interested in Bonhoeffer in his own context of Nazi Germany and his contemporaries: 'Exploring Bonhoeffer's life through that broader lens might give us some new information, and it could also be a corrective to some of the things we've gotten wrong', suggests Barnett (College Institute 2018). One of the things that we have 'gotten wrong' is the hagiography that has emerged around Bonhoeffer, which has led to uncritically accepting parts of his theology, ethics and the emerging political theology of his work. By situating Bonhoeffer in the context of his peers, his own concrete time, the political challenges he faced and the decisions he had to make under pressure, we gain a better insight into the human Bonhoeffer. This insight then also provides a way to critique the popular tendency to form a mystical connection between events of our own age, and Bonhoeffer's life and times.

THE IMPACT OF WAR: CRISIS AND THE DECLINE OF *BILDUNG*

Neo-Kantianism had been the dominant philosophical movement in Germany from 1870 until the First World War.[3] Neo-Kantian philosophers, theologians and other scholars were typically systematic and comprehensive thinkers, who saw themselves as inheritors of Immanuel Kant's intellectual legacy, although they did not accept all of Kant's philosophy uncritically. Of particular importance to Neo-Kantians was the belief that apriori concepts and principles made knowledge possible, and that the object of this knowledge is culture, itself thematically approached through the areas of knowledge, ethics and aesthetics (Heis 2018). In this context, education was understood as the pinnacle of character development and formation of the individual, a project that was aimed at the progressive self-liberation of humanity. Education understood as *Bildung* was considered essential to both self-cultivation and the pursuit of truth, united in personal knowledge or wisdom.[4] Those educated in this tradition formed a social and cultural elite, shaped by the 'deeply-rooted obligation to be guardian of a great historical legacy and intellectual tradition' (Bethge 1977: 4).

Following the end of the First World War, the Neo-Kantian generation of scholars tended to continue to advocate for the Kantian ideal of humanity as autonomous and rational subjects. But for a younger generation of intellectuals, the empirical reality of the war came to signify the abrupt and fierce terminus to the faith in reason's self-legislating and regulative functions. The younger generation believed that the old approach of the past and its emphasis on inward cultivation of character was no longer capable of addressing the urgent needs of the present, of the new 'crisis' age. For them, the social and political upheaval required a more robust response from Germany's intellectuals.

The first example of the impact of a crisis culture on the academic landscape is the disagreement between Karl Barth and Adolf Harnack. The place of Harnack in late nineteenth- and early twentieth-centuries German Protestant theology cannot be overstated. He has been described as a 'Renaissance man translated into the early twenty century' and is considered one of the 'greats' of European historical scholarship with a bibliography of 1611 works, under whose guidance liberal theology reached its pinnacle (Frend 2001: 84, 101).[5] In addition to being a theologian, Harnack had training as both a philologist and historian. As part of the

Neo-Kantian educated elite, Harnack, who held a professorship at the University of Berlin, can be seen to represent the high point of *Bildung*. Yet, despite his intellectual brilliance and high moral sense, Harnack also understood Prusso-Germany was God's Hammer (*Got strafe Engeland*) and its culture as superior German *Kultur*. Staunchly patriotic and a committed imperialist, Harnack had been the Kaiser's 'ghost writer', rallying the support of the industrial masses to the cause of war in 1914 (Moses 2009: 33).[6] According to John Moses, Harnack was typical of the theologians of Wilhelmine Germany who 'had incorporated the history of the state into their theology to such an extent that they could virtually equate the foreign policy of the *Reich* with the kingdom of God on earth' (1999: 18–19).[7] Indeed, during the Great War, the Protestant churches were amongst those conservative Germans who saw a union between 'throne and altar' as fundamental for a state under God.[8] Even after the failure of the Great War, the view of war as providential remained the norm amongst the Protestant *Bildungsbürgers* or the educated middle class and their intellectuals.

While some of the established intellectual elite, such as Harnack, promoted the war in their academic capacity, a new generation of young German intellectuals came of age in the brutal reality of the battlefield, or experienced that reality directly in their family. For the younger generation that was affected by the experience of war, the war came to signify the abrupt and fierce terminus for the confident assumptions of nineteenth-century intellectuals, particularly those who had confidently invested human knowledge with a progressive and unitary character (Howard 2006: 304).

The loss of confidence in their teachers can be powerfully shown through the young Swiss theologian Karl Barth's attack on Harnack, in the years following the close of the war. Barth argued that it was Prussian nationalism that led him to doubt 'the teaching of all my theological masters in Germany. To me they seemed to have been hopelessly compromised by what I regarded as their failure in the face of the ideology of war' (cited in Howard 2006: 121). Barth felt he could no longer 'follow either their ethics and dogmatics or their understanding of the Bible and of history. For me at least, 19th-century theology no longer held any future' (cited in McCormack 1995: 79). Far from developing good character and high moral sense, Barth believed that the liberal Protestantism of the German academies had made theology and the Christian gospel complicit with the political ambitions of the state. Because Harnack had equated God's hand with Germany's imperial ambitions, Barth argued that he had failed to see God as transcendent to human ambitions and Christianity as a critique of culture and the actions of the state. For Barth, a theology in service to the state presented the greater threat to both the church and the world.

Karl Barth's public attack on Harnack began in 1920, following the publication of *Commentary on the Romans* (1919). In a lecture on April 17th at a student conference in Aarau, Switzerland, Barth emphasised the dependence of humanity on God's grace, beginning with the Bible, rather than human knowledge. Somewhat poignantly in light of the debate that would unfold, Harnack also gave an address at this lecture that he hoped would help 'the post World War generation which longed for firm answers along lines of renewed certainty' (1989: 45–46).[9] Harnack believed that the answers for this troubled generation could be found through disciplined historical research. Such research was 'the one great majestic crystal' which enabled the elimination of subjectivity, to 'construct an edifice of the greatest objectivity' in order to provide a secure and firm foundation of knowledge (Harnack 1989: 47–48). For Harnack, historical analysis of culture, and institutions in particular, enabled a prediction of future events with some confidence. While error was possible, Harnack considered it analogous to the mistakes made in forecasting the weather (1989: 53). Thus, historical-critical analysis could lead to sufficient knowledge to enable humanity to influence future events through emancipation from the past, acting in the present, with regard to the future.

Barth critiqued Harnack's historical approach, as he argued all historical thought was tainted by sin:

[T]he moment when religion becomes conscious of religion, when it becomes a psychologically and historically conceivable magnitude in the world, it falls away from its inner character, from its truth to idols. Its truth is its otherworldliness, its refusal of the idea of sacredness, its non-historicity. (Barth 1928: 69)

Truth for Barth is found in its testimony to a non-historical 'otherworldliness', and it is this that should be the beginning of theology. Upon hearing Barth's 1920 student conference speech, Harnack later said that the effect of 'Barth's lecture was just staggering ... Not one word, not one sentence could I have said or thought. I saw the sincerity of Barth's speech, but its theology frightened me' and comparing Barth's thinking to a meteor 'rushing toward its disintegration', Harnack declared that 'this sort of religion is incapable of being translated into real life' (cited in Dorrien 2000: 60).

A debate followed through a published exchange in 1923, in the Liberal Protestant theological journal *Christliche Welt*.[10] Barth continued to argue in favour of *autopistia* or the autonomy of faith, which restored the absolute transcendence of God, a God who could not be distilled by critical science and reduced to a moral teacher of truth. For Barth, God's revelation must be understood 'as a mighty, historical process, a movement, a victorious struggle which must end with the renewal of all things' (1968: 41). In revealing himself in this way, God communicates in a way that is contrary to that valued by the world, suggested Barth. Having witnessed theology in service to war, Barth argued that the gospels showed that the relation between God and the world was indeed, inexplicable, an opposition that could be 'overcome only through the miracle of the eternal God himself' (cited in Harnack 1989: 89). Barth placed revelation front and centre of his new theology to ensure that God's ordering of the world would not reflect that of worldly powers.

For his part, Harnack showed deep concern for this prioritising of revelation; he believed this would lead to 'naïve biblicism' and 'subjective experience' (1989: 85). Harnack thought Barth showed an apparent disdain for critical analysis, thereby devaluing the critical question of truth. In place of this, Barth showed a tendency to draw on one's own understanding of the material from one's soul, which for Harnack meant, the free creation of truth for oneself (Rumscheidt 1972: 22). Harnack believed Barth's understanding of theology would open 'the gate to every suitable fantasy and to every theological dictatorship', a 'withdrawal from the world' and 'uncontrollable fanaticism' (1989: 87, 94). In the final analysis, the separation of reason and science from the divine, for Harnack, could only be interpreted as a victory of the irrational or demonic over the individual. The turn of young Barth against his teachers is a particular striking example of the general shift between the older intellectual *Bildung* shaped generation and the younger generation shaped by the experience of war. Barth's critique appears perhaps justified to us because of Harnack's failure to separate faith from culture in his support of the war. But not all intellectual battles could be considered defensible on comparable grounds.

A similar debate took place in philosophy, between 'the acculturated and well-to-do German Jew' Ernst Cassirer and the 'lapsed Catholic of provincial petit-bourgeois origin', Martin Heidegger (Gordon 2010: 37).[11] Cassirer and Heidegger represented two philosophical generations, and the famous dispute was understood by many present as a conflict between the old and young generation or as one reporter for the *Frankfurter Zeitung* declared, it was 'a confrontation between representative figures of two epochs' (cited in Gordon 2010: 50). Unlike Harnack, Cassirer had not supported Germany's war, but had instead remained 'apolitical', as was more typical of the intellectual elite who had tended to be politically disinterested. Cassirer was the embodiment of European liberal culture, his scholarship 'bespoke a robust attachment to the rationalist spirit of the *Aufklärung* and the cultural legacy of German classicism' (Gordon 2010: 11). As a Neo-Kantian, Cassirer saw historical knowledge as 'a bright clear mirror' (cited in Gordon 2008: 234) that enabled the development of the autonomy of reason.

Similar to Barth's critique on Harnack's critical-historical theology, Heidegger attacked the older Neo-Kantian generation of philosophers, arguing that the sovereignty of reason was much less secure than they claimed. For Heidegger, the freedom of the individual does not lie in good moral order, but in the nothingness of her *Dasein* (existence):

This nothingness is not the occasion for pessimism and melancholy. Instead it is the occasion for understanding that authentic activity takes place only where there is opposition and that philosophy has the task of throwing man back, so to speak, into the hardness of his fate from the shallow aspect of a man who merely uses the work of the spirit. (Heidegger 1990: 182–183)

Heidegger viewed the 'nothingness' that confronts the new generation positively for it enabled a new form of existence that was only possible in 'crisis' or in a situation of opposition. For the older generation, such as Cassirer, the new language of 'crisis' signalled a break that *endangered* the Enlightenment belief that humanity through transcendent reason could bring about a good and ordered society.

Gordon describes the disagreement as grounded on two normative images of humanity: Heidegger emphasised human receptivity or our 'thrownness', while Cassirer prioritised human spontaneity as the basis on which humanity could realise its free and self-determining nature, particularly through scientific and cultural achievements (Gordon 2008: 233). To his critics, Heidegger came to represent existential nihilism in his claim that there is no security to be had in this world. Heidegger, on the other hand, viewed the crisis that faced humanity as not only reveal- ing the deeper reality of the human condition, but also as the opportu- nity to clear away the sedimentation of Western metaphysics perpetuated by philosophers of whom Heidegger believed Cassirer was an emblem- atic example.[12]

The final example of the impact of a crisis culture on the aca- demic landscape is the disagreement between the jurists, Carl Schmitt and Hans Kelsen. Schmitt arguably began the war as a Neo-Kantian. While he served only in an administrative capacity, the realities of the First World War affected the Neo-Kantian abstraction evidenced in his earlier writing as an 'apolitical' *Staatsrechtslehrer* (state jurist) and 'he began to veer toward a starker political realism', characterised by 'the ever-present possibility of conflict' (Schwab 2005: xxxviii).[13] While he never openly criticised the Weimar Constitution, nevertheless he considered the Republic futile in addressing the problems of a mod- ernising mass society (Preuß 2014). In his book *Political Romanticism* (1919), Schmitt argued the Republic was capable of only 'passive gov- ernment', as it lacked the necessary precondition to all political action: the ability to make the either/or decision. Three years later in *Political Theology* (1922), Schmitt mounted a frontal assault on one of the lead- ing Neo-Kantian state jurists who defended the Weimar Republic, the Austrian Hans Kelsen. Much like Harnack's stature amongst liberal the- ologians, Kelsen was considered by his contemporaries to be 'unques- tionably the leading jurist of the time', during the Weimar years, an influence that extended in the following decades (cited in Paulson 1992: 311). As a Neo-Kantian, Kelsen believed legal reasoning was similar to a sound theory of knowledge, and required no other basis than rea- son itself. For Kelsen, the law could be established by appeal to norms, where the constitution was the basic norm, or in Kelsen's view, 'highest norm' or 'ultimate norm' beyond which no higher appeal was possible (Paulson 1992: 325).

Schmitt argued that in taking this view, Kelsen had ignored the foun- dation of law: the concept of sovereignty that is founded as an analogy to the theological concept of 'miracle', the exceptional or unpredictable event, as discussed in Chapter 5. By beginning with the miracle, Schmitt hoped to wrest political discourse away from what he perceived to be the pernicious influences of the Enlightenment, which had banished the miracle or the exception from theology and political structures and thereby, according to Schmitt, destroyed the very possibility for political organisation. Kelsen, as a positivist, believed that the unity of the state rested on a collective submission to the rule of law, a rule that was guaranteed by the juridical sphere, while Schmitt, as an anti-positivist, believed that the unity of the state depended on the political decision of the sovereign. This meant that Kelsen viewed the constitutional court as the guarantor of the state, while Schmitt saw the dictator or president as interpreting the executive's emergency powers, as granted in the Weimar Constitution under Article 48 (Jabloner 2000: 70–71). Kelsen was highly critical of Schmitt's attempt to make the state independent from law. In all his writing and discussion up to 1934, he concluded his positions by affirming the impossibility of arriving at a clear distinction between state and law, rejecting any basis for the state other than juridical law.

The three exchanges between the younger generation and older generation of 'mandarin intellectuals' emerge within different intellectual disciplines. Yet all three exchanges can be seen as emblematic of a broader struggle in intellectual life. The elder generation of scholars continued to believe and advocate for the Kantian ideal of humanity as 'self-contemplating and self-willing intellectual beings' (Hunter 2001: 308) that could overcome the limitations of the empirical world through regulating and ordering thoughts and behaviours, as captured by the notion of *Bildung* as character formation. While hesitant to speak directly to the political challenges of his time,[14] Cassirer urged others to remember the achievements of the Enlightenment: 'The age which venerated reason and science as man's highest faculty cannot and must not be lost even to us' (cited in Gordon 2008: 229) For Cassirer, retrieving the Enlightenment as the philosophy for modernity meant to hold up 'a bright clear mirror' to a troubled age, similar to Harnack's idea of historical research as 'the one great majestic crystal' that would eliminate excessive subjectivity. Yet, by the early 1930s, Kantian and Neo-Kantian philosophies were 'increasingly out of favor' (Gordon 2008: 234). Far from gazing into a bright clear mirror, the new generation saw itself as engaged in struggle that was itself part of life's natural condition.

REVELATION, REVOLUTION AND THE CREATIVE STRUGGLE

While only being able to give a cursory overview of the three exchanges, similar themes emerge in all three debates. The concepts of revelation in Barth and nothingness in Heidegger are similar in that both 'confront' the individual, in Barth as a 'mighty ... movement' that leads to a 'victorious struggle', in Heidegger, this is framed as 'opposition' that enables 'authentic activity'.[15] Conflict also plays a key role in Schmitt's emerging political theology, grounded in the exception analogous to the theological concept of the miracle that subsequently becomes the basis of his notion of sovereignty. Moreover, Barth's answer to Harnack's Christendom is a radically divine God whose sovereignty appears as contrary to human understanding, irrupting into the world as unexpectedly as Schmitt's exceptional event. All three critics of the 'mandarin intellectuals' engage in demolition and subversion of their intellectual forebears, radicalising faith, thinking and political life.

Yet, there is something more significant about the preceding discussion, as crisis thinking was not limited to the halls of academia. The language of crisis and an accompanying sense of fatalism pervaded intellectual life in post-war Germany, extending to the arts, religion, psychology, natural science, culture and politics. This language of crisis was often framed in terms of a 'historical moment' of generational conflict, of the sons murdering their Weimar fathers (Gordon 2010: 48).[16] In this context of generational conflict, Harnack said of the younger Karl Barth's theological rebellion, 'the sons of today are more hostile to their fathers than their grandfathers' (cited in Rumscheidt 1972: 20). The 'mandarin intellectuals' had once claimed the right to speak for the educated classes and frequently also to articulate the cultural aspirations of the nation (Ringer 1989: 195). This time was now past. The political implications of this were significant.

Amongst intellectuals, crisis thinking led from the lecture theatre into the political arena, where 'crisis' language provided a bridge for uniting theory with practice. Indeed, the simplified division between old and young, pre-war and post-war, teachers and students proved especially convenient because it mirrored the increasingly factious character of politics in the Weimar Republic.[17] Weimar politicians were increasingly viewed by their critics as engaging in shabby political compromises and self-seeking deals, the republic's democratic political order seen as a sign of weakness, indecision and an inability to rule

(Henig 1998: 5; Müller 1991: 695).[18] Those critics can be broadly grouped under the umbrella of 'conservative revolutionaries', a disparate number of political positions that all shared certain basic attitudes that included a critique of the supremacy of rationality, the rejection of party-political activity and a desire for an authoritarian, hierarchical '*Volksstaat*' (Bullivant 1985: 52). It is here amongst the 'conservative revolutionaries' who ultimately undermined the fragile democracy of the Weimar Republic and paved the way for National Socialism, that Carl Schmitt finds his own place. [19]

Conservative revolutionaries is an apt term, for it captures the developing tension that have been outlined in this chapter. For the younger conservative revolutionaries, the outbreak of war in 1914 was decisive. Those born between 1885 and 1905 had volunteered in large numbers, 'hoping to find a life at the front, which freed from the constraints of the society they hated, contained the seeds of a new and more meaningful existence' (Bullivant 1985: 48). While for many the subsequent post-war experience of crisis led to a feeling of pessimism, it is significant that Barth and Heidegger interpret the experience of crisis in terms of a necessary precondition to future change that makes possible what Heidegger would term a turning or *Kehre*, towards a new beginning.[20] The younger generation were strongly shaped by the image of a revolutionary force that was neither ideological nor a military struggle, but more akin to a 'creative chaos' made possible through the dialectic process of destruction and creation (cited in Bullivant 1985: 53).[21] The conservative revolutionaries fostered a belief that they must exist in the 'secret Germany', nurturing a 'heroic faith', while waiting for a 'potentially decisive historical mission' (Bullivant 1985: 54).

It seems that crisis was not just considered the reality of the political and cultural situation. For the new generation, 'crisis philosophy' itself was seen as the way forward; it was not only descriptive of their time, but had a normative role. It was increasingly believed that the individual experiences a new beginning only as a result of crisis. Crisis was therefore seen as *necessary* for political and social change. Schmitt captures this understanding of crisis very well when he optimistically declared that: 'In the exception the power of real life [*Kraft der wicklichen Lebens*] breaks through the crust of a mechanism that has become torpid by repetition' (Schmitt 2005: 15). For the younger generation, being, God and the event had the power to break into the world with unexpected but regenerative force. Crisis was not only their reality, but expressed the hope and possibility of a future. It was an ideology for a generation that grew up in the shadow of conflict and war.

Finally, mention must be made of Kierkegaard's influence on this interwar generation, as his influence contributed much to the 'crisis' philosophy and theology that emerged during this period.[22] The initial Kierkegaard reception in Germany was largely confined to theologians who were moved by Kierkegaard's 'devastating critique of Christendom and the mediocrity of a worldly church' (Malik 1997: 220). These theologians were exposed to the 'Christian' Kierkegaard, the image of the lone protestor against the Danish Lutheran Church. Throughout the 1920s and 1930s, Kierkegaard would influence the 'dialectical theologians', including Karl Barth,[23] Emil Brunner, Friedrich Gogarten, Rudolf Bultmann and Paul Tillich.[24] These theologians did not publish or write much about Kierkegaard himself (Schulz 2009: 334). Their use of Kierkegaard was more 'indirect'. That is, they came to read Kierkegaard with a feeling of personal affinity.

With the publication of some of Kierkegaard's pseudonymous writings, the readership broadened to a new audience who responded more strongly to Kierkegaard's perceived individualism, style of communication and also developed a strong personal affinity with the philosopher.[25] Franz Kafka wrote in a journal entry of 1913—'Today I received Kierkegaard's *Buch des Richters*. As I suspected, his case is very similar to mine despite essential differences. At least he is on the same side of the world as myself. He corroborates me like a friend' (cited in Malik 1997: 366). The Catholic philosopher, essayist, cultural critic and physiognomist Rudolf Kassner praised Kierkegaard as one of the greatest artists and humourists, who discovered 'the form or the idea of the single individual (*der Einzelne*)' (Schulz 2009: 322). Wittgenstein came to call Kierkegaard 'by far the greatest philosopher of the nineteenth century' (testimony of Wittgenstein's student Maurice Drury, cited in Malik 1997: 380). Heidegger himself minimally acknowledged Kierkegaard, but he borrowed Kierkegaard's notion of inwardness (Huntington 1995). And, as briefly noted in Chapter 5, Schmitt had also used Kierkegaard in developing his idea of the state of exception.[26]

Significantly, for these readers Kierkegaard served to heighten a sense of crisis that eventually found expression in a variety of ways in their philosophies. The reception of Kierkegaard emerged on the eve of the First World War, and Kierkegaard's vivid depiction of the individual's state of anxiety and despair would prove deeply influential for a generation that grew up in the shadow of war (Malik 1997: 379). The highpoint of Kierkegaard's influence came during the 'interwar' years, the years shaped by the language and imagery of 'crisis' in Weimar Germany. So pervasive was Kierkegaard's influence during the 'interwar' years that Hannah Arendt declared in the *Frankfurter Zeitung* (1932):

> The most varied and heterogeneous schools of thought look to Kierkegaard as a prime authority; they all meet on the ambiguous ground of radical scepticism, if, indeed, one can still use that pallid, now almost meaningless term to describe an attitude of despair towards one's own existence and the basic principles of one's own scientific or scholarly field. (Arendt 1994: 46)

While this overview of Kierkegaard's influence on the interwar generation is by necessity cursory, it is clear that the influence was extensive and included key intellectual figures such as the 'sons' featured in this chapter, Barth, Heidegger and Schmitt, who all in various ways have also emerged in Bonhoeffer's writing.

BONHOEFFER IN A TIME OF CRISIS

Themes that have appeared throughout this chapter in the context of intellectual and political life in Weimar Germany echo key Bonhoeffer themes explored in this book, including revelation, crisis and confrontation. Likewise, Kierkegaard's influence on Bonhoeffer was established in previous chapters. Yet, Bonhoeffer's turn to 'crisis' theology and philosophy has its own illuminating narrative.

As a child of his time, Dietrich Bonhoeffer came of age in the tumultuous years of post-war Germany. When Bonhoeffer was born in 1906, *Der Kaiserreich*, founded by Bismarck in 1871, was at the peak of its military and industrial power, his childhood was shaped by this empire and its self-destruction in the years 1914–1918 when Bonhoeffer was twelve years old. Like so many of his contemporaries, the war years and the death of his older brother Walter (on the battlefield) ended Bonhoeffer's idyllic childhood. Bonhoeffer's turbulent teenage years into adulthood took place in the Weimar Republic, his university education shaped by the political and economic chaos from 1929 to 1933. Bonhoeffer entered the world of adult responsibility with the ascension to power of Adolf Hitler. As Schlingensiepen notes:

From 30 January, the day on which Reich President Hindenburg named Adolf Hilter as Reich Chancellor (Prime Minister), 27-year-old Pastor Bonhoeffer was caught up in a whirlwind of events which at times called upon him to make new decisions from one day to the next. (2010: 114)

Yet, despite 'coming of age' in a politically turbulent time, Dietrich's own faith and intellectual formation remained embedded in the culture of the German aristocracy that flourished under the *Kaiserreich*. This was in part due to his family background[27] and in part due to the place of the Bonhoeffer family in society. The family moved to the German capital in 1912, becoming neighbours of the physicist Max Planck and the historians Adolf von Harnack and Hans Dellbrück (Rumscheidt 1999: 50–51).[28] Indeed, some years later Bonhoeffer began his university education under Harnack, with whom he developed a close relationship.[29] At the close of their three semesters together, Bonhoeffer wrote to Harnack, 'What I have learned and come to understand in your seminar is too closely associated with my whole person for me to be able to ever forget it' (cited in Rumscheidt 1999: 55). Harnack embodied all the worldly values of Dietrich's father: middle-class humanistic learning and the reconciliation of theology with empirical science.

But Bonhoeffer had already begun to question his teachers and their worldly values. Bonhoeffer was not to remain Harnack's pupil. When he discovered Karl Barth, in the winter of 1924–1925, he was initially pulled between the conservative theology of Harnack and the radical ideas of the younger Swiss theologian (Bethge 1977: 50).[30] Bonhoeffer began his own critique of Harnack's humanist theology in his doctoral thesis *Sanctorum Communio—A Dogmatic Investigation of the Sociology of the Church*, completed in 1927 at the University of Berlin. Reinhold Seeberg's report on Bonhoeffer's dissertation mentions there are references to Barth and censures Bonhoeffer for 'his critical comments on church practice [...] his hopeful optimism regarding the proletariat along with his contempt for the middle class [...] they do not arise out of the principles of the thesis but are merely subjective value judgments' (Seeberg cited in Green 2009: 8). The turn away from the humanism of both Harnack and Seeberg appeared to be final with Bonhoeffer's second dissertation, *Act and Being* (1930)[31] which contains extensive references to another emerging radical intellectual of his generation, Martin Heidegger.[32] Thus, Bonhoeffer can be seen to have made a turn away from the humanist values of his 'fathers' towards a new way of thinking, pioneered by Heidegger and Barth. Indeed, Bethge's biography notes that Bonhoeffer saw 'Seeberg and his friends as incapable of understanding the post-war collapse and crisis and interpreting them to his generation' (Bethge 1977: 49).

An image appears of a young Bonhoeffer, initially steeped in an education tradition that embraced the highest humanist values of *Bildung*, a form of education that aimed at self-cultivation and the pursuit of truth gained through reason. Yet, Bonhoeffer like his intellectual contemporaries was sensitive to the sense of crisis that emerged from Germany's war experience, a sense that deepened during the turbulent years of the Weimar Republic. In this 'crisis', the 'old' tools of the past, the tradition of *Bildung*, was considered no longer capable of addressing the urgent needs of the present. Bonhoeffer, too, finds his place here within the last generation to be shaped by the Weimar intellectuals, the sons destined to murder their fathers.

This chapter has provided a sense of the intellectual, cultural and political climate of Bonhoeffer's time through tracing the decline of the unique tradition of *Bildung* and the Neo-Kantian liberals, and giving voice to a new generation shaped by the war years and defeat of Germany in 1918. Neo-Kantianism would lose the intellectual and political fight. Many Neo-Kantian philosophers were Jewish, including Ernst Cassirer, who was forced to flee to England and then Sweden in 1933, and Hans Kelsen, who relocated to Geneva, Switzerland in 1933 and the USA in 1940.[33] Barth, Heidegger and Schmitt emerge as scholars who represent a new generation that had lost faith with the Kantian ideal of *Bildung* as cultivation of the human beings.[34] They are the 'sons' turn away from their 'fathers' towards a new method of philosophy, theology and political governance, one shaped and defined by the new language of crisis. Bonhoeffer, too, finds his place here, at least for a time, within the last generation to be shaped by the Weimar intellectuals, the sons murdering their fathers.

NOTES

1. In that time, Berlin changed from the imperial state of the German empire or *Der Kaiserreich*, first founded by Bismarck in 1871, to a republic with the constitution of Weimar after 1918, to National Socialism by 1933.
2. For the purposes of contextualising key Bonhoeffer ideas in Weimar Germany, no reference is made to Bonhoeffer's year at Union Theological Seminary (1930–1931), which changed Bonhoeffer, both personally and intellectually.

3. There were two separate main schools of Neo-Kantian philosophy: Marburg and the Southwest School (also known as Baden and Heidelberg school), the two schools did not see themselves as part of a common movement, but according to Jeremy Heis, the two shared important fundamental doctrines. Ernst Cassirer had trained under Hermann Cohen at Marburg and was considered Cohen's heir and a leader of Marburg Neo-Kantianism (Heis 2018). Karl Barth had studied under Wilhelm Herrman at Marburg, while Adolf Harnack taught at Marburg for two years (1886–1888).

4. This form of education included the humanities: classic languages, literature, art, music and theatre and the Christianity of German culture, as well as the sciences: mathematics, physics, and chemistry, history and modern languages. For an extensive discussion on *Bildung*, see (Ringer 1969).

5. Harnack was the champion of the Protestant University and heir to Schleiermacher's task of modernizing German theology, defending theology's scientific credentials against a host of progressive intellectuals, managing to furnish theology with legal protection in the Weimar Constitution.

6. Harnack was not an isolated example of theologians who divinely sanctioned imperialist ambition. A number of Karl Barth's teachers had signed the agreement to the Kaiser's war policy, the *Manifesto of the Ninety-Three* (*Aufruf: An die Kulturwelt*), published on Oct 4, 1914 (Oakes 2012: 45).

7. However, not all 'intellectual elite' were 'militaristic' in their ambitions. As Durst points out, many of the 'mandarins' of German intellectual life showed a political disinterest that often crossed into outright apathy, preferring the German ideal of individual *Bildung* over the valorisation of public and political life (Durst 2004: 51).

8. It was not just the theologians who were unable to critique the militarism of their nation. Ringer argues that the three groups of 'mandarin intellectuals' as a whole owed their comprehensive education to their close relationship to the state, a relationship that is characterised by obedience and the outcome of Germany's own heavily bureaucratic monarchy (Ringer 1969: 7).

9. Harnack's address was titled 'What has History to offer as certain knowledge concerning the meaning of world events?' Harnack was one year from retirement when giving this address.

10. The 1923 exchange lasted just over four months and consisted of five letters, three by Harnack and two by Barth.

11. Such was the impact of the contrasting cultural background of the two speakers. Gordon further notes that the family name Cassirer itself

marked a connection between merchants and cashiers, while the name Heidegger carries a trace of woodsmen and uncultivated terrain.

12. Gordon views the Cassirer-Heidegger exchange in the context of a larger tension that emerged 'as yet another stage in the interwar struggle between Neo-Kantianism and existentialism' (Gordon 2008: 225).

13. On Schmitt's involvement in the war: he delayed entry into the military until he passed his final assessor's examination at Berlin (Feb 15, 1915) then found himself unfit for combat duty following a vertebra injury during basic training. Subsequently, he spent most of the war in Munich in an administrative capacity, simultaneously continuing his academic career, a career in which he became increasingly critical of the Catholicism and Neo-Kantianism of his idealistic youth, and the republic that arose after the abdication of the Kaiser (Nov 9, 1918).

14. Unlike Harnack, Cassirer had not supported Germany in the First World War, but had instead remained 'apolitical', as was more typical of the intellectual elite who had tended to be politically disinterested. However, Cassirer had been offered professorships at two new universities founded at Frankfurt and Hamburg under the auspices of the Weimar Republic, and he gave a defense of Weimar in 1928 at the University's celebration of the tenth anniversary of the Republic (Friedman 2018).

15. For a comparison between Barth's theological ontology and Heidegger's onto-theological project, see Stanley, Timothy and Peter Candler. 2010. *Protestant Metaphysics After Karl Barth and Martin Heidegger*. London: SCM Press.

16. This idea of generational conflict, born with the Weimar intellectuals themselves, was also understood by many as an essential part of interpretation, cultural creation and accumulation as new individuals overturn past ideas: 'Productive misunderstanding is often a condition of continuing life' stated the sociologist Mannheim in 'The Problem of Generations' (1923) (Gordon 2010: 48).

17. It is beyond the scope of this chapter to do justice to the political complexities that led to the formation and fall of the Weimar Republic, save to say that despite its ideal as an institution based on the best German tradition, that of *Bildung*, combined with a new parliamentary democracy, and the attempts by its educated elite and politicians to engage the population, 'the silent majority regarded democracy as an imported product implanted in Germany under allied pressure in 1919' (Hans Mommsen cited in Henig 1998: 15). The Weimar Republic as a 'liberal, democratic, capitalist, welfare state' ultimately succumbed to the economic and social circumstances and its critics, the 'radical conservatives' who saw the republic's democratic political order as a sign of weakness, indecision and an inability to rule (Müller 1991: 695).

18. A number of prominent Neo-Kantian scholars were supporters of the Weimar Republic. This included Ernst Cassirer, who was a dedicated liberal and played a small role in promoting the constitution for the fledging Weimar Republic (Gordon 2003: 128) and Hans Kelsen.

19. Keith Bullivant differentiates between the 'older generation' of conservative revolutionaries, represented by Thomas Mann, Ernst Troeltsch and Friedrich Meinecke, who believed the desired 'middle way' could be found by working within the Republic, and the 'younger generation', who either aided those who worked against the Republic, or distanced themselves from the political arena (Bullivant 1985: 56).

20. Indeed, crisis, in its original Greek meaning, suggests a sifting or separation that leads one to a judgement or point of decision (Bambach 1995: 6). In German, the linguistic play with *Scheidung* (separation) and *Enscheidung* (decision) fosters the idea of a 'decisive judgement'.

21. A sentiment found, for example, in Ernst Jünger's understanding of 'unconditional destruction that will transform itself into unconditional creation', in *The Adventurous Heart* (*Das abenteuerliche Herz* (1929)).

22. For a more in-depth examination of Kierkegaard's reception in Europe, see Habib C. Malik's in-depth study *Receiving Søren Kierkegaard: The Early Impact and Transmission of His Thought* (1997).

23. Particularly through Barth's *Der Römerbrief* (1922).

24. Karl Barth saw in Kierkegaard a welcome ally in his fight against German Protestant culture and conservative Lutheranism. Yet, the later Barth in *Church Dogmatics* would become more critical of Kierkegaard, arguing Kierkegaard promoted a private Christianity.

25. The serious reception of Kierkegaard in the German-speaking world occurred after 1894, with the translation of the pseudonymously written 'Diary of a Seducer', published independently from its context in *Either/Or*. As it was published independently of its context, a trend emerged, sensationalizing Kierkegaard into an image of 'Søren and sex' (Malik 1997: 339).

26. In all, Schmitt makes three explicit references to Kierkegaard in his work. There is one direct reference in each of three published texts, *Political Romanticism* (*Politische Romantik* 1919), *Political Theology* (1923) (noted in Chapter 5) and *The Concept of the Political* (1932). Schmitt's published diaries refer to Kierkegaard far more frequently, as Schmitt read Kierkegaard for his personal edification. It is this combination of personal and academic that accounts for a deeper Kierkegaardian influence than first appears at a superficial reading of Schmitt. See (Burkhard 2009).

27. Bonhoeffer's Christian values were a legacy primarily of his mother, Paula Von Hase (1874–1951), who was responsible for instilling the Christian values of German culture through hymn singing and Bible stories. Dietrich's humanist values came from his father, Karl Bonhoeffer

who, although he provided Scriptural readings at festive occasions, was informed by progressive scientific and humanist values (Bethge 1977).

28. Karl Bonhoeffer, Professor of Psychiatry and Neurology, was offered the most highly regarded chair in his field at the University of Berlin.

29. As well as a family friend, Bonhoeffer was one of a group of students personally selected by Harnack to work with him after his retirement (Rumscheidt 1999: 53–54).

30. In reality, Bonhoeffer was not uncritically accepting of all of Barth and the two kept up a dialogue 'equally friendly and full of tension' (Tödt 2007: 2). Bonhoeffer was pulled between Harnack and Seeberg's 'genetic-historical' method and Barth's 'theological-dogmatic' method, abstracting the church from history altogether (Moses 2009: 37).

31. In his introduction to the English edition of *Act and Being*, Wayne Whitson Floyd Jr. declares that 'this work begs to be interpreted within the concrete historical context of the cultural crisis in Germany between the world wars, which eventuated in the National Socialist rise to power in 1933' (2009: 7).

32. Particularly Heidegger's *Being and Time* (1927). His director during this time considered Bonhoeffer a 'Heideggerian' (Rumscheidt 1999: 65). However, as Zimmermann has pointed out, the degree of Bonhoeffer's familiarity with Heidegger's work and the depth of its influence on Bonhoeffer are difficult to assess. In his assessment of Heidegger's influence on Bonhoeffer's work, Zimmermann concludes that aside from the references in *Act and Being*, Bonhoeffer ultimately judges Heidegger's hermeneutic ontology as being of limited use for his own theological work (2009: 106–107).

33. Following the war, he served as a legal adviser to the United Nations War Crimes Commission (Encyclopedia 2017).

34. Heidegger and Schmitt joined the National Socialist party on the same day, May 1, 1933, and both initially achieved some recognition and standing. Heidegger was elected Rector at Freiburg University (although this occurred several weeks before he joined the Nazi party), Schmitt was appointed State Councillor for Prussia, and became editor-in-chief of the Nazi publication, the *German Jurists' Journal*. Karl Barth spoke out against the Nazi regime and was very active in challenging the German *Reichs Kirche*, together with Bonhoeffer.

REFERENCES

Arendt, Hannah. 1994. *Essays in Understanding: 1930–1954.* New York: Schocken Books.

Bambach, Charles R. 1995. *Heidegger, Dilthey, and the Crisis of Historicism.* New York and London: Cornell University Press.

Barth, Karl. 1928. *The Word of God and the Word of Man*, trans. Douglas Horton. London: Hodder and Stoughton.

Barth, Karl. 1968. *The Epistle to the Romans*, trans. Edwyn C. Hoskyns. London: Oxford University Press.

Bethge, Eberhard. 1977. *Dietrich Bonhoeffer: Theologian, Christian, Contemporary*, trans. Eric Mosbacher, Peter and Betty Ross, Frank Clarke, and William Glen-Doepel. London: Fountain Books.

Bullivant, Keith. 1985. The Conservative Revolution. In *The Weimar Dilemma: Intellectuals in the Weimar Republic*, ed. Anthony Phelan, 47–71. Manchester: Manchester University Press.

Burkhard, Conrad. 2009. Kierkegaard's Moment: Carl Schmitt and his Historical Concept of Decision. In *Redescriptions: Yearbook of Political Thought, Conceptual History and Feminist Theory*, 145–171. Berlin: LIT Verlag.

Collegeville Institute. 2018. *Theology in Uncertain Times: An Interview with Bonhoeffer Scholar Victoria J. Barnett*. Bearings Online. https://collegevilleinstitute.org/bearings/theology-in-uncertain-times/. Accessed 10 Nov 2018.

Dorrien, Gary. 2000. *The Barthian Revolt in Modern Theology*. Kentucky: Westminster John Knox Press.

Durst, David C. 2004. *Weimar Modernism: Philosophy, Politics, and Culture in Germany 1918–1933*. Lanham, MD: Lexington Books.

Encyclopedia, New World. 2017. Hans Kelsen. http://www.newworldencyclopedia.org/p/index.php?title=Hans_Kelsen&oldid=1005846. Accessed 7 Sept 2018.

Floyd, Wayne Whitson, Jr. 2009. Editor's Introduction to the English Edition. In *Act and Being*, ed. Wayne Whitson Floyd Jr., 1–24. Dietric Bonhoeffer Works English. Minneapolis: Fortress Press.

Frend, W.H.C. 2001. Church Historians of the Early Twentieth Century: Adolf von Harnack (1851–1930). *The Journal of Ecclesiastical History* 52 (1): 83–102.

Friedman, Michael. 2018. Ernst Cassirer. In *Stanford Encyclopedia of Philosophy*, ed. Edward N. Zalta. Stanford: Metaphysics Research Lab.

Gordon, Peter Eli. 2003. *Rosenzweig and Heidegger: Between Judaism and German Philosophy*. Ewing, NJ: University of California Press.

Gordon, Peter E. 2008. Neo-Kantianism and the Politics of Enlightenment. *Philosophical Forum* 39 (2): 223–238. https://doi.org/10.1111/j.1467-9191.2008.00292.x.

Gordon, Peter Eli. 2010. *Continental Divide: Heidegger, Cassirer, Davos*. Cambridge, MA: Harvard University Press.

Green, Clifford J. 2009. Editor's Introduction to the English Edition. In *Sanctorum Communio: A Theological Study of the Sociology of the Church*, ed. Clifford J. Green. Dietrich Bonhoeffer Works English. Minneapolis: Fortress Press.

von Harnack, Adolf. 1989. *Adolf von Harnack: Liberal Theology at Its Height*. London: Collins.

Heidegger, Martin. 1990. *Kant and the Problem of Metaphysics*, 4th ed. Indianapolis: Indiania University Press.

Heis, Jeremy. 2018. Neo-Kantianism. In *Stanford Encyclopedia of Philosophy*. Stanford University: Metaphysics Research Lab.

Henig, Ruth. 1998. *Weimar Republic, 1919–1933*. London, GBR: Routledge.

Howard, Albert. 2006. *Protestant Theology and the Making of the Modern German University*. Oxford: Oxford University Press.

Hunter, Ian. 2001. *Rival Enlightenment: Civil and Metaphysical Philosophy in Early Modern Germany*. New York: Cambridge University Press.

Huntington, Patricia J. 1995. Heidegger's Reading of Kierkegaard Revisited: From Ontological Abstraction to Ethical Concretion. In *Kierkegaard in Post/Modernity*, ed. Martin Beck Matuštík and Merold Westphal, 43–65. Bloomington: Indiana University Press.

Jabloner, Clemens. 2000. Hans Kelsen. In *Weimar: A Jurisprudence of Crisis*, ed. Arthur J. Jacobson and Bernhard Schlink, 67–109. Philosophy, Social Theory, and the Rule of Law, vol. 8. Berkeley: University of California Press.

Malik, Habib C. 1997. *Receiving Soren Kierkegaard: The Early Impact and Transmission of His Thought*. Washington, DC: The Catholic University of America Press.

McCormack, Bruce L. 1995. *Karl Barth's Critically Realistic Dialectical Theology: Its Genesis and Development, 1909–1936*. Oxford: OUP Premium.

Moses, John A. 1999. Bonhoeffer's Germany: The Political Context. In *The Cambridge Companion to Dietrich Bonhoeffer*, ed. John de Gruchy, 3–21. Cambridge, New York: Cambridge University Press.

Moses, John A. 2009. *The Reluctant Revolutionary*. New York and Oxford: Berghahn Books.

Müller, Jan Werner. 1991. Carl Schmitt, Hans Freyer and the Radical Conservative Critique of Liberal Democracy in the Weimar Republic. *History of Political Thought* 12 (4): 695–715.

Oakes, Kenneth. 2012. *Karl Barth on Theology and Philosophy*. Oxford: Oxford University Press.

Paulson, Stanley L. 1992. The Neo-Kantian Dimension of Kelsen's Pure Theory of Law. *Oxford Journal of Legal Studies* 12 (3): 311–332. https://doi.org/10.1093/ojls/12.3.311.

Preuß, Ulrich K. 2014. Carl Schmitt and the Weimar Constitution. In *The Oxford Handbook of Carl Schmitt*, ed. Jens Meierhenrich, Oliver Simons, and Ulrich K. Preuß. Oxford: Oxford University Press.

Ringer, Fritz. 1969. *The Decline of the German Mandarins: The German Academic Community, 1890–1933*. Cambridge, MA: Cambridge University Press.

Ringer, Fritz. 1989. Bildung: The Social and Ideological Context of the German Historical Tradition. *History of European Ideas* 10 (2): 193–202.

Rumscheidt, Martin. 1972. *Revelation and Theology: An Analysis of the Barth-Harnack Correspondence of 1923*. London: Cambridge University Press.

Rumscheidt, Martin. 1999. The Formation of Bonhoeffer's Theology. In *The Cambridge Companion to Dietrich Bonhoeffer*, ed. John W. De Gruchy, 50–70. Cambridge: Cambridge University Press.

Schlingensiepen, Ferdinand. 2010. *Dietrich Bonhoeffer 1906–1945: Martyr, Thinker, Man of Resistance*, trans. Isabel Best. London and New York: T & T Clark International.

Schmitt, Carl. 2005. *Political Theology: Four Chapters on the Concept of Sovereignty*, trans. George Schwab. Chicago and London: The University of Chicago Press.

Schulz, Heiko. 2009. Germany and Austria: A Modest Head Start: The German Reception of Kierkegaard. In *Kierkegaard's International Reception: Northern and Western Europe*, ed. Jon Stewart, 307–419. Farnham, UK: Ashgate.

Schwab, George. 2005. Introduction. In *Political Theology: Four Chapters on the Concept of Sovereignty*, xxxvii–lii. Chicago: The University of Chicago Press.

Tödt, Heinz Eduard. 2007. *Authentic Faith: Bonhoeffer's Theological Ethics in Context*, trans. David Stassen and Ilse Tödt. Grand Rapids, MI: Eerdmans.

Zimmermann, Jens. 2009. Dietrich Bonhoeffer and Martin Heidegger: Two Different Visions of Humanity. In *Bonhoeffer and Continental Thought—Cruciform Philosophy*, ed. Brian Gregor and Jens Zimmermann, 102–155. Bloomington: Indiana University Press.

CHAPTER 10

Conclusion: Bonhoeffer the Conspirator—A Dangerous Heroism?

It seems to be the *rigueur* that anyone who writes on Bonhoeffer shares their own 'Bonhoeffer moment' in a short anecdote. I first encountered Bonhoeffer through an illustrated and abridged version of *Letters and Papers from Prison*, while on a retreat in a beautiful and tranquil bushland setting. The contrast between my own concrete situation and that of Bonhoeffer's at the time of his writing could not have been starker. And in many ways, my ongoing engagement with Bonhoeffer has continued to be expressed in symbolic contrast. It was not the saint and martyr that I encountered in that first reading. Indeed, as I began to read the vast secondary literature on Bonhoeffer, I found the deference and sanctified air of scholarship grating, to say the least. Just as I was not moved by the accounts of martyrdom, so I was not impressed by scholarship that insisted on describing Bonhoeffer and his choices in a straightforward way as moral and good, in contrast to the murderous brutality of the Nazis. At times, it felt as though I was viewing a documentary/drama of brave resistors against evil regimes, of outstanding and heroic individuals who sacrificed themselves to save the world from the clutches of evil maniacs and their henchmen. I had to turn to various feminist critiques of the narratives of war to realise that Bonhoeffer too had been co-opted into a deeply masculinist story.

On that first reading of *Letters and Papers in Prison*, what drew me to Bonhoeffer were three things: Bonhoeffer's engagement with and descriptions of his own intellectual and cultural heritage, the very prosaic and ordinary descriptions of his daily life in prison and his personal

© The Author(s) 2019   189
P. Brown, *Bonhoeffer*,
https://doi.org/10.1007/978-3-030-05698-8_10

exchanges with family and friends. In short, it was the very human Bonhoeffer who inspired me and has contributed so richly to my own ongoing education. Given my initial reading of Bonhoeffer, the subsequent encounters with various hagiographies and all too frequent attempts to ask 'how would Bonhoeffer respond to [insert issue] today?' were something of a shock. Any early tendency I may have had to effuse about Bonhoeffer's life quickly disappeared and was replaced by a more critical distance. I quickly had to overcome my own inclination to find 'inspiration' in Bonhoeffer and to view him as part of a wider story, history and set of ideas. When I became aware of Bonhoeffer's popularity amongst American evangelicals and discovered that Bonhoeffer had been used to justify acts of violence, the need to critically investigate Bonhoeffer's writings through the lens of his decision to become a conspirator became more urgent. I began to view the various attempts at theological justifications in the secondary literature as a stumbling block, rather than an explanation. I asked myself could someone, who believes themselves to be a Christian and believes themselves to be at war with the world, find in Bonhoeffer's writing something that would enable them to justify violence in the name of Christ?

To this, I would now give a qualified yes. Through following the concept of exception in Bonhoeffer's writing, a narrative has appeared in which Christian identity or discipleship is portrayed as radically isolating and as formed primarily in opposition to the world. Consequently, for the disciple of Christ, the forms of ethics based on general or universal principles are dismissed for an immediate relationship with Christ and a willingness to obey Christ and to see his will done on earth as it is in heaven. When faced with confrontation, the disciple may see herself as beyond good and evil, no longer bound to principles, fundamental rules or laws. Without the guidance of ethical principles, the disciple must be open to Christ's will revealed to her anew at each 'decisive moment'. While the isolated Christian in *Discipleship* is commanded to love her enemies, the isolated Christian in the 1929 lecture may well be commanded to murder. And because she is obedient to that command, even murder can be 'sanctified'. In the law of radical freedom, there is no right or wrong, only faithfulness to or deviation from God's will. Bonhoeffer's rejection of ethical principles in favour of a crisis point that leads to decision, in his early writings and *Discipleship*, sets a dangerous opposition between reflection, critical analysis and shared judgment on the one hand, and action, obedience and individual decision on the other hand. The isolated disciple who finds herself in an 'extraordinary situation' must ultimately retreat from the very principles and tools that might nevertheless guide action and mediate the crisis in a situation of *necessità*. Far from Christ's command to love her enemies, the reader who turns to Bonhoeffer to find a model of Christian action applicable to a state of exception may well find herself endorsing violence in the name of Christ.

Some of Bonhoeffer's writings can therefore seem to support evangelicals who are encouraged by his emphasis on commitment to Christ and the cost of discipleship. For them, Christ as the centre of one's life requires obedience and loyalty against competing interests and idols. This is a key theme throughout Bonhoeffer's writings, from the late 1920s to *Discipleship*, and echoes continue to be heard in *Ethics*. The tone of his writing might not quite portray the 'muscular Christianity' hoped for by former Australian Prime Minister Kevin Rudd, nor does his piety necessarily appear as 'manly, bracing, and rugged in every way', as Huntemann claimed. However, it is clear that parts of Bonhoeffer's writings support Huntemann's emphasis on Christ's sovereignty that makes the Christian responsible 'not to a law, but to the Lord who gives the command', as Huntemann puts it. Moreover, some of Bonhoeffer's writings do lend themselves to facilitating a sense of contemporaneity with the unreflective reader who looks for an emotional connection that transcends historical context, secure in the knowledge that God is in control. His own Christologically shaped writings seem to encourage this.

However, I do not believe that the isolated disciple who obeys Christ in a state of exception is Bonhoeffer's final view what discipleship means, nor does Bonhoeffer provide what evangelicals might hope is a Christian justification for last resort violence. Bonhoeffer's understanding of the place of Christ in his life, in the community and the world did not emerge as a single doctrine, but developed overtime. Gregersen describes Bonhoeffer as combining an existential approach (Christ for me), with a community-oriented approach (Christ for us) that would towards his later writings culminate in a more universalist approach (Christ for the world) (Gregersen 2007: 136).[1] Thus, Bonhoeffer's theology changes over his too-short life, in response to the concrete events and challenges that face him. While the book has focused on the concepts of discipleship, obedience to Christ and the extraordinary situation as these emerge in Bonhoeffer's earlier and middle periods of writing, his later reflections while in prison show a different image of what discipleship might look like.

On the day that he learnt of the failure of the July 20th plot to kill Hitler, Bonhoeffer wrote that he no longer saw himself as separate from the world: 'one only learns to have faith by living in the full this-worldliness of life'; it is only when a person stops trying to make something of oneself, such as a saint or a church leader, that one can embrace this worldliness, by which Bonhoeffer means 'living unreservedly in life's duties, problems, successes and failures, experiences and perplexities' (Bonhoeffer 2010b: 486). The phrase that one must abandon to attempt to make something of oneself echoes Arendt's critique of revolutionaries who believe institutions, laws and people can be made in the same way as furniture.[2] The term 'this-worldliness' refers to the actual events that challenge a person in life and to the choices made in concrete experiences in taking up duties and responsibilities. If we read this as an autobiographical reflection, it suggests that Bonhoeffer's change from pacifist pastor to conspirator was finally one in which his own identity changed from someone attempting to *make* something of himself, to someone accepting duties in response to what was needed in a particular time and place.

Bonhoeffer describes his own actions as a shift from what he calls the 'phraseological to the real' (Bonhoeffer 2010b: 358). This can be seen as turning away from the abstract expressions of theological ideas to an active involvement in the concrete events of his own life. While in prison, Bonhoeffer critiqued his own church-based ethics developed in *Discipleship*, particularly for the way this separated the Christian disciple from the concerns of the world. For Bonhoeffer, being responsible meant living in faith amongst all of life's tasks, questions, successes, failures, experiences and perplexities, action and guilt, health and happiness, as well as suffering and harassment.

While in prison, Bonhoeffer requested a book by his former teacher and mentor, Adolf Harnack. Upon having read the four-volume work, Bonhoeffer wrote to his parents:

> Harnack's *History of the Academy* has made a deep impression upon me; it made me feel partly happy, partly regretful. There are so few people today who still want to have an inner and spiritual connection with the 19th and 18th century ... who still have an idea of what our grandfathers laboured on and achieved and how much of what they knew is already lost to us! (cited in Rumscheidt 1989: 217)

In reflecting on Bonhoeffer's turn to Harnack and other intellectual greats, Bethge writes that: 'He [Bonhoeffer] wanted to become better acquainted with particular aspects of nineteenth-century literature and *rehabilitate* the tradition of the forefathers [...] over against more modern existentialist tendencies' (Bethge 1977: 747). It seems that Bonhoeffer, given time to reflect in prison, found much to retrieve from the past and his forebears, in particular as he sought to rediscover its theological themes in order to address the 'present reality that had abandoned all values, a time that was so empty and wasted' (Rumscheidt 2008: 215). The promise and hope of a mighty movement or victorious struggle that had emerged in intellectual life and found its way to the popular rhetoric of the 1930s had clearly failed Germany, in Bonhoeffer's estimation. Retrieving Harnack would prove key to Bonhoeffer's prison writings, and Harnack's influence is evident in new theological themes that Bonhoeffer developed while in prison.[3] These include key ideas such as 'world-come-of-age', 'non-religious interpretation of Christian concepts' and the 'arcane disciplines' or mysteries of Christian faith. These ideas are generally associated with the later Bonhoeffer, who envisions a new mode of living out Christian faith in the world that acknowledges the existence of the world, the church that must live in the midst of the world. To be a Christian doesn't signify identification as sinner or saint, but 'it means being human', and poignantly, Bonhoeffer contrasts the 'human' Jesus with the religiously named and identified John the Baptist (Bonhoeffer 2010a: 480, 485). A very human portrait of Bonhoeffer emerges in the prison writings, as he seeks to breathe new life into ideas of the past, tries his hand at more creative expressions of writing and engages in wide correspondence with friends and family as he tried to live out what it meant to be a 'decent human being' in the face of 'the horrid dehumanization' that was the Nazi regime (Rumscheidt 2008: 223).

We need not view Bonhoeffer's involvement in conspiracy as a simple act of obedience to Christ's mystical command, heard by the disciple alone. Bonhoeffer's attending to the worldly or natural duties of responsibility to family and loved ones stand as a check to hubristic claims of divine inspiration. His decision for conspiracy can be viewed as Bonhoeffer properly attending to his worldly duties, in particular his responsibility towards his family, as living fully immersed in the 'penultimate sphere' of recognising and affirming God's created world, which cannot simply be ignored as we believe we are doing the work of furthering God's kingdom. Whether the latter is understood as evangelistic preaching, attending a protest rally or becoming involved in law-breaking acts of resistance, Christian action does not take place apart from this world. If there is salvation or redemption to be found, it 'passes through and depends upon the world as well as our bodies with which we are bound to the world' (Manoussakis 2009: 239). Bonhoeffer's desire to be 'this-worldly' is an affirmation of our embodied life in the world that affirms the existing and enduring inter-relationality of one's concrete world.

It has been over 100 years since the start of the First World War, and we live in a continuation of its shadow, scholars suggesting there is much resonance between today's global political and social volatility and that other great 'crisis' age of the twentieth century, the volatile and short-lived interwar period of the Weimar Republic.[4] In a world rocked by constant images of extreme weather events, terrorism, refugee crises and a destabilising global political milieu, the future seems marked, not by hope, but by apocalyptic visions of a doomed humanity. Bonhoeffer appears to have something to say to this present generation that finds itself in an increasingly destabilised age, facing unprecedented crises that challenge, not just one group of people, but the global community as a whole. For many, Bonhoeffer is an exemplar faith who doesn't simply retreat from the world, but courageously seeks to enact change. In a climate with a heightened sense of crises, Bonhoeffer seems to be a model of the decisive and 'extraordinary' action that will increasingly be required of future generations.

Yet, the failure of the Weimar Republic and the historical events that occurred are not simply the result of a divine hand unfolding in history. The 'generational gap' in Weimar Germany, together with the factious character of politics, led to the polarisation of debate and the radicalisation of discussion that discouraged individuals and parties from moderation and mediation. When a cultural-political situation is framed in the language of crisis, the conventional methods are no longer considered adequate and the only solution is swift and decisive action. The overarching danger of crisis language leads to 'thinking in a time of need' (Bambach 1995: 256).

Those who accept Bonhoeffer as an example of Christian violence in a situation of 'last resort' may wish to become more familiar with the historical events and ideas that shaped the Weimar years. Christians who wish to read Bonhoeffer as an example of what it means to get one's hands dirty as an act of love modelled on Christ's example would do well to read Carl Schmitt, the architect of dictatorship, before appealing to such a justification for violence. They may find that they are led to a Schmittian view of the world, a view that prioritises the decision over established law and process, that appeals to strong sovereignty in place of measured forms of governance and that sees the friend–enemy distinction as the foundation of all human relations.[5]

Evangelicals, who see the world in apocalyptic terms as a fight between good and evil and a battle to be waged in the name of Christ, may wish to consider Schmitt's judgment that conflict cannot be settled by a general norm or judgment, but is an indication of the friend–enemy relation that is at the heart of politics. Troublingly, Christians who would argue that violence as a last resort is acceptable may, just like Schmitt, conflate the individual decision with the exceptional event, nullifying the authority of the law as law (impartial in application), rendering it dependent on the absence of peril and the good will or prudence of the sovereign. As with Schmitt, they may be tempted to attribute to their sovereign quasi-divine powers to make *ex nihilo* decisions that are outside the governance of law. Yet, in doing so, they are blind to the dangers of separating decisions from norms. The critique applied to Schmitt may well apply to the political views of evangelical Christians who praise Bonhoeffer for obeying Christ's command, a command that is 'clear, definite and concrete to the last detail' and 'comes from above', to put it in Huntemann's terms (1993: 233, 234).

Conservative evangelicals should reconsider their own desire for authority in light of Schmitt's political theology. Instead of clamouring to 'dirty their hands', evangelicals may wish to take note of Agamben's claim that the state of exception 'tends to increasingly appear as the dominant paradigm of government in contemporary politics' (2005: 2). One does not need to agree with all of Agamben's pronouncements to recognise that last resort vocabulary is rarely conducive to rational analysis. A culture of crisis demands an immediate response, a decision and a commitment from those who have the ears to hear and heed the apparent danger in the warning. As Agamben notes, in such a climate, force without real reference will necessarily threaten to become its own justification. Without a sense of ratio, or measure, such Christians may very well come to mirror the violence they are seeking to prevent. Force, far from preserving the world, as Christians may wish, may equally lead to the loss of the world through a disregard of other forms of relationship and other possibilities of communication between human beings.

Existential confrontations based on an apocalyptic worldview fail to see that communities and people are shaped by ever-changing historical circumstances and events. As with the exception's neglect of mediating institutions, the good–evil disjunction is blind to the power of diplomacy in complex situations and relationships that can prevent the need for force in the first place. If Bonhoeffer's decision to participate in conspiracy becomes understood in terms of a *normative theory* of Christian action, then subsequent generations who interpret Bonhoeffer's participation in conspiracy in order to theorise potential 'states of exception' may well find themselves with a form of Schmittian 'political theology of despair' (Huysmans 1999: 325).

By turning Bonhoeffer's decision for conspiracy into a normative model, self-sacrifice and vulnerability are open to being put into the service of claims to sovereignty in which other human beings are finally treated as mere obstacles to self-creating power. The danger lies in a growing combination of religious and political fervour that could potentially lead to a Christ-sanctified case for war based on a Bonhoeffer/Schmittian political theology of 'Christ's command in a time of exception', no longer addressed to the 'individual' as with Bonhoeffer but to the 'personhood' of the sacred nation/state.

Instead of retrieving Bonhoeffer as the exemplary model of Christian action in a time of crisis, it is important also to commemorate others who acted courageously in an 'extraordinary action'. The Lutheran pastor Paul Schneider was arrested for removing his beret in tribute to the Swastika flag on Hitler's birthday in 1938. He became known as the 'Preacher of Buchenwald' because he would preach with a loud voice to prisoners in the yard, despite numerous orders to be silent and beatings to enforce the order. He was eventually executed because he could not be silenced.[6] Schneider showed courage in proclamation, in speaking out against power.

News of Schneider's death reached Bonhoeffer when he was ministering to a German congregation in England, following his return from New York. When Bonhoeffer heard of Schneider's death, he had already decided against this kind of martyrdom. According to Rasmussen, pacifism of this kind, while a courageous witness, for Bonhoeffer would have been a private act of pietism (Rasmussen 2005: 62). Such 'pietism' appears to appeal little to those who would wish to invoke Bonhoeffer in their own 'extraordinary situations', such as those who seek to defend America's 'unborn children' or those who seek to embark on a 'war on terror'. Yet those who give Bonhoeffer the epitaph of martyr and Protestant saint, and see him as an expression of 'authentic Christian character' may not wish to efface other types of sacrifice, such as that demonstrated by Schneider.

There are ways that we can challenge those who see in Bonhoeffer some kind of legitimisation of Christian violence. Bonhoeffer's own historical circumstances and concrete relationships can serve as a sober check for those who claim a 'mystical union' or connection between Bonhoeffer and themselves or his time and their own. Bonhoeffer's own decision for conspiracy involved close family connections and more prosaic reasons that may not fully come through in his own writing during his time. Drawing attention to the human Bonhoeffer avoids a simplistic reading of a particular passage of his work in order to justify violence for an abstract goal, whether this is understood as 'unborn children' or the 'nation', or indeed, 'American' or 'Christian' values. And while there has been limited scope to do so within this book, considering Bonhoeffer in his own historical context, the events and relationships of his own time, develops an appreciation for the complexity of individual actions within multifaceted cultural and historical situations.

Finally, this book has considered three possible ways to test the claims to acts of violence as a 'last resort' through the role of the church, the ultimate/penultimate distinction and the manifestation of conscience and guilt. Of these three motifs, the role of guilt should be considered a rich resource for Bonhoeffer scholars. It is a theme that recurs throughout Bonhoeffer's writing, particularly during his conspiracy involvement as he is required to choose between 'wrong' and 'wrong', and it is highly relevant to contemporary issues in political philosophy. Michael Walzer's account of 'dirty hands' actions and the role of guilt challenges straightforward attempts to justify immoral actions on the grounds of necessity. It is also in the context of guilt that the figure of Iphigenia emerges in Bonhoeffer's key conspiracy text, as a reminder that Bonhoeffer was required to make moral decisions strictly on the mortal plane, amongst flawed human beings in situations that were deeply and thoroughly compromised.

This book began as a protest against the sanctification of Bonhoeffer. For this reason, I introduced Dhanu, the Tamil Tiger suicide-terrorist and the 'exceptional' violence of one individual. I want to draw again attention to the person, not the terrorist, Dhanu: an individual who came of age in a time of crisis and acted to stop the destruction of her own people and culture against the claim of a sovereign nation state. Both demonization and sanctification ultimately strip individuals of their humanity and threatens to place them in service of a militarism that is encouraged in an environment of friend–enemy relations. In such a world, one's own extreme acts are all too easily justified and forgiven while the extreme act of the other is judged as the unjustified and unforgivable crime. The concept of political exception leads to violence without reference enacted against what is ultimately most deeply our own: a shared humanity and a common world.

NOTES

1. Gregersen argues that in Bonhoeffer's developing Christology, the world that is cast away in his early writings, such as *Creation and Fall*, by the later writings, is preserved: 'The new creation (*creatio nova*) is now seen as emerging out of the old creation (*creatio nova ex vetere*), for also the fallen creation is both preserved, accepted and reconciled in the comprehensive reality of Jesus Christ' (Gregersen 2007: 156).

2. For a direct comparison between Bonhoeffer and Arendt's view on the world, see Brown, Petra 2016. Reading Bonhoeffer Through Arendt: Bringing Worldly Christianity into the Common World. *The Bonhoeffer Legacy: Australasian Journal of Bonhoeffer Studies* 4 (1): 19–37. Also see Bernauer (2007) who argues that both Bonhoeffer and Arendt embrace worldliness, Bonhoeffer in the *Letters and Papers from Prison* through the concept of 'religionless Christianity'; Arendt through her classic work, *The Human Condition*, for which she had considered the alternative title, 'Amor Mundi' or 'Love of the World'.

3. As Marty argues, it is because Bonhoeffer is placed between Harnack and Barth that scholars often read him as either a lineal descendent of the nineteenth-century liberal tradition or a Lutheran Karl Barth, a neo-orthodox 'radical conservative' (1963: 13).

4. See for example Sharpe, Matthew, Rory Jeffs, and Jack Reynolds. 2017. *100 Years of European Philosophy Since the Great War: Crisis and Reconfigurations*. Philosophical Studies in Contemporary Culture: Vol. 25: Springer.

5. It is worth noting that Schmitt, since his death in the mid-1980s, has become increasingly quoted and studies by North American political scientists, who find in Schmitt a useful and convincing political theorist that meets the need of the current sense of global turmoil, and whose language of 'exception' provides a model for American politics in what is perceived

to be a time of global instability. Concurrently, a different group of North Americans since the 1980s have turned to Bonhoeffer, whose act of obedience to Christ in a time of exception led him to a form of violence that can be broadly conceptualised in terms of 'violence as a last resort'. For this second group, Bonhoeffer's political action is a call for every Christian who would be faithful to Christ in the godless influence growing in America itself.

6. See Foster, C.R. *Paul Schneider: The Buchenwald Apostle: A Christian Martyr in Nazi Germany: A Sourcebook on the German Church Struggle.* SSI Bookstore, West Chester University, 1995; Wentorf, R. *Paul Schneider: The Witness of Buchenwald.* American Eagle Publications, 1993.

REFERENCES

Agamben, Giorgio. 2005. *State of Exception,* trans. Kevin Attell. Chicago and London: University of Chicago Press.

Bambach, Charles R. 1995. *Heidegger, Dilthey, and the Crisis of Historicism.* New York and London: Cornell University Press.

Bernauer, James. 2007. Bonhoeffer and Arendt at One Hundred. *Studies in Christian-Jewish Relations* 2 (1): 77–85.

Bethge, Eberhard. 1977. *Dietrich Bonhoeffer: Theologian, Christian, Contemporary,* trans. Eric Mosbacher, Peter and Betty Ross, Frank Clarke, and William Glen-Doepel. London: Fountain Books.

Bonhoeffer. 2010a. *Letters and Papers from Prison,* trans. Isabel Best, Lisa E. Dahill, Reinhard Krauss, and Nancy Lukens. Dietrich Bonhoeffer Works English. Minneapolis: Fortress Press.

Bonhoeffer. 2010b. *Letters and Papers from Prison,* trans. Isabel Best, Lisa E. Dahill, Reinhard Krauss, and Nancy Lukens. Dietrich Bonhoeffer Works in English. Minneapolis: Fortress Press.

Gregersen, Niels Henrik. 2007. The Mysteries of Christ and Creation. In *Mysteries in the Theology of Dietrich Bonhoeffer,* ed. Kirsten Busch Nielsen, Ulrik Nissen, and Christiane Tietz, 135–158. Göttingen: Vandenhoeck & Ruprecht.

Huntemann, George. 1993. *The Other Bonhoeffer: An Evangelical Reassessment.* Grand Rapids: Baker Publishing Group.

Huysmans, Jef. 1999. Know Your Schmitt: A Godfather of Truth and the Spectre of Nazism. *Review of International Studies* 25 (2): 323–328.

Manoussakis, John Panteleimon. 2009. "At the Recurrent End of the Unending": Bonhoeffer's Eschatology of the Penultimate. In *Bonhoeffer and Continental Thought: Cruciform Philosophy,* ed. Brian Gregor and Jens Zimmerman, 226–244. Bloomington: Indiana University Press.

Marty, Martin Emil. 1963. *The Place of Bonhoeffer.* London: SCM Press.

Rasmussen, Larry. 2005. *Dietrich Bonhoeffer: Reality and Resistance*. Louisville: Kentucky Westminster John Knox Press.

Rumscheidt, Martin. 1989. *Adolf Von Harnack: Liberal Theology at Its Height*. London: Collins.

Rumscheidt, Martin. 2008. The Significance of Aodlf von Harnack and Reinhold Seeberg for Dietrich Bonhoeffer. In *Bonhoeffer's Intellectual Formation*, ed. Peter Frick, 201–224. Tübingen, Germany: Mohr Siebeck.

Index

© The Editor(s) (if applicable) and The Author(s), under exclusive license to Springer Nature Switzerland AG 2019
P. Brown, *Bonhoeffer*,
https://doi.org/10.1007/978-3-030-05698-8